Across the Waves

THE HISTORY OF COMMUNICATION

Robert W. McChesney and John C. Nerone, editors

A list of books in the series appears at the end of this book.

Across the Waves

*How the United States
and France Shaped the
International Age of Radio*

DEREK W. VAILLANT

UNIVERSITY OF
ILLINOIS PRESS
Urbana, Chicago, and Springfield

For Jane, Ty, Devin, and Sarah

Contents

Acknowledgments

A number of conversations that occurred early during this project come to mind at this happy moment of completion. I am grateful to Jean-Jacques Cheval, Charles Rearick, Gabrielle Hecht, Raymond Grew, and Joshua Cole for their insights. Susan Douglas read innumerable drafts, wrote letters, and offered wise counsel. Michele Hilmes and Francis Couvares offered critical support early on that helped launch the project. Victoria De Grazia, Kate Lacey, and Gabrielle Hecht read an early draft of the manuscript and offered invaluable and perceptive feedback. I also gratefully acknowledge those who read or commented on parts of this book as a work in progress, including Herrick Chapman, Judith G. Coffin, Suzanne Moon, Aswin Punathambekar, Rebecca Scales, Emily Thompson, Katherine Sender, Paddy Scannell, Liz Anderson, and Jason Loviglio. Conferences for the American Historical Association, International Communication Association, Society for Cinema and Media Studies, Society for French Historical Studies, and Society for the History of Technology all provided a forum for presentations and dialogue, as did the Science, Technology, Medicine and Society Speaker Series and the Communication Studies Colloquium at the University of Michigan. Research support came from the Council for International Exchange of Scholars (CIES), the U-M Associate Professor Support Program, and the National Endowment for the Humanities.

I owe an extraordinary debt to Jean-Jacques Cheval, who sponsored my first trip to France on behalf of the Franco-American Commission and the Fulbright Research Scholar Program. Steeped in French media sociology with formidable expertise in the Chicago electric blues tradition, culinary concerns, and all matters Breton, Jean-Jacques continues to be an extraordinary colleague and friend. Through his efforts, I came to know the faculty at the Maison des sciences de l'homme d'Aquitaine at the University of Bordeaux III, particularly Annie Lenoble-Bart and André-Jean Tudesq. Before his untimely death, André-Jean graciously fielded queries from a neophyte and generously shared his vast knowledge.

Thank you as well to past and present members of the *Groupe de recherches et d'études sur la radio (GRER)* who welcomed me to their merry band, especially Christophe Bennet, Étienne Damome, Béatrice Donzelle, Jean-Jacques Ledos, Pascal Ricaud, Blandine Schmidt, and Bernard Wuillème. In Paris, Pascal Griset, Denis Maréchal, and Cécile Méadel shared thoughts and suggestions.

I gratefully acknowledge colleagues and friends in the North American Radio Studies Association and the field of sound studies for your inspiration and camaraderie, especially Kathleen Battles, Art Blake, Dolores Inés Casillas, Christine Ehrick, David Goodman, Michele Hilmes, Bill Kirkpatrick, Jason Loviglio, Elena Razlogova, Alex Russo, Joshua Shepherd, Susan Smulyan, Michael J. Socolow, Christopher Sterling, Jonathan Sterne, David Suisman, Shawn VanCour, Neil Verma, and David Weinstein.

Current and former colleagues in the Department of Communication Studies helped make this a better book. I thank particularly Scott Campbell, Tony Collings, Jimmy Draper, Rowell Huesmann, Shazia Iftkhar, Nojin Kwak, Robin Means-Coleman, Russ Neuman, Scott Selberg, Katherine Sender, and Julia Sonnevend. In the Department of History, Howard Brick, Kathleen Canning, Jay Cook, Jean Hébrard, Gabrielle Hecht, Matt Lassiter, Gina Morantz-Sanchez, and Geoff Eley offered collegiality and inspiration.

I wish to thank my dedicated readers at the University of Illinois Press: Kate Lacey, James Schwoch, and an anonymous reviewer for your excellent comments and suggestions that sharpened this project. My editor, Daniel Nasset, championed this project from the start and did a great job of author whispering and running interference when needed. Marika Christofides, Tad Ringo, and Geof Garvey offered their production expertise. I am proud to be a part of *The History of Communication* series, which exists thanks to the enterprise of Robert W. McChesney and John C. Nerone. I also gratefully acknowledge the Johns Hopkins University Press and the University of Pennsylvania Press for permission to adapt material previously appearing in Derek W. Vaillant, "At the Speed of Sound: Techno-Aesthetic Paradigms in U.S.–French International Broadcasting, 1925–1942," which appeared in *Technology and Culture*, and "Occupied Listeners: The Legacies of Interwar

Radio for France during World War II," in *Sound in the Age of Mechanical Reproduction*, edited by Susan Strasser and David Suisman.

I cannot begin to acknowledge all of the archivists and specialist librarians who aided this project over the years, but I will single out Michael Henry at the Library of American Broadcasting, Lee C. Grady at the State Historical Society of Wisconsin, Karen King at the National Public Broadcasting Archives, David Langbart at the National Archives, and Andy Lanset at WNYC. Corinne Gaultier and Christine Barbier-Bouvet served my research needs at the Bibliothèque nationale française and the Institut national de l'audiovisuel in Paris. Bertrand Cousin, Thierry Lefebvre, and Aurélie Zbos at the Musée de Radio France helped obtain an elusive photographic image. University of Michigan librarians and media specialists Barbara Alvarez, Charles Antonelli, Jennifer Bonnet, Shevon Desai, Annette Haines, Phil Hallman, Michael McLean, and Bryan Squib offered their considerable expertise. Justin Jocque of the Stephen S. Clark Library created the maps in this book and patiently supervised my students Elena Lamping and Henry Duhaime as they geocoded and constructed an ARC/gis radio carriage map. Andrea Comiskey, Christopher Decou, Helena Javier, Julia Lippman, Edward Sloan, and Edward Timke contributed research assistance. Annemarie Iddins provided crucial editorial assistance and offered insights from her work on radio in Morocco.

Judith Bate Acheson, E. N. Brandt, Paulette Sabarthe, and Douglas Siler generously shared memories with me. Sadly, not all of you have lived to see this book completed. I hope I have faithfully retold your stories. I gratefully acknowledge the contributions of Miriam Crénesse, who answered questions, exchanged emails, and helped me obtain copies of photographs with the able assistance of Thierry Boccon-Gibod. Miriam became a long-distance friend over the many years I worked on this project. Her dedication to her husband's memory and his work left a deep impression.

To all who generously made France a home for me and my family over a span of many years, I wish to recognize Marie-Claude and Régis Arnauld, Jean-Jacques and Angelina Cheval, Isabelle Delorme, Christophe Delorme, and Loraine Kennedy and Pascal Weil. Deep thanks, too, to Annie and François Bart, Hervé and Alexandra Bourhis, Maria Santos-Sainz, Chris and Virginie Skoczen, Delphine and David Perrais, and Joël Zanouey.

To Bettina, (Wilde) Bill, Bill S., Bipin, Dave, David L., Dean, Dörte, Gisela, Hazel, Josephine, Karen, Liz A., Liz D., Lorel, Lourdes, Peter, Pratt (mon grand ami), Lourdes, Rachel, Rob, Sophie, Stu, and the boys making soup in the basement (Mike G., Mike R., and Bob M.): who's like you? Damned few.

I want to acknowledge my parents. Dr. Janet G. Vaillant traveled unaccompanied to Senegal in the mid-1970s to produce a landmark biography of Léopold Séder Senghor. Dr. Henry W. Vaillant brought medical aid to Haiti and stood up for socialized medicine decades before it was fashionable to do so. Thank you, Eliza and Marian, my dear sisters. And thank you Andy, for your support of them. Here's to the memory of Dev. Thank you Julia, Peter, Matty, Gené, and Ryan for being wonderfully supportive. Finally, this book is dedicated to my children and to Sarah H. Kennedy. So many rely on you, Sarah. We are grateful beyond words.

List of Acronyms and Abbreviations

BBC	British Broadcasting Corporation
BFA	Broadcasting Foundation of America
BNF	Bibliothèque nationale française
CBS	Columbia Broadcasting System
CAEC	Comité de l'action extérieure et de la coopération
DAEC	Direction des affaires extérieures et de la coopération
EIS	European Intelligence Section
FBS	French Broadcasting System in North America
IGN	International Goodwill Network
INA	Institut national de l'audiovisuel
NAEB	National Association of Educational Broadcasters
NBC	National Broadcasting Company
OIC	Office of International Information and Cultural Affairs
OIE	Office of Information and Educational Exchange
ORTF	Office de radiodiffusion-télévision française
OSR	Office of the Special Representative
OSS	Office of Strategic Services
OWI	Office of War Information
PCF	Parti communiste français
PTT	Postes, télégraphes et téléphones; Ministry of Posts, Telegraphs, and Telephones
PWB	Psychological Warfare Branch
PWD	Psychological Warfare Division
RCA	Radio Corporation of America
RDF	Radiodiffusion française
RTF	Radiodiffusion-télévision française
SHAEF	Supreme Headquarters Allied Expeditionary Force
USIA	United States Information Agency
USIS	United States Information Service

Introduction

At the Border of U.S.–French Broadcasting

It was a broadcaster's nightmare. In spring 1953, Simon J. Copans, the seasoned announcer for the Voice of America (VOA) radio network in Paris, fumbled for words. Fortunately, the problem did not occur in front of a microphone, but in front of a typewriter, as he struggled to complete a restricted memo to the U.S. State Department summarizing the condition of U.S.–French broadcasting. "It is very difficult," Copans admitted, "to list separately what the French radio does for the [VOA] and what the [VOA] does for the French radio."[1] The state of affairs defied easy description partly because it contradicted the definition of international broadcasting as one nation-state transmitting programs to another. Since the end of World War II, Copans had watched a procession of French and U.S. radio producers, announcers, technicians, and talent stream through the Roosevelt Studios, built near the Champs-Élysées by the United States Army. The VOA shared the studios with Radiodiffusion française (RDF), French national broadcasting. U.S.–French radio represented a curious mechanism of Cold War geopolitics in which the making and distribution of national radio programs had parted company with clearly identifiable sovereign origins and control.

To begin to understand Copans's quandary when separating the work of the VOA from the RDF, one need only switch on the radio. On any given evening in Paris, he could hear the national newscast, *Ce soir en France* (France Tonight). It blanketed metropolitan France, Europe, and French North Africa (Algeria, Morocco, Tunisia). To achieve such wide coverage, however, the RDF required a discreetly furnished power boost from the multinational transmitters of the VOA. With an all-band receiver, Copans could also hear the VOA's daily French-language program *Ici New York* (This Is New York), broadcast directly to France via shortwave. (French law prohibited foreign powers from broadcasting on French soil.) If only an AM set was available, the VOA's *Ici New York* was courteously relayed on the RDF's national Chaîne Parisienne. The RDF also broadcast popular music programs hosted by Copans with acknowledgment to the VOA. Finally, on *Paris-Inter*, a one-station "network" serving greater metropolitan Paris, Copans and others could enjoy French popular and classical music and talk programs produced in English by the French Broadcasting System in North America (FBS), a unit of the RDF staffed by U.S. and French nationals in Paris and New York and supported with funds from the French and U.S. governments. FBS programs circulated on hundreds of U.S. radio stations from coast to coast, along with other types of RDF-produced content.[2]

The arrangements producing such a scramble of content, producers, production locales, target audiences, and distribution methods resisted precise assignment of national responsibility because they often bypassed official diplomatic and legal agreements. The understandings between French broadcasting and the U.S. State Department were obscure by design and rarely, if ever, publicized. Some were classified. To a historian, such arrangements and the programs that resulted provoke numerous questions: Who was speaking to whom via U.S.–French radio, and to what end or ends? Why had the sovereign boundaries between France and the United States grown so indistinct in the field of broadcasting? Above all, who stood to gain (or lose) through such arrangements, and what consequences did this entanglement have for U.S. and French sovereignty and cultural expression in the twentieth century?

Decades before satellite television and the Internet, radio broadcasting, the world's first instantaneous mass medium, catalyzed new processes of cultural production, consumption, and distributed communication on an international, even global, scale.[3] Between 1931, when regular U.S.–French transatlantic broadcasting began, and 1974, when France dissolved its public broadcast monopoly, the United States and France shaped international radio into a multifaceted cultural and political medium. Over time, broadcasting contributed to the accelerating pace of the transatlantic circulation of information, ideas, and cultural expression, and to the aesthetic embodiments of such material.[4] Transatlantic radio constituted a field in which modern U.S.–French relations could be instituted and transacted through the production, circulation, and consumption of forms of cultural capital.[5]

During the 1920s and 1930s, U.S.–French transatlantic encounters produced contrasting models of radio's technical and cultural usage that shaped the future of broadcast interaction.[6] The U.S. techno-aesthetic ideal stressed power, abundance, and high-speed execution; it could be quantified in kilowatts (kW), stations, transmitters, and program hours. The French techno-aesthetic emphasized quality, scarcity, and deliberate pacing; it prized the artistic and aesthetic merits of a program, valorized the disciplining effect of making do with finite resources, and celebrated deliberation over speedy results. These archetypes served as shorthand for U.S.–French radio producers, boosters, listeners, and critics assessing one another's interrelated cultural and technical capacities in a new communications environment. They marked a complicated tension that resurfaced in different forms as U.S.–French broadcasting developed over the span of the twentieth century.[7]

Like the electrical telegraph, suboceanic cable, and the telephone, France and the United States developed international radio communications with an eye toward expressing power, expanding influence, and exercising and preserving control.[8] Challenges of modernization, world war, and cultural diplomacy spurred such development further. By the early Cold War, however, the conditions arising in U.S.–French broadcasting marked what many believed was a brazen U.S. intrusion into French and global affairs. The European Recovery Plan (i.e., the Marshall Plan, 1948–51), masked ulterior motives to skeptics. In exchange for foreign aid, France found itself struggling to manage not only its sovereign diplomatic affairs, but also wave upon wave of commercial forms of "Americanization" that threatened French cultural production and identity from food customs to cinema. Members of the French Left complained especially that France's alignment with the United States came at too high a price to national sovereignty and cultural self-determination.[9]

This book studies the users and developers of U.S.–French broadcasting to illuminate the complexity of international broadcasting and reveal its consequences for cultural affairs and geopolitics. It acknowledges the persistent appeal of the "Americanization" versus "remaining French" binary and the critical framework of cultural imperialism in assessing U.S.–French history.[10] These models are only so useful, however, in answering the question of what U.S. broadcasting did for France and what France did for U.S. broadcasting. This book resists the overhasty conclusion that the seeming amalgamation of U.S.–French broadcasting that Simon Copans observed signaled encapsulation of French media culture by U.S. power. Radio's transatlantic production and distribution generated a form of cultural flow in which accommodation as well as resistance could be entertained, and in which appropriation of dominant messages about the United States and France was entirely possible.[11] To be sure, U.S.–French radio exchanges popularized fables and idealized representations of states, cultures, and peoples that could be informative and entertaining, but also prejudiced and misleading. Nonetheless, radio's aesthetic properties supported active listening and interpretation. Without transatlantic interdependencies, French-influenced perspectives would not have found their way to U.S. radio listeners as they did. French listeners would not have learned to listen to the United States in fresh and new capacities.[12]

International broadcasting has suffered marginalized status in media and communications history.[13] It tends to be treated theoretically and institutionally as a modular add-on to broadcasting and studied as a specialized service rather than a dynamic constituent of the character of the broadcast medium.[14] Remedying the isolated condition of international broadcasting is important because of radio's remarkable contributions to everyday life and nation-state formation within and across national borders. Scholars have charted the discursive formation of radio nations, national audiences, and radio publics and counterpublics. They have explored the medium as an aesthetic domain, as well as an embodiment of social and political power that embraced disaggregated populations, but also sometimes excluded groups from the symbolic nations it constituted. International outreach, in-flow, exchange, and cooperative production were processes of broadcasting from its earliest days, but the implications for the formation of national broadcast cultures and radio nations remains understudied by the field. How did historical processes unfolding simultaneously within and across nation-state borders affect how radio and national identity grew up together?[15]

Across the Waves argues that treating international connectivity as central rather than peripheral to the rise of modern broadcasting can shed light on the formation of radio nations, that is, nationally bounded broadcast cultures. Viewing broadcasting both within and outside the nation-state frame makes cross-border phenomena easier to recognize. It becomes possible to model national broadcast systems as something more than rigid political economic structures and artificially bounded cultural systems, but as dynamic elements of regional, international, continental, intercontinental, and global cultural and technological networks. Bringing international broadcasting in from the margins makes it easier to appreciate radio's linkages to antecedent and subsequent instantaneous, cross-border communication technologies associated with the circulation of cultural actors and products, the promotion of cosmopolitanism, new modes of political regulation, new features of geopolitical competition and presence, and the creation of technological infrastructure and use protocols that have connected the planet with and without wires.[16]

This book draws from U.S. and French manuscript and archival collections, primary and secondary documents, newly discovered recordings, and program scripts. It borrows insights from sound studies and science and technology studies to investigate how broadcasting, sound, and listening helped constitute a mass-mediated geopolitics.[17] In addition to thinking about transatlantic broadcasting as a field of interaction, this book takes up the technological development of U.S.–French broadcasting as a "mode of politics" whose development unfolded in conjunction with, but not simply determined by, parallel historical forces.[18] Finally, it considers the mutability of radio as essential to contextualized historical analysis. Technological innovations, such as directional antennae systems, mobile radio trucks, sound-on-disc transcription recordings, wax nets, reel-to-reel magnetic tapes, and bicycle networks transformed the nature of radio and its potential impact.

Part 1 of this book examines the rise of U.S.–French broadcasting through case studies of international shortwave broadcast projects from the mid-1920s to the end of World War II. It follows the successes and setbacks of transatlantic interconnection and the effects of the European political crisis, World War II, and the German Occupation of France on U.S.–French program production and exchange. Part 2 shifts to post-Liberation France, the Marshall Plan era, and the conditions of enterprise and entanglement that characterized changes in U.S.–French broadcasting as a broad manifestation of Cold War geopolitics. It focuses on French broadcasting in the United States, and includes close analysis of English-language radio programs produced in Paris in the late 1940s and 1950s, and their dramatic evolution by the late 1960s and early 1970s.

The history of U.S.–French broadcasting demonstrates how instant communication between continents and across oceans on a mass scale shook up conventional understanding of national borders, spaces, and cultures. The shake-up continues. Alongside contemporary long-distance media and communication tools, radio remains a hardy medium that can be produced and consumed easily and inexpensively. In France, where household penetration of television did not reach 50 percent until the mid-1960s, the passion for radio and sound media persists as it does in the United States.[19] Understanding radio's historical importance to these two allied but starkly different societies can help us more clearly apprehend the roots, structure, and implications of international and global media in the modern world.

PART I

The Rise of U.S.–French Broadcasting, 1925–44

1 At the Speed of Sound

Techno-Aesthetic Paradigms in
U.S.–French Broadcasting, 1925–39

In summer 1924, David Sarnoff, chairman of the Radio Corporation of America (RCA) returned to New York following talks with English, French, and German radio officials. "The era of transoceanic broadcasting is near at hand," he predicted jubilantly. Soon the medium's destiny, "to bring the Old and New worlds a little closer together," would be fulfilled.[1] In the coming years, experimental shortwave broadcasts crisscrossed the Atlantic in growing numbers. In September 1929, U.S. listeners heard reports of the Schneider Cup seaplane races from the British Broadcasting Corporation (BBC). In December, British, German, Dutch, and U.S. broadcasters exchanged holiday wishes in a series of live two-way shortwave exchanges. RCA reported that advances in international radio circuitry had now "brought all the nations of the world within broadcasting distance of one another." In fall 1930, the National Broadcasting Company (NBC), an RCA subsidiary, broadcast news to Paris of the successful transatlantic flight of French aviators Dieudonné Costes and Maurice Bellonte. (Charles Lindbergh's 1927 accomplishment came too soon for transatlantic broadcasts from Paris.) On May 6, 1931, France made its first official broadcast to the United States with the government's new Poste Coloniale (Colonial Station). The opening of the French Colonial Exposition outside Paris offered the perfect showcase for pairing imperial ambition and new world communications.[2] As the station's name indicated, the government planned to use international broadcasting chiefly to influence France's overseas colonies and départements. It also intended to radiate French culture globally, which included broadcasting to the United States. RCA and NBC assisted at both ends in the special programs sent to the United States, which were relayed from New York to a national audience.[3]

Amid the excitement, however, the unknown implications of regularized, instantaneous transatlantic mass communication via radio raised concern. There were many unanswered questions about the nature of this new method of communication and its possible effects on individuals, groups, and the integrity of nation-states and nationally identified cultures. The prospect of international exchanges between private U.S. networks and French national broadcasting (controlled by the government) suggested intriguing opportunities, but it also stirred apprehension in France about managing such encounters. U.S. broadcasting embodied the leading edge of global electronic communication. It readily conjured images of U.S. influence spreading in pervasive, and perhaps inexorable, ways.[4]

This chapter sketches the history of U.S.–French electronic communications prior to broadcasting and then follows the simultaneous national and international emergence of interwar radio broadcasting in the United States and France. Focusing primarily on the French side of the story, it analyzes the anticipatory and reactive discourses to live mass connectivity between the United States and France, as well as reaction to early U.S. transatlantic broadcasts. It examines how French broadcast officials approached the question of U.S.–French broadcast ties and the steps they took to develop international broadcast capability.

The interwar period of U.S.–French broadcast interaction produced two contrasting national techno-aesthetics defining excellence in radio production and the value of radio as an aesthetic form.[5] For U.S. broadcasters, technological power, abundance, and high-speed execution demonstrated professional competence and efficiency. Quantity and swift production and distribution were valued. The French paradigm emphasized quality, accepted scarcity, and valued deliberate speed. Many actors and institutions developing U.S.–French broadcasting shaped these emergent models, including public and private broadcasters, electronics firms, the radio press, politicians, and listeners.[6] More than mere extensions of preexisting differences in U.S. and French conventions (though these clearly exerted important effects), the broadcast paradigms emerged relationally and cross-nationally. They took shape in popular discourse and in professional settings where U.S. and French radio technicians and producers came in contact with each other to undertake transatlantic projects. The misunderstanding and friction these encounters sometimes produced revealed unacknowledged assumptions about the universality of modern communication. In 1930, RCA announced a corporate mission to build an international and global broadcast "community of sound and vision." The envisioned community assumed the terms of technical mastery and expertise of broadcasting to be universal and self-evident rather than outcomes of historical and cultural processes that differentiated U.S. and French broadcasters.[7]

The techno-aesthetic differences of interwar U.S.–French broadcasting were not historically inevitable or without variation and contradiction; they were neither necessarily mutually exclusive nor limited to shortwave broadcasting.[8] Some of their characteristics antedated broadcasting entirely. Pascal Griset observed that executives of nineteenth-century private U.S. telegraph and telecommunications firms sometimes fumed over what they perceived as plodding French governmental processes, which clashed with speedy transactions, rationalized systems, and corporatism in the U.S. style.[9] Such differences in business and regulatory cultures could not alone explain the contrasts affecting radio. Unlike the case of England and Germany, both public *and* private stations operated in France during the interwar years. Most French stations used commercial advertising to a greater or lesser extent for about half of the 1930s. Tastes varied sufficiently at the subnational level in France and the United States, such that these paradigms should not be mistaken for reflections of innate national characteristics or a reductive binary of "modern" versus "antimodern" systems or mentalities. Nonetheless, they emerged as powerful forces that characterized the reflexive nature of U.S.–French radio and the kinds of interaction that resulted.[10]

U.S.–French Electronic Communication before Radio Broadcasting

During the late nineteenth century, the development of submarine telegraphy—undersea cables connecting landmasses—elevated the stakes of communications in service of imperial power and geopolitics. British cable cartels dominated the laying and management of submarine cable lines, which fit into the plans of Great Britain to bind and maintain its imperial territories and peoples. Competitor firms jockeyed with the cartels to develop a French stake in the growing international system of submarine cable, but with limited success. Like many others, France found itself dependent on British firms.[11] Anglo–U.S. interests established the first viable transatlantic system in 1858. A submarine cable between France and the United States was laid in summer 1869, but it, too, operated through a pool arrangement outside direct Franco-American control.[12]

Experiments in wireless telegraphy and wireless telephony at the turn of the century contributed to the rise of a major competitor to cable. In 1901, using a detection device invented by Édouard Branly of France, Italian physicist Guglielmo Marconi executed a one-way transatlantic wireless signal.

Spark-generated signaling technology permitted point-to-point communication through coded pulses of electricity and freed the telegraph from the necessity of a wired connection. Radiotelephony enabled wireless point-to-point transmission of speech and continuous sound. By 1906, Canadian Reginald Aubrey Fessenden had accomplished two-way transatlantic wireless signaling, as well as voice and musical transmission experiments. In 1907, U.S. physicist and research scientist Lee De Forest patented the Audion tube, which became a critical component in detection and amplification of continuous-wave transmission of vocal and musical signals. The elements of radio broadcasting were now in place.[13]

Scientific associations and amateur organizations in France, the United States, and elsewhere played a critical role in developing early radio. French organizations supporting experimental point-to-point wireless communication included the Société française d'études de TSF (the French Society for Wireless Studies), established in 1914, and the Radio-Club de France, established in 1920. Their members communicated among themselves and with international counterparts, including members of the American Radio Relay League (ARRL), established in 1914 in the United States. After World War I, these organizations coordinated transatlantic point-to-point communication involving scores of enthusiasts. An International Amateur Radio Union composed of members from twenty-three nations met in Paris in April 1925. Nine nations subsequently formed the Union Internationale de Radiodiffusion (International Broadcasting Union) to coordinate spectrum allocation for international broadcasting. As Rebecca Scales demonstrates, the IBU policy debates stirred extensive political discussion in France about the ideal national and cosmopolitan parameters of the emerging "radio nation" relative to its neighbors.[14]

These technical innovations, social networks, and political discussions took shape within an atmosphere of feverish competition involving corporate and political interests in Europe and the United States. The Marconi Company, based in Britain, controlled essential patents for wireless communication and developed multinational operations dealing in proprietary radio systems. These operations included a growing U.S. subsidiary, popularly known as American Marconi. British Marconi showed every sign that it would extend England's dominance of international telegraphic communications into wireless communications.[15] As it happened, however, unforeseen international events disrupted the agenda.

Adam Tooze argues that World War I changed France in ways that ultimately tipped the balance of U.S.–French power toward the United States. France entered the war with a large army and as the second leading creditor in Europe. It exited victorious, but with a drained population and an economy in shambles. The Third Republic (1870–1940) struggled to recover in the face of economic setbacks and political division. Short-lived coalitions governed France, led mostly after 1900 by the center-right anticlerical party known as the Radicals. The coalitions suffered from ideological polarization, including right-wing extremism and a political left antagonistic to conservative nationalists and suspicious of America's increasingly powerful status abroad.[16]

The United States, by contrast, entered the war in April 1917 and suffered heavy losses, but not nearly at the catastrophic scale of France and other major combatants. The United States suffered an estimated 323,000 casualties in comparison with France's 6.2 million.[17] U.S. diplomats worked through the Paris Peace Conference and beyond in support of France's postwar recovery. During the 1920s, however, difficulties in managing the payment of Germany's war-debt reparations, France's fiscal and political problems, and stress across Europe created U.S.–French tension and contributed to isolationism in the United States. In France, postwar trauma, frustration over the nation's slow recovery, and apprehension about the future, included an undercurrent of resentment toward the United States, an apparent victor in the war. These circumstances shaped the brittle atmosphere in which international shortwave emerged, and in which U.S. and French radio pioneers came together to build transatlantic broadcast connections.[18]

The war created an opportunity for the United States to check the momentum of Marconi radio communications. The U.S. Navy's wartime emergency annexation of private radio communications in 1917 included the acquisition of numerous Marconi marine radio systems. The government legally transferred ownership of the equipment to General Electric (GE), which created RCA in 1919. By 1922, Owen D. Young, a lawyer and corporate executive for GE and RCA, had devised a radio patent pool that included RCA, GE, American Telephone and Telegraph, and Westinghouse. The deal permitted the wholesale U.S. manufacture of radio equipment under ideal conditions for business that catapulted U.S. radio and broadcast communications manufacturing and technology to the forefront of the international scene. RCA expanded internationally and made deals with la Compagnie Générale de Télégraphie sans Fil (General Wireless Company), a holding firm with a controlling stake in France's wireless telegraphy market.[19]

The French government pursued ties with RCA and other U.S. radio firms partly to build ties with an ally, but also to ease French dependence on British-controlled intercontinental cable lines. Relying exclusively on British lines could be costly in monetary, but also strategic, terms, as Germany discovered when England severed the Kaiser's cable links into and out of Europe at the start of World War I.[20] For such diplomatic and security reasons, France remained motivated in cooperatively advancing the state of transatlantic broadcast connectivity with the United States.[21]

U.S. networks saw ample reasons to invest in long-distance transmission and reception technology, despite the fact that international communications law prohibited the use of shortwave for direct advertising or other commercial purposes. Broadcasters desired goodwill with foreign governments, which controlled the telecommunications infrastructure essential to making two-way international broadcasting possible. Building up shortwave exchange and partnership projects garnered the networks publicity and prestige. Listeners in the United States and abroad were intrigued at the thought of hearing (even if imperfectly) a European concert performance live from Salzburg, Berlin, Paris, or New York. The prospect of rapid intercontinental news broadcasts by correspondents in the field also interested the networks. Should such programs and exchanges with international partners prove popular with U.S. listeners, commercial broadcasters would reap rewards from domestic advertisers. Finally, by underwriting the expense of transatlantic broadcasts and exchanges, networks demonstrated to federal regulators that they were fulfilling the "public interest" requirement for licensing renewals by expanding broadcasting beyond the United States.[22]

The Rise of National Broadcasting in the United States and France

Radio broadcasting exploded across the United States after World War I, and licensed broadcasters numbered some 550 by 1922. Station operators included well-capitalized electronics firms and private entities developing the medium for promotional and commercial reasons; low-power metropolitan and region stations operating nonprofit educational, religious, and community services; wealthy eccentrics, who enjoyed the exposure; and many others. Soaring demand for airtime and spectrum scarcity compelled the U.S. Congress to create the bipartisan Federal Radio Commission in 1927 and then the Federal Communications Commission in 1934 to regulate the airwaves. Under the new regime, the so-called American system of advertiser-supported broadcasting dominated by corporate communications giants achieved supremacy by the mid-1930s.[23]

After World War I, the French military transferred development and oversight of national broadcasting to France's Ministry of Posts, Telegraphs, and Telephones (PTT). In 1921, the PTT's Eiffel Tower station became France's first permanent civilian broadcaster. In 1923, a sibling station, Paris-PTT, joined the Eiffel Tower. Together they furnished news, weather, market reports, and occasional concerts. The PTT added relay stations and transmitters in Rennes, Toulouse, and Bordeaux. These affiliates also produced local programs. In the 1920s, the PTT national newscasts garnered regular listeners, but cultural programs from Paris failed to win widespread enthusiasm, most likely because of their literary and cultural pretensions, which emphasized themes of cultivation and uplift over excitement and diversion.[24]

André-Jean Tudesq observed that what was most political about interwar French radio was not what listeners heard over the air so much as the rancorous process to agree on the form of the national broadcast system. Gabrielle Hecht proposes the term *techno-politics* to describe "the strategic practice of designing or using technology to constitute, embody, or enact political goals."[25] During the 1920s, with broadcasting roaring to life in the United States, England, and Germany, France struggled to forge techno-political consensus. The PTT operated French telegraph and telephone networks as public monopolies, but control of broadcasting was an unsettled issue. Coalition governments formed, dissolved, and reformed with dizzying rapidity, and the government could not decide on a model for the nation to pursue, which left one analyst to lament in 1925, "Must each change in the composition of the French political cabinet lead to a sweeping change in radio policy?"[26]

Despite the PTT's apparent control of broadcasting, several enterprises had obtained governmental permission to broadcast commercially. The electronics firm Radiola and the international news and advertising agency Havas launched a station in 1922, which operated as Radio Paris from 1924 to 1932 before it was annexed by the PTT. The Poste-Parisien, owned by *Le Petit Parisien*, a daily newspaper, began operations in 1923.[27] A handful of unauthorized parties jumped into broadcasting, too, in Lyon, Toulouse, Bordeaux, and several other cities. The public seemed to welcome these independent stations because they furnished music, news, and entertainment programs of a popular character not found on PTT stations.[28] Private interests and the French government invested in the independent, commercial foreign station Radio Luxembourg, which served as a peripheral broadcaster (périphérique) transmitting popular content over the border into France. In 1928, the government froze further private station expansion and legally recognized the thirteen independent stations in operation. The PTT now held full responsibility for growing French national broadcasting.[29] A public network model had been chosen, but funding its growth remained a chronic problem, which had direct implications for what would be possible for U.S.–French interaction.[30]

Steps toward Transatlantic Broadcast Connectivity

In 1920, a wireless station erected by the U.S. Navy in Bordeaux (later, the PTT station Bordeaux-Lafayette) began transmitting signals to North America.

RCA established its first permanent radio circuit to France that year and co-operated with British Marconi in experimental transatlantic vocal broadcasts. "Each country should—and in my judgment, ultimately will—be equipped with a high-power radio station, capable of international communication," declared RCA chairman David Sarnoff. He lobbied European nations to invest in shortwave transmission equipment to support long-distance international broadcast exchanges, "so that the programs of London, Paris, and Berlin might be easily heard by the American listening public." Sarnoff described international broadcast development as an almost inexorable force that "will come about for national reasons if not for purely commercial reasons."[31] How private broadcasters and foreign governments should work together to realize Sarnoff's vision remained to be determined.

Shortwave radio signals traveled immensely farther than medium- and long-wave amplitude modulation (AM) signals. Shortwave signals traveled via "sky waves" rather than following the contour of the Earth. Beamed upward rather than outward, and at calibrated angles, shortwave signals "bounced" (sometimes more than once) between the Earth's ionosphere and the ground. Traveling at high frequency, shortwave signals could reach a reception area thousands of miles from the transmission point. Terrestrial signals, even powerful ones, lost energy to terrain and distance traveled. Shortwave broadcasting faced a host of technical issues, however. Atmospheric conditions, solar activity cycles, and times of day had to be aligned for a broadcast to succeed perfectly. Shortwave transmitters were most effective when linked to multidirectional adjustable antennae systems and to transmitters capable of fine-tuning of frequencies to compensate for atmospheric fluctuations. Live shortwave broadcasts typically reached listeners in two ways. They could be heard directly using an all-wave radio set or picked up on a conventional radio if a terrestrial AM transmitter relayed the shortwave signal. In the United States, the networks operated facilities using shortwave transmitters and receivers, radio circuits, and dedicated AT&T phone lines to circulate signals from all over the world to international listeners and to local affiliates.[32]

Power Matters: Techno-Aesthetic Difference and Critique

By the mid-1920s, with news of experimental shortwave broadcasts implying an instantaneous and mass-connected future for France and the United States, French observers began to reflect on France's status in a new era. In April 1926, Michel Walter, of the French Chamber of Deputies, noted that

Germany had twenty domestic stations of one kilowatt or more and Great Britain had eighteen; France, by contrast, had all of three. "Why this inferior position?" he demanded. The disparity was even greater when comparing the roughly two dozen radio stations in France with the many hundreds of U.S. stations, which on average transmitted at higher rates of power than French stations.[33]

Le Petit Radio (LPR), France's weekly guide to public broadcasting, lamented the significant technology gap between the two countries. The relative quantity of stations, cumulative daily and weekly program hours, and effective radiated power (a rough measure of how far a station's signal traveled) revealed a consistent French disadvantage. Manifestations of the U.S. technological abundance took visual form, too, such as a photograph that LPR described of U.S. president Herbert Hoover speaking before a bank of eleven (!) microphones, which could only be taken to mean that the United States had "passed us in their radio productions."[34]

To offset such quantifiable indicators of France's alleged "inferior position" required turning the measures of technical accomplishment upside down and inside out. Ambivalence toward modern trends in France often translated into harsh criticism of the United States as a technologically dependent and culturally underdeveloped nation.[35] French critics developed an alternative interpretation of the radio data showing a U.S. technological edge. True, they argued, the U.S. broadcast system bristled with hundreds of high-wattage stations, but its announcers and programs rarely had something of significance to communicate. When U.S. broadcasters reportedly lowered a waterproof microphone into the foamy tumult at the base of Niagara Falls, LPR hooted with derision. The thrill of this stunt broadcast—primitive, cacophonous, and with no particular purpose other than to seize attention—needed little explanation for LPR readers, who expected greater things from French radio. "This feat surely amuses Uncle Sam," sniffed one commentator, "but as far as we are concerned, it's certain that we prefer more interesting broadcasts."[36]

The image of U.S.-style radio as a cudgel wielded by clumsy, unsophisticated people offered French nationalists an irresistible stereotype of a U.S. public in thrall to industrial technology and cheap thrills.[37] The French techno-aesthetic of quality, scarcity, and deliberate speed turned the seeming "inferior position" on its head. It represented the hidden virtue of finite resources, which imposed discipline onto French radio and stimulated ingenuity, efficiency, and artistry. Laments about inadequate funding for the PTT or governmental restrictions of private enterprise could be divisive, whereas this critique of U.S. techno-power and abundance offered a redemptive and unifying counterexample. What the counteraesthetic might lack in subtlety, it made up for in moral currency as it recharacterized scarcity as the precondition for the virtuous pursuit of quality productions.[38]

Abundance and choice sold the U.S. public on commercial broadcasting, but to skeptics in France (and elsewhere), the market model exacted costs of its own at the level of quality and craft. During the 1920s, on hundreds of U.S. stations, a good portion of musical programming came directly from the stages of commercial halls and auditoriums. When radio producer and engineer Hans Bodenstedt visited the United States on behalf of German public broadcasting, LPR published excerpts from his field notes. Bodenstedt praised the quantity of U.S. programming and the power of networks to consolidate listeners into large audiences for fine music. He felt dissatisfied, however, with the variable quality of U.S. broadcasts, which he felt frequently suffered from acoustical irregularities and slipshod production methods that failed to guarantee a high artistic standard.[39]

Bodenstedt voiced concern about the shift to studios for concert performances in response to the problems that rapid growth, proliferation of U.S. stations, and thousands of program hours to fill appeared to be creating for U.S. broadcasters by the late 1920s. Concert performers accustomed to unamplified theater stages and music hall settings sometimes had trouble, in Bodenstedt's words, "adjusting to the studio." The aesthetic implications of the artist compelled to adapt to technological dictates and potentially alter or compromise the performance mirrored concerns over the commodification of music and broadcasting in the United States. The sovereignty of the artist over technologies of commerce became a problem, Bodenstedt believed, when schedules and program slots required the use of low-quality venues for radio music, which pressured singers and instrumentalists to play and perform differently than in the well-tempered acoustical concert palaces of Europe.[40]

Bodenstedt portrayed U.S. technological abundance as a symptom of a culture overly reliant upon compensatory technology to "correct" the inherent acoustic flaws of the typical music hall, which he found inferior to those in Europe. He criticized U.S. radio's compensatory use of low-sensitivity microphones to capture the voices and instruments of performers, which, he argued, failed to deliver pleasing results to the radio listener's ear. Despite the impressive abundance of programs, commercial halls, and listeners that characterized the U.S. broadcast techno-aesthetic, lax standards and indifferent production produced a mediocre product. By contrast, the limited number of European concert halls designated for broadcast on a limited number of public channels, and the cultivated forms of music performed in them—namely, symphonic and choral music—imposed and reinforced a craft aesthetic that valued quality and prudent management of scarcity.[41]

La réception européenne devient de plus en plus difficile à cause de la puissance et du nombre sans cesse croissant des nouveaux émetteurs. Le RADIOLA 545, grâce à son montage Super - Inductance à 4 circuits vous servira "à la carte" le programme

CHOISI

RADIO-PARIS
PRAGUE
DAVENTRY
LANGENBERG
MILAN
Radiola

SERVI

désiré avec une qualité et une facilité merveilleuses. 5 modèles RADIOLA Super-Inductance à partir de 1.375 francs. Les postes RADIOLA sont garantis un an. Demandez une démonstration gracieuse à votre domicile.

Radiola

le compagnon de
tous les instants

125

This popular 1934 radio receiver allowed French listeners to choose among a variety of international services. (Courtesy *Bibliothèque Nationale de France*)

The Temple of Radio City

The December 1932 gala opening of Radio City Music Hall—the crown jewel of RCA's Radio City complex—and the opening of the NBC studios in Radio City the following year celebrated commercial entertainment in the United States and the U.S. broadcast techno-aesthetic. Radio City garnered attention in the French radio press. The five-story CBS broadcasting center might charitably be termed "a radio skyscraper," and Westinghouse's KDKA signal from Pittsburgh be dubbed "stronger than Marius," but French commentators agreed that no foreign competitor rivaled Radio City.[42] The BBC studios "were nothing, or almost nothing, next to the still more modern palace that is NBC," commented journalist Michel Ferry. "Everything is grander, more vast, more luxurious, more carefully designed."[43] Tourists were reportedly flocking to Radio City at a greater rate than to the Statue of Liberty or the Empire State Building. "The [RCA Building] is 240 meters tall," Ferry marveled; "it has 5,804 windows. NBC alone occupies an area of more than 100,000 square meters, and there are 74 elevators." For all its soaring majesty, however, the

RCA Building was only "*almost* as tall as the Eiffel Tower."[44] In the celebratory spirit of future long-distance radio connections between NBC and France, NBC producer Fred Bate used the network move-in to present a transatlantic broadcast, "France Greets Radio City," which featured testimonials and music beamed live via shortwave from Paris to New York.[45]

Not everyone found Radio City so impressive and intoxicating. To French skeptics of U.S. culture industries, gigantism and technological abundance were obnoxious. They gave the impression that what David Nye called the technological sublime had mesmerized the U.S. public to the exclusion of all else. RCA compared its facilities to a beehive rather than a temple, but some disagreed. New York–based French journalist Raoul Roussy de Sales was among the foreign observers questioning the U.S. faith in technology and commercial mass communications. A colleague of his observed, "In building your Radio Cities, your Boulder and Grand Coulee dams [Americans] seem to be making a dedication as did those ancient builders to a divinity."[46] Another called out the ideological work of U.S. popular media abroad. "The slum districts of an American city are no cleaner than those in China," he noted, "only I never remember seeing a picture of the Bowery; all the photographs we had of America being those of Radio City and other beautiful places."[47] The critic implied that the architects of the mediated sights and sounds of the United States ought to circulate representations of both the limitations and the accomplishments of the United States abroad. To such detractors, RCA's pledge of fostering an international "community of sound" contained self-aggrandizing and imperial overtones.[48]

In Europe, the mounting use of international broadcasting by political propagandists in Germany and Soviet Russia suggested that technological power and abundance hardly guaranteed a harmonious future. They could just as easily drive nationalist provocations and antidemocratic agendas.[49] As French socialist Paul Campargue observed of competition in international broadcasting, the total of "kilowatts has become part of national prestige. . . . What's more, the race for [broadcast] power, like the race for arms, is little but a mirage and a sophism. . . . [T]he same old and traditional politics of prestige are, in Europe today, more alive than ever!"[50] From New York, Roussy de Sales reluctantly agreed: "the disrupting force of nationalism such as we know it today is so great that modern facilities of communication and the shortening of distances, instead of checking it, seem rather to give it more virulence and more reality."[51] Under such circumstances, transatlantic broadcast expansion could not be treated casually or regarded as synonymous with freedom's advance and wireless communitarianism.[52]

There were even signs in France of fatigue over commercial radio hype and political posturing over the international airwaves. In a 1934 cartoon, published in *Le Petit Parisien*, two passersby stand outside an electronics shop listening to a blaring sidewalk radio. An advertising placard next to the radio reads "Come Hear: Mussolini, Pilsudski, Hitler, Stalin, etc." One listener declares, "What a racket!" to which a clerk standing in the doorway brightly replies, "Madame, it's all of Europe on the loudspeaker!" Mocking the supposed power of radio to foster international and intercultural understanding and alluding to the fractious politics of the period, the cartoon spoofed fast, noisy, high-wattage hucksters and pitchmen, be they selling radio sets or instant political solution sets such as communist and fascist ideology.[53]

It was Georges Duhamel, however, who presaged key objections to the emerging U.S. broadcast aesthetic. In the acerbic 1930 bestseller *America the Menace: Scenes from the Life of the Future* (*Scènes de la vie future*), Duhamel savaged the United States for its allegedly voracious appetite for material goods and indolent pleasures, ranging from Hollywood cinema to commercial radio listening. The U.S. population, he wrote,

> yearn desperately for phonographs, radios, illustrated magazines, "movies," elevators, electric refrigerators, and automobiles, automobiles, and once again automobiles. They want to own at the earliest possible moment all the articles mentioned, which are so wonderfully convenient, and of which, by an odd reversal of things, they immediately become the anxious slaves. . . . There are on our continent, in France as well as elsewhere, large regions that the spirit of old Europe has deserted. The American spirit colonizes little by little such a province, such a city, such a house, and such a soul."[54]

Radio City had not been erected when Duhamel visited the United States, but his exposure to U.S. radio and popular music convinced him that broadcasting was among the most objectionable embodiments of the imperial "American spirit." Duhamel perceived cultural outflow from the United States, such as international broadcast boosters proposed, to threaten refined Old Europe. His elitism qualified him perfectly for the cultural gatekeeping that defined French public radio culture. Indeed, Duhamel became an advisor to the PTT. Although a political conservative, Duhamel's critique of U.S. culture also resonated with voices on the French Left, who regarded commercialized amusements as eroding authentic workers' culture and weakening socialist expression.[55]

Gathering Speed in France

Technology, modernity, and speed (taken to refer broadly to rapidity of events, sequences, or moving objects) form a familiar trinity in analyses of modernism and modernity.[56] Historians of premodern Europe, France, and

North America have shown how perceptions of speed are closely tied to natural and human-built cycles, which could be affected by environmental conditions, including the introduction of new technologies and labor systems.[57] Such relationships varied across regions, social settings, and cultures, however, even when correlated with technological advance.[58] Thinking about reactions to the advent of transatlantic broadcasting as a problem of relative speed relates to the critical concept of time-space compression most often associated with accelerated technologized mobility, instantaneous electronic communications, global processes, and digital fields of living and being.[59]

Noting the contrasting techno-aesthetics of speed in U.S.–French broadcasting, it is important to stress that despite what some U.S. critics of French radio alleged, appreciation of speedy execution was abundant in France. Auto racing, cycling, and skiing were among the nation's sanctioned speed cultures, which celebrated skill, strength, efficiency, and daring. In the sensitive interwar climate of U.S.–French broadcast encounters, however, U.S.-style speed registered as hasty, reckless, disrespectful, and even mildly threatening. U.S. speed as a national characteristic disturbed traditional French cultural mores. U.S. speed in broadcast communication reflected a culture's apparent impatience to acquire ever more goods, experiences, and sensations that clashed with the disposition of the stewards of French public broadcasting and the guild of technicians and producers responsible for French programs (see chapter 2).[60]

The PTT fastidiously transposed the conventions and tastes of France's cultural elite to the interwar public airwaves. It broadcast cultivated music, talks, and dramas drawn most frequently from a classical literary canon. The PTT also supplied educational programming. The aesthetic accepted scarcity as a hallmark of selectivity and cultivation. Gravitas and restrained pacing contrasted with the hurly-burly of French private broadcasting (and commercial culture generally), where market conditions created turbulence, risk, and error.

France's independent commercial stations embraced the popular, lively styles of programs that the PTT rejected. It is risky, however, to overdraw the distinctions between French public and private stations, especially prior to 1935.[61] Just as turning the radio dial in the United States revealed motor-mouthed announcers and hot jazz one moment, and lugubrious roundtables and extra-inning baseball games the next, French airwaves carried domestic and international programs of various speed registers, with a range of valuations inhering to them.[62] A symphonic music festival might be as fast-paced and thrilling to a PTT listener as a jazz orchestra's improvisations were to a listener of the private station Radio Paris. French politicians made dramatic national addresses using the PTT network. Likewise, heavy courses of advertising on independent stations could stupefy audiences as well. In a 1932 newspaper cartoon, a middle-aged male radio listener, slumping in his armchair before the radio set, calls to his partner seated next to him, "Aglaë, you wake me when the advertisements are over," only to discover ("Say!") that she's already succumbed to their narcotic effects.[63]

"The Speed with Which the Program Unfolds": The Techno-Aesthetics of Difference

U.S. network broadcasts to France and elsewhere did more than bring programming in English (and other languages) to a wider international audience. They exposed listeners to a U.S. broadcast techno-aesthetic circulating beyond the nation-state. These signature traits of difference complemented, but were independent from, the verbal or written information a listener might obtain about where a program originated (e.g., New York, Chicago) or what it would contain (music, drama, news). These "extra" elements concerned the techno-aesthetics of radio production. Transatlantic shortwave broadcasts began to expose French and European audiences to the particular technical production grammar and rhythm of U.S. radio. Whether consciously or not, listeners to international radio experienced the "foreignness" of the transmission in part through the cues that marked the assembly points of the presentation, such as the scripted recurring introductions and exits of a program, switches between studios and remote locations, and transitions from one scheduled program to the next. Timed pauses, test tones, spoken phrases, station identifications, and musical themes were examples of elements that imparted a flavor to the program and the experience of listening to it. These technical elements served a practical function to engineers, performers, and announcers, and they were passed forward to listeners, too, who through them were growing habituated to what was happening, how to react accordingly, and what to anticipate next.

Some French and European listeners encountering transatlantic programs from the United States noticed a telltale difference that bound these many elements together: an unfamiliar rate of speed that signaled the likelihood that the program was a U.S. broadcast. Speed differences underscored previously unrecognized norms of time's passage and the local or national cultural conventions of radio speaking and listening. The novelty of transatlantic broadcasts probably explains some of the attention paid to seemingly minor technical differences. For listeners trying to extract maximum cultural information from these programs, even subtle variations mattered. Speed constituted one of the messages of the medium for those curious about the implications of U.S. technological and cultural expansion and how it might affect the way that national, regional, and cultural boundaries, differences, and personal predispositions were perceived.[64]

Le Petit Radio reported that listeners in Switzerland hearing their first shortwave programs from the United States were struck that the announcer's intro and outro were butted up unusually tightly against the classical musical performance. "Imagine for an instant that a program from one of our national stations unfolded at this express speed for an entire evening," remarked LPR, "What a scramble it would make of our poor European brains!" The comment poked fun at U.S. announcers and their (mis)handling of classical material; more broadly, however, it identified the perceptual shock that listening to transatlantic shortwave radio could deliver along with the scheduled program. Commenting on "the speed with which the program unfolds" was a message in and of itself, which added a layer of significance to how the program was interpreted by non-U.S. listeners.[65]

Interwar international broadcasting tested the stability of what Emily Thompson identifies as a hegemonic and Western "soundscape of modernity" marked by efforts at total control of sound and engineered signal in the manner of Radio City and the network broadcast techno-aesthetic. The French approach suggested the existence of alternative soundscapes of what Herrick Chapman has called "modernities," associated in this case with practices of radio production. The possibility that U.S.-led transatlantic shortwave might substitute (or even impose) an alien or imperial techno-aesthetic atop European or French conventions under Duhamel's "American menace" scenario reveals how processes of international communication and exchange right down to the perceptual decoding of technical details could stir national competitiveness and status anxiety and vice versa.[66]

Acceleration and Modernization of the French Airwaves, 1935–39

During the 1930s, French devotees of power, abundance, and speed began making their mark on France's independent airwaves. Peppy announcers, fast-paced comedy-drama-variety programs, and the presence of other crowd-pleasing diversions catalyzed the medium's breakout from the bourgeois parlor into hundreds of thousands of ordinary homes, cafés, and public spaces throughout France.[67] One enthusiastic appropriator of U.S. radio style was Marcel Bleustein-Blanchet, founder of the advertising firm Publicis. In 1935, he acquired private station Radio L-L in Paris, and in homage to the

Manhattan original, renamed it Radio-Cité.[68] The station added U.S.-style quiz and talent programs, popularized "the mike in the street"—a stark contrast to the staid talk on the PTT—and sent mobile recording trucks careering around Paris, seeking news or just creating it on the spot. By the late 1930s, French national broadcasting served a spectrum of listener tastes, from PTT cultural conservatives to consumers of a French variant of U.S. commercial broadcast techno-aesthetics.[69]

In 1934, an ambitious reformer shook up French public broadcasting. PTT chief Georges Mandel was a political conservative from a prominent Jewish family. He had served as an aide to former prime minister Georges Clemenceau, and also as a deputy to the National Assembly.[70] He centralized administration, abolished commercial advertising on public stations, and created a new revenue stream by requiring annual radio set license fees.[71] As PTT coffers filled, Mandel doubled the daily hours of national programming to sixteen. He introduced a national news roundup from Paris that pleased the public because, as one listener put it, the show "quoted the Monarchists as well as the Communists."[72] In fall 1935, France announced a planned shortwave center to consist of four high-power transmitters with directional antennae affording "colonial and global" transmission and reception capability. A serious impediment to France's participation in the burgeoning field of international shortwave to this point lay in the fact that while the Poste Coloniale could *transmit* to the colonies, the United States, and elsewhere, the antiquated site lacked adequate capacities to *receive* shortwave programs and relay them to other PTT stations.[73]

Setbacks delayed construction of the center, however, and Mandel did not remain in power long enough to see his plan bear fruit. In 1936, after years of center-right and conservative governments, the Popular Front (PF), a Socialist-Left, antifascist coalition led by Léon Blum, took office. "From here on," promised Robert Jardillier, the new PTT chief, public broadcasting would strive "to be an exact and true mirror of all of the forms of French life" and "the image of living France."[74] Vowing to dismantle entrenched elitism at the PTT and invigorate French national broadcasting, Jardillier fired hundreds of PTT employees and embarked on a campaign that promised new, social-realist cultural programs.[75]

Jardillier dusted off the popular critique of U.S. broadcasting and its techno-aesthetics to fire enthusiasm for his reform agenda. He linked the development of public broadcast infrastructure to the future of French art and culture. "It's not necessary, to tell you the truth," Jardillier told his colleagues, "to proclaim that the defense of quality will be the first of [the revamped PTT's] preoccupations: how could it be otherwise? *Are we not, and do we not wish to remain the country of quality?*" The allusion to countries of inferior quality threatening France seemed directed toward the United States. The nationalist appeal appeared designed to resonate across France's political landscape. "Between technical operations and artistic expression," Jardillier continued, "there can be no solution, except through continuity. It is not the least of radio's merits that it *establishes a connection between the artist and the technician,* and it does so under condition in which one cannot proceed without the other. And the two cultures are so much associated that the same man must more and more master both."[76] Jardillier proposed a PF variation of the techno-aesthetic of quality, scarcity, and deliberate speed that synthesized socialist art and modern technique in service of a unified society. The vitality of French radio and its techno-aesthetic depended on a sensibility that could unite urban-industrial and rural-agricultural sectors and overcome political divides. Its core characteristic would remain artisanal quality and valued tradition applied to the new artistic medium of radio broadcasting.

When it came to the resulting programs, however, the PTT's efforts to synthesize Socialist-Left political ideals, modern broadcast techniques, and artisanal aesthetics did not succeed. As Joelle Neulander and Cécile Méadel have argued, the ideological messaging weighed down the content and ultimately failed to excite listeners or lure them away from private stations in significant numbers. The PF's brief reign could not substantively alter a PTT techno-aesthetic of quality narrowly understood to mean a cultivated, classical orientation toward music and literary style; scarcity, another hallmark of the "selective" process of classical culture formation; and restrained pacing, which is to say, a preference for nuance, reflection, and exegesis. The outcome confirmed the contention of Jacques Attali and Yves Stourdze that "Communication, as understood by the French centralized state, was primarily a *lecture* which the State with professorial wisdom delivered to society."[77] For the greater part of listeners, the bubbly, fast-paced, and flexible attitude of independent French radio instilled greater passion.[78]

In June 1937, Léon Blum resigned, and the PF yielded to a series of right-center political coalitions. With heightened concern about a war in Europe, officials viewed the shortwave center more as a military installation than a beacon of enlightened internationalism. Services to the United States and elsewhere continued, but the focus lay closer to home. Marcel Pellenc, the PTT inspector general, explained the challenge facing France's international broadcast policy. "In times of peace," he began, the Poste Coloniale "is a station to deliver culture across continents and French expression in all of its aspects. Furthermore, it is a station which in the event of danger or European conflagration will constitute in some sense the sole means of connection

French public and private broadcast stations, ca. 1939. (Map courtesy of Justin Jocque)

between France and the other countries of the world—and so the only means of *enlightening world opinion*."[79] The late 1930s were hardly "times of peace," however, and faced with a need to counter aggressive propaganda attacks, the French government of Édouard Daladier established an information service in 1938, and the following year took control of radio from the PTT. The Poste Coloniale became Paris Mondial as France prepared its defenses for war.[80]

"Accustomed to Thinking in Terms of Quality"

In the United States, the discovery of techno-aesthetic differences in French and U.S. ideals of radio broadcasting generated notice among industry observers, particularly as they appeared to apply to French preferences for news and information programs. French criticism of U.S.-style broadcasting and its commercial artifices could be unsparing, but evidence suggested that the French techno-aesthetic of quality did not preclude heavy production and packaging of news. The insight would become extremely important to the future of U.S.–French broadcasting, though no one yet knew how important until World War II began.

During the interwar period, Fernand Auberjonois, a well-traveled Swiss journalist, worked for the French news agency Havas and as a French-language announcer for NBC's International Division in New York. During World War II, he became an intelligence analyst and operative for the U.S. Office of War Information (OWI; see chapter 3). While at NBC, Auberjonois studied the dynamics of French and U.S. broadcasting in hopes of bridging the techno-aesthetic divide. He discovered that polls made by "the big French (commercial) stations" in the late 1930s, revealed that when it came to news and information, French listeners preferred detailed, packaged news shows rather more than vivid, up-to-the-moment, news specials and "round-ups" that became the signature of U.S. commercial broadcasting in that period. As Auberjonois explained,

> The French public is used to, and likes, special events programs, built in a studio, with the help of actual sound effect recordings and with a running commentary by the announcer.... This is what the French call radio-reportage.... *A program that is free from artifice doesn't please the French half as much as the composite show does.* The audience is accustomed now to this formula and likes to listen to the description of a special event condensed into a half-hour program rather than follow it for several hours while it is in progress.[81]

Auberjonois discerned a relationship connecting resource scarcity, news production methods, and the techno-aesthetic trait of deliberate speed and quality sensitivity, which produced the style of "radio reportage" apparently favored by French audiences. Some years later, a training manual for OWI field broadcasters moving with the Allied troops into Occupied France explained the importance of techno-aesthetic differences and national listening habits: "There has been a tendency [in the United States] to judge and criticize French broadcasting," it read,

> owing to France's relatively underdeveloped technological infrastructure compared to peer European nations and the U.S. The French, mainly because they have to make the best of their limited facilities, did a great deal of experimental work on scripts, sound, and production. As a result of their constant quest for

new ideas, the audience grew accustomed to thinking in terms of quality rather than quantity and stunts.[82]

By this interpretation, material scarcity and deliberate pacing had nourished French creativity in broadcasting and allowed producers to succeed despite material and technical limitations. It is not clear that the "constant quest for new ideas" and ways of "thinking in terms of quality" emerged exclusively from the challenges of producing radio, but they certainly shaped the interwar approach to broadcasting in France that set it apart from, but also in relation to, the international expansion of U.S. radio networks with their own preferred methods and techniques.

The contrasting paradigms of U.S.–French interwar broadcasting emerged out of discourses and practices linked to the interrelated rise of national and international broadcasting. RCA's corporate prediction of a frictionless consolidation of an "international community of sound" through modern technological means collided with different political and cultural perspectives on the meaning of modernity and the place of broadcasting in domestic and international affairs. Differences in U.S. and French production practices and genre forms, and the embrace in certain cases of U.S.-style radio by independent French broadcasters, showed that even with increasing technological standardization, at least, in radio broadcasting, cultures of national and subnational difference remained not only possible but likely as the interface point of international broadcasting made different expectations and practices impossible to ignore.

At points during the interwar period, the techno-aesthetic contrasts of U.S.–French broadcast development conjured the figure of the artisan, an iconic figure in French social history and cultural memory. In a classic study of French nationalism, Eugen Weber noted the "highly ambiguous" status of the rural artisan of late-nineteenth- and early-twentieth-century France. "His presence helped keep his community apart from the national traffic. But it also helped clarify—that is, teach the community—how it was linked to the nation, slowly developing the formulas of political, that is adversary, relationships." Weber conceptualized the artisan as a regional cultural manager and temporal mediator of the "new" manifested in economic and technical production methods, forces, and widening circulations, which included contending with the problem of national, and now international, "traffic." The interwar French broadcast techno-aesthetic with the radio-artisan as its avatar emerged within what Weber might have termed the "highly ambiguous" circumstances of early U.S.–French transatlantic broadcast encounters. The French techno-aesthetic marked an alternative route to international broadcast engagement that skirted isolation at one extreme and technical and cultural homogenization at the other. Techno-aesthetic production marked a struggle for position within the evolving field of international broadcasting in which alliances, as well as "adversarial relationships," often closely resembled one another.[83]

The next chapter follows the U.S. radio network managers who moved across France and Europe after World War I to develop a transatlantic broadcast infrastructure. The labors of U.S., French, and European broadcasters transpired against a climate of political crisis, which contributed to the inherent challenges of establishing reliable modes of transatlantic broadcast connectivity. The chapter traces the formation of the transatlantic working relationships necessary to support international radio's expansion, the programs that resulted, and the challenges of managing the different interests and motives shaping the U.S.–French radio partnership.

2 We Won't Always Have Paris

U.S. Networks in France and Europe, 1932–41

In 1932, NBC and CBS defied the uncertainties of the Great Depression by stationing full-time managers overseas to produce international broadcasts for U.S. audiences. Working from Paris and London, NBC's Fred Bate spent the following decade developing international broadcasting into a viable enterprise. Along with counterparts at CBS and elsewhere, Bate and his colleagues struggled to establish network operations on foreign soil, report news in Europe's delicate political climate, and contend with the administrative uncertainties of the interwar PTT. Over time, these efforts made it possible to deliver broadcast news from Europe to millions of radio listeners across the United States.[1]

The work of Bate and the pioneers who built the foundations of transatlantic international broadcasting often gets overshadowed by accounts dedicated to radio's celebrated role during the European crises of 1938, such as the German-Austrian *Anschluss* and the Munich Agreement that ceded the Sudetenland of Czechoslovakia to Adolf Hitler's Germany. Attention often focuses on the international news roundup, which became a signature of network news reports at CBS and NBC in the late 1930s. The roundups pieced together live reports in rapid succession from announcers in various European cities. Roundups personified the trinity of technological power, abundance, and speed for which U.S. broadcasting prided itself. Flowing across the Atlantic via shortwave, the networks relayed the reports to a national audience that discovered radio as the best source for up-to-the-minute international reportage.[2]

Celebrating the roundup as a landmark invention of U.S. broadcasting can have the unintended consequence of reinforcing a nation-centered way of thinking about media history that obscures the cross-national web of inter-connection upon which the news roundup and programs like it depended. For CBS and NBC to perform their wizardry required creativity and innovation but also partnership and struggle to harmonize European and U.S. radio techniques and methods. The stunning reports out of Munich in 1938 and the captivating stories from the 1940 Battle of Britain were more than "effects" of newsworthy events. Breaking stories could become radio news thanks to the unsung efforts of Bate and the European managers, whose efforts, setbacks, and successes had implications for what could (and sometimes could not) become broadcast news in the early phases of transatlantic broadcasting.

This chapter follows the career of Fred Bate and his colleagues abroad, particularly their projects that involved France. The chapter highlights the ways in which techno-aesthetic differences affected transatlantic news reporting. I argue that it would have been impossible for international broadcasting to expand as rapidly as it did in the late 1930s without years of painstaking effort by an interwar generation of U.S. radio producers and correspondents in France and other places, shaping, sometimes painfully, the art of the possible in foreign news broadcasting.

The BBC provided the most reliable means of routing transatlantic radio communications to the United States. U.S. broadcasters also depended on cordial relations with the governments of Europe that controlled broadcast communications abroad. They relied on technical assistance in foreign studios and in the field to produce and transmit reports. Shortwave transmissions originated from all corners of Europe, including France, and the location of events often influenced whose national equipment would be used. In the domain of breaking news, public broadcasters such as the PTT controlled the ebb and flow of news and information on behalf of the French government. The restraint and deliberate pacing would prove a frequent source of frustration for U.S. radio reporters.[3]

To manage its European broadcasts, CBS hired César Saerchinger, a German-born naturalized U.S. citizen, print journalist, and radio stringer. NBC, however, selected two quite different representatives. Max Jordan was raised and educated in Switzerland, Italy, and Germany and handled those countries and Eastern Europe. Jordan previously worked in Berlin as a journalist and in New York for the Hearst information service. NBC's second representative handled programs from London and Paris. The unlikely candidate was a college dropout from the Midwest, a failed painter, and a well-known bon vivant with no journalism experience, who at age forty-six was no youngster.[4]

Frederick Blantford Bate had a laconic air that concealed a fierce competitive streak. A photograph of the schoolboy baseball player showed Bate sliding into a base with spikes aggressively extended in the manner of Ty Cobb. Born in 1886, Bate grew up on Chicago's West Side and matriculated at the University of Chicago. In 1912, he quit school after three mediocre quarters and sailed for Europe, hoping to become a painter. In Paris, Bate enrolled at the prestigious Académie Julien, but his career went nowhere. During World War I, he volunteered for the U.S. Army's Ambulance Corps. He met and married Sarah Gertrude Arkwright, an English nurse, with reputed blood ties to the British aristocracy. After the war, Vera, as she was known, worked briefly for Parisian designer Gabrielle "Coco" Chanel, and the couple moved in glamorous circles. The marriage ended in divorce, but not before the Bates produced Bridget, who later became a successful artist.[5]

Bate moved to Vienna to work for the Reparation Commission, the international body charged with managing Germany's war debts under the 1919 Treaty of Versailles. Quick with languages, including French and German, and described as "suave and convivial," Bate mixed with Europe's business elite, the international press corps, French politicians, and members of the British royal family, including the Prince of Wales, who became a personal friend.[6] In 1929, Bate connected with the RCA founder, Owen D. Young, who headed a second reparation commission bearing his name. In 1930, Bate returned to Paris. He went to work for RCA and was appointed NBC's European manager in summer 1932, slightly before CBS appointed Saerchinger.[7]

The choice of Bate over more experienced journalists suggests that NBC wanted a polished ambassadorial figure in London and Paris.[8] It remained to be seen, however, whether ambulance driving, working for a troubled French bank, running errands as a Reparation Commission "bellhop," and hitting the occasional golf ball with the Prince of Wales qualified Bate to effectively build NBC's brand overseas. His biggest challenge in France would be to develop productive relations with French politicians and PTT officials, who would naturally be wary of an emissary of a major U.S. corporation associated by many Europeans with jazz music and selling toothpaste.[9]

A Game of Risk

Bate moved to NBC as the economy battled the effects of the U.S. stock market crash. In 1931, for the first time in corporate history, RCA reported an annual loss blamed on "worldwide subnormal business conditions."[10] NBC relocated Bate from a plush home office in Paris to London. He went to work at Electra House, the nerve center for England's major communications company, Cables and Wireless, along with numerous international firms, including RCA. Bate began meeting regularly with BBC and PTT broadcast officials and foreign diplomats. He also recruited freelance reporters in the French and Anglophone press to assist with stories and ideas for programs. As NBC's representative to the International Broadcasting Union (IBU), Bate networked with the heads of public broadcast systems throughout Europe to envision how NBC and RCA could help develop a cooperative system of access and technical support to enable intra-European communication and transatlantic transmission.[11]

At the moment that the European managers took their posts, NBC enjoyed an advantage over CBS in prestige and international contacts. RCA's presence in Europe since the war gave it privileged access to the heads of European public broadcasting. William S. Paley, the head of CBS, aggressively closed the gap, however, by paying his on-air correspondents and news stringers more than NBC did. Writer A. J. Liebling once joked, "The most lavishly accoutered man I have seen in France turned out to be an employee of the Columbia Broadcasting System." As they did at home, NBC and CBS fought constantly for the best overseas talent, the best foreign press coverage, the best studio times, and above all, an "exclusive" with a prominent politician or internationally recognized figure. Bate fretted constantly about what "Columbia" might do next, and César Saerchinger, CBS's representative, spoke of NBC only as "the Opposition."[12]

Peace Signals: The International Radio Forum and the Committee on International Broadcasting

The inaugural U.S.–French shortwave broadcasts transmissions in 1931 resulted partly through the efforts of an internationally active group of private citizens and U.S. foundations hoping to shape international broadcasting into a vehicle of peace and global understanding. As Michele Hilmes has noted, these interwar humanistic efforts reflected parallel work in U.S. domestic broadcasting to develop the airwaves for public, educational, and nonprofit purposes rather than exclusively commercial ones.[13]

The first U.S.–French broadcast series was born in summer 1931 when Ira Nelson Morris, son of a Chicago meatpacking magnate, and the former U.S. envoy and minister to Sweden, addressed U.S. listeners via shortwave from France. "The night before I was to speak, I slept but little," Morris recalled, "For I felt a great sense of responsibility . . . [and] it seemed to me to indicate an obligation to use the radio to further the cause of international understanding and world peace."[14] Morris had recently proposed an exchange program with the French foreign minister, the PTT, and NBC president Merlin H. Aylesworth. Morris offered to curate a two-way, bilingual radio

Ira Nelson Morris. His International Radio Forum hoped to promote global understanding through transatlantic broadcasting. (Library of Congress)

series consisting of English-language programs from France to the United States and French-language broadcasts from the United States to France.

To promote the exchange and recruit speakers for it, Morris established the International Radio Forum (IRF), whose sixty-five members were from Austria, England, France, Germany, Sweden, and the United States. Its ranks included the duke de Broglie, a French physicist; the marquis de Chambrun of the Chamber of Deputies, the lower house of the French parliament; Madame Paul Dupuy, partner of the owner of *Le Petit Parisien*; and Jules J. Jusserand, former French ambassador to Washington. Morris also recruited the joint winners of the 1931 Nobel Peace Prize, Jane Addams and Dr. Nicholas Murray Butler, president of Columbia University and head of the Carnegie Endowment for International Peace.[15]

Over the course of the next year, IRF members presented more than thirty transatlantic talks for U.S. audiences originating from Paris, London, Berlin, Amsterdam, and Stockholm.[16] Sir Winston Churchill and German chancellor Franz von Papen both participated. André-Gustave Citroën, André Maurois, Pierre Étienne Flandin, Wellington Koo, Pierre le Comte du Noüy of the Pasteur Institute, André Lefebvre de la Boulaye, and André Siegfried spoke from Paris.[17] On April 10, 1931, Jules Jusserand defended France's policy on German war debt reparations from attacks in the U.S. press. The ailing Jusserand called upon journalists and the U.S. public to use "less sarcasm and more brotherly love" in understanding France's resistance to ending Germany's required war payments.[18]

Keeping pace, CBS formed the Committee on International Broadcasting to coordinate international programs designed "to provide an intelligently planned interchange of ideas throughout the world, through the medium of transoceanic broadcasting." The group intended to work with foundations and organizations committed to internationalism, such as the Rockefeller and Carnegie foundations, the Academy of Political Science, and the Council on Foreign Relations. The committee pledged its programs would be "entirely nonpartisan and free from all national propaganda." Somewhat awkwardly for NBC, however, CBS named Dr. Nicholas Murray Butler as chair of its new organization. Even if an "exclusive" to win the transatlantic competition wars had been lost, and even if NBC had to share Dr. Butler with CBS, the network initiatives supported the larger principle of promoting international conversations via broadcasting.[19]

"The American Networks Cannot Be 'Crashed'"

During the early 1930s, the Radio-Club France-Amérique (RC), a Paris-based production company authorized by the French Foreign Ministry and the PTT to represent French public broadcasting in the United States, approached NBC. Because most U.S. listeners tuned only to amplitude modulation (AM) programs, the RC requested NBC's help in relaying a new weekly English-language shortwave program sent from Paris via the Poste Coloniale across NBC's Blue national network.[20] The RC stands out because its two principals were female, which was unusual in French broadcasting. Franka Gordon, scientist, president, and artistic director of the RC, had worked for Western Electric and maintained a research laboratory at the Sorbonne. A soprano, she also ran a voice-training studio in Paris for aspiring film and radio announcers. The host and announcer for RC programs was Alice Langelier, a U.S. journalist with ten years of experience in Paris working for the International News Service, where she had gotten to know Frank E. Mason, who was now an NBC executive in New York.[21]

Business with NBC initially got off on the wrong foot, however, when Langelier and Gordon approached the French ambassador in Washington about broadcasting to the United States under the mistaken assumption that private U.S. networks took instructions from the federal government about international programs.[22] When the gambit failed, Langelier wrote Fred Bate a letter wondering coyly if he "would be so kind to play Cicerone," to help the RC get its programs picked up by NBC. Forgiving the botched attempt to bypass his authority, Bate warned the RC about the further "injection of officialdom into the picture," which could only complicate matters between the PTT and NBC. He reassured Langelier that he would do whatever he could to assist the RC in meeting its goals. Material from France "would be of genuine interest to American listeners," and "no [governmental] intervention [would be] necessary" as long as the proposed RC programs met NBC quality standards.[23]

As accommodating as NBC wanted to be with prospective international partners, the network's identity rested on the uniform quality of its programs and its independent editorial control. "*First and foremost it is program value that counts,*" Bate declared. "Whereas the PTT [control] the programs and messages of broadcasts in France, American listeners ultimately [dictate] the character of what commercial networks produce. Every broadcasting possibility is brought to the air—the best remain on the air. As far as international programs are concerned, they are no longer a novelty and, like domestic programs, are judged by their quality."[24] Moreover, NBC's credibility as a partner of other public broadcast systems across Europe required vigilance to avoiding any sign of favoritism or political manipulation. NBC had to remain a neutral party lest it antagonize the governments it relied upon to make its transatlantic transmissions.

From a commercial broadcaster's perspective, ideologically encoded material tended to produce mediocre programs. "My own feeling," Bate confided to Langelier, "is that most of the talks and articles which attempt to 'sell' one country to another are paid no attention to."[25] In his estimation, the refined intellectual and artistic presentations of the PTT stood little chance of overcoming the limited attention span of the average U.S. listener.[26] Merely delivering a PTT-style program from France to the United States would fail in Bate's estimation. Nor would it inspire the "press and public to get up on their hind legs and talk about 'that broadcast from France last night'"[27] The spirit of goodwill and cultural exchange could never justify ordinariness. Low standards in programs would doom the enthusiasm for U.S.–French radio in the United States that both NBC and the PTT wanted to cultivate.

Bate explained to Langelier that he imagined the future of U.S.–French broadcasting as a medium channeling the natural and human-built sounds of France as well as the ideas and cultural expressions of the population. He suggested that the RC send a recording engineer to capture the coastal soundscape of Concarneau in northwestern France with "the herring fleet coming in and the noise of selling catches, yelling from boats to quay as they enter the inner harbor." He proposed gathering sound of "a service from Rheims Cathedral with the bells, or the organ from St. Sulpice, or a broadcast from a typical French cabaret, padded by using someone *really* good—Lucienne Boyer (or any present top-notcher) etc., etc." As idiosyncratic as his suggestions might have appeared, they exemplified the ways in which radio producers were already searching for a "sound of France" and French cultural difference that would have mass appeal beyond national borders.[28] Bate reiterated that NBC supported talks by French authors, thinkers, and journalists provided that the speakers "not allow their talks to be tinged by nationalism."[29] The network's sensitivity to content perceived as nationalistic echoed the concerns of Ira Nelson's IRF and the CBS Committee on International Broadcasting, which sought to keep propaganda off the airwaves.

Bate realized that the PTT system was starved for resources and that Langelier and Gordon were under pressure to deliver programming at the lowest cost possible. "If I know what you are up against, the ideas which I have in mind probably exceed the budgetary provision which has been made for your service," Bate wrote sympathetically. "Here again, provided you agree with my general ideas on this matter, you can help Pierre Comert [head of the information and press service for the French Foreign Ministry] by proving to those who, in the end, must be convinced, that the American networks cannot be 'crashed' without time, thought and money being spent."[30]

Stretched to pay for its European managers and the bulk of the transmission costs of transatlantic exchanges, NBC took a firm position on the message it sent to the RC and to the PTT. No commercial network wanted to be mistaken for an extension of the U.S. government or a public service vehicle for France's benefit alone. "France has so much to give," Bate told Langelier, if only the government would invest time and resources. "As far as broadcasting is concerned [the government] has conservatively (or rather impecuniously) hid her light under a bushel—or still more economically—under a quart! It's wrong!"[31] Bate expressed cautious optimism to executives in New York about the overtures from Langelier, but admitted that the situation would require close monitoring. "Unless we help by suggestion and argument," he wrote to John F. Royal, NBC vice president for programming, the PTT "will never go so far as to get started. They will try to do it on a shoestring and never offer anything that our networks would want. We will keep at them, however, and I now think we can see some interesting material ahead out of France at little or no cost to us."[32]

Bate and the RC eventually struck a deal that recognized the club as a regular client of NBC and promised assistance to the RC for "programs which merit relay" on NBC's domestic network. Not wanting to be exposed politically for supporting a direct relationship between the government and a U.S. corporation, the French foreign minister gave no funds to the RC. Instead, he authorized the club to recruit commercial sponsors in France, such as hotels and travel agencies, which would be interested in reaching NBC listeners by buying commercial time on the programs sent to the United States. NBC felt pleased because the burden to sell the series in advance fell on the program developers. NBC avoided upfront financial risk and could charge a commission for the advertising time sold by the RC.[33] Following some of Bate's suggestions, the RC series brought the sounds of large and small French orchestras, choir and organ concerts from cathedrals in Rouen and Paris, and musical segments from music halls, cabarets, and other festive settings with voiceover commentaries to NBC listeners across the country. Bate expressed satisfaction: "This is the first time the French have made any serious [effort] to really help an organization provide programs which might merit network time. . . . The move requires encouragement."[34]

Between 1931 and 1935, NBC international shortwave broadcasts jumped from several dozen to more than one hundred fifty.[35] The RC relays expanded the forms and cultural interest of transatlantic broadcasts from France. But interwar domestic political travails weighed on French broadcast policy. Public investment in French radio was insufficient for the system to grow as vigorously as it might. French communications infrastructure also needed updates to produce high-quality sound all the way from the studio to the transmitter. U.S. engineers grumbled when well-planned and executed transatlantic programs sounded substandard because of technical issues beyond the control of NBC that could be easily fixed with a bit of directed investment. As one NBC engineer observed ruefully, "The best combination of transmitter, antenna, etc. in the world will not be satisfactory if its connection with the microphone is as bad as most French telephone lines."[36]

"Not Ready in Paris"

On a beautiful spring morning in Manhattan, almost three years to the day after U.S.–French broadcasters inaugurated the Poste Coloniale, hopes of reaching new heights in U.S.–French broadcasting were soaring at Radio City. The year 1934 marked the centennial of the decease of the Marquis de Lafayette, and NBC and Fred Bate had planned a live shortwave broadcast linking New York, Washington, D.C., Paris, and listeners across the United States to honor his memory. In the sunken plaza in front of Rockefeller Center, the French ambassador, two battalions of the U.S. Army Seventh Regiment, a marching band, and assorted VIPs waited for the celebration to begin. In the nation's capital, U.S. secretary of state Cordell Hull waited to salute the great champion and benefactor of the American Revolution. And, more than three thousand miles away in Paris, foreign minister Jean-Louis Barthou was booked to speak live on the importance of Franco-American unity in the face of diplomatic tension over German war reparations. Diplomacy, international news, state-of-the art communications wizardry, and a touch of Radio City razzle-dazzle were set to converge.

The program started brilliantly as RCA circuits flashed Secretary Hull's address to New York for network transmission. Down on the plaza, the French ambassador, André Lefebvre de la Boulaye, no stranger to transatlantic broadcasts, delivered prefatory remarks and introduced the foreign minister in Paris. There was an expectant pause, and then, silence. Quickly, the conductor queued the regimental band, which struck up a tune to fill the dead air, while NBC engineers hunted for Barthou on a backup shortwave frequency. Hearing the sound of spoken French, they switched live, accidentally sending a Parisian radio comedy sketch rocketing across the plaza and out over the national network. Barthou could not be found. New York did not have Paris. The transatlantic segment had to be scuttled.[37]

For reasons that were never exactly clear, Barthou arrived late to the microphone. A French newspaper reported that officials "explained that the foreign minister, who was in Paris, had thought his speech was to start ten minutes later than the scheduled time."[38] NBC officials did not believe the explanation, however, and the "Barthou incident" as it was grimly termed at Radio City, chilled some of the good feeling for France and the PTT that Bate had worked so hard to cultivate at NBC.

The New York press jumped on the snafu as a telling example of the unreliability of a competitor medium. "There was difficulty in the timing and [Barthou] was not heard. . . . the Foreign Minister was not ready in Paris," reported the *New York Times*.[39] Another report mocked NBC's attempt to expand into international news reporting, which remained dominated by wire services, news syndicates, and, of course, newspapers. "Many of those attending the ceremonies were French," wrote the reporter, "and they were considerably astonished, but amused, when from the loud-speakers there came the voices of a woman and a man arguing about whether the man loved the woman. It turned out that he did."[40] Surprise entrances and exits, amorous declarations, and pratfalls belonged on NBC's entertainment schedule, not on its international news reports. A reader of the press coverage might conclude that the incident marked the latest episode of a farce in which the bumbling (yet canny) French public broadcast establishment had duped NBC, keeping the network colossus off balance, and leaving the U.S. audience wondering who held the power to determine the terms and tempo of transatlantic broadcasting.

From London, a chagrined Fred Bate scrambled to reassure NBC officials that Barthou's lack of punctuality reflected a misunderstanding and not a deliberate slight to the network (and possibly the United States). Bate wrote, "The trend [in France] is to cooperate and extend relations. . . . We will require patience." As if trying to explain what he was up against, Bate continued, "Instinctively [the French] are not mixers. Instinctively they want to know whys and wherefores. Instinctively they tend to be suspicious. I am convinced that the 'trend' is in the right direction. Gradually things will work out there."[41] Failures of coordination between U.S. networks and the PTT could be rationalized and forgiven as technical mistakes. They also might be taken, however, as danger signals of "instinctive" and intractable differences that might never be reconciled.

Contending with Flux

NBC officials applauded PTT chief Georges Mandel's efforts to place the PTT on a surer administrative and financial footing. Mandel's planned shortwave transmitter center, while not yet operating, would boost inbound and outbound reception and transmission capacities, which would allow the PTT to become a more active U.S. partner should it choose. In the interim, France lagged behind England and Germany in distributing broadcast content to the United States. In 1935, NBC received and retransmitted 324 international programs. More than one-third of them came from England; the BBC was a reliable and popular supplier of programs.[42] France relied exclusively on the Poste Coloniale for international broadcasting to all parts of the world, which imposed severe limits on output to the United States. NBC's own international exports totaled 178 events, mostly broadcasts using W3XAL, NBC's shortwave transmitter. Various countries received these transatlantic broadcasts, including Germany, Sweden, Italy, Russia, Denmark, Norway, Poland, Finland, and Czechoslovakia.[43]

Bate and John F. Royal hoped that Mandel's reforms would produce a breakthrough in two-way U.S.–French exchanges, but there were skeptics elsewhere at NBC. In spring 1935, Alfred H. Morton, a former Paris-based RCA engineer and veteran of the 1931 Colonial Exposition broadcasts, shared a discouraging technical assessment with Royal: "The general broadcasting situation [in France] shows no improvement," Morton reported. "There is still no real coordination among the many independent [PTT] stations, and nothing yet in the form of a real network." Morton noted the positive impact of Mandel's nationalization efforts, but he doubted that the costly shortwave center would be ready as soon as the PTT claimed. Morton also questioned the cultural fit between PTT programming and NBC listener tastes. "At the moment I should say that in France there is less broadcasting material of interest to us than in almost any of the European countries."[44] Morton was hardly the only naysayer either. Some French officials privately advised NBC to give up on the PTT entirely. They suggested that NBC approach commercial Radio Luxembourg about reaching a French audience. In a private meeting, Mandel assured Bate and RCA chief David Sarnoff that he favored an increase in exchanges, but that the continued shortage of resources and resulting technical inadequacies made this a prospective ambition. With the interwar political flux in France, NBC thought it unlikely but not inconceivable that a more business-friendly government might emerge in France. Executives decided to remain patient with the PTT because, in Morton's words, "the time is not yet ripe [to switch loyalties]."[45]

When the Popular Front swept to power in 1936, the optimistic Bate averred that he had hopes for the "new crowd" at the PTT. Under Mandel's successor, Robert Jardillier, however, the situation hardly improved. Jardillier showed interest in NBC's facilities at Radio City but offered no fresh proposals for PTT-supported broadcasts to the United States. RCA, like NBC, played a long game by providing consulting services to the new PTT administration in the area of international communications infrastructure. Working with the PTT, NBC did manage a series of reports tracking the French luxury ocean liner *Normandie* on its first voyage across the Atlantic, which included reports en route from Fred Bate that used a variety of technologies, including ship-to-shore radio, AT&T receiving stations, and an onboard shortwave transmitter. The series include interviews with passengers and crew, and a performance of one of the ship's dance orchestras. NBC also ran a simple two-way transatlantic broadcast in December to celebrate the inception of direct telephone communication between France and the United States. But the fact remained that the Popular Front government showed little interest in bolstering its international broadcast capabilities to reach the United States.[46]

"Furriners" and the Powers of Obstruction

From as early as 1926, the International Broadcasting Union (IBU), the body charged with international radio communications guidelines, had, in the starchy words of one official, "negotiated a gentlemen's agreement to the effect that the member organizations would adopt all possible guarantees against transmissions which would harm the spirit of cooperation and good international understanding." This pact had direct consequences for international journalists using the broadcast facilities of an IBU member nation. As A. E. Burrows, secretary-general of the IBU in 1933, explained, "most broadcasting organizations, certainly those in the highly complex and politically sensitive European area, found it necessary to ask for a previous submission of the manuscript from all invited to broadcast from their studios."[47] The convention of screening came under increasing pressure, however, as the number of U.S. radio journalists seeking access to foreign studios grew with the growth of NBC's and CBS' international operations and Europe's intensifying political problems.

As a ministry of government, the PTT embraced the IBU script convention and remained wary of controversial foreign or domestic speakers on French airwaves. The PTT and the foreign ministry would never knowingly cede control of France's facilities to a journalist insensitive to the government's definition of French interests. As Jacques Attali and Yves Stourdze have argued, the developmental and regulatory philosophies toward the telegraph, railroad, and telephone reflected a French governmental tendency toward "a republic of one-way media" and more than a little "nervousness about the rise of an authentic communication *network*."[48] The observation certainly held true in this instance, particularly as ideological clashes between the Left and the Right began to tear France apart and influence French news reporting.[49]

The way that U.S. broadcast journalists were gaining the technological means to report on breaking news around the world and expecting to have access to microphones overseas created friction in France and Europe over policies toward foreign reporters. National precedent made a huge difference in this instance. Paul Starr argues that new media tools and practices, such as broadcast journalism, develop within a historical "communications framework" that is often shaped decisively by the "constitutive choices" of prior technological and information policies. The occupational ethos of budding U.S. radio journalists abroad followed that of their U.S. print colleagues, whose industry had developed over many generations with the support of the principles of free speech, information flow as a democratic good, and liberal economic ideals.[50] In the Third Republic, by contrast, press freedoms were contingent on constitutional provisions and precedents that gave more limited rights to correspondents and news organizations.[51] The techno-aesthetic differences of U.S.–French radio, themselves a partial legacy of intersecting yet distinctive national communications frameworks, had a bearing on the reception of U.S. radio reporters in France. U.S. radio journalists began finding themselves in awkward situations with uncomprehending or unsympathetic international colleagues and government officials over their journalistic practices.

One instance of the circumstances in which friction could occur came in the unlikely domain of international fashion reporting. May Birkhead, a *Chicago Tribune* fashion writer, who had broadcast reports on Parisian haute couture on NBC since the early 1930s, took offense when officials at the PTT and French foreign ministry began demanding advance copies of her scripts. NBC wanted to ensure the liberties of any network correspondent using French studio facilities for any purpose, especially in the event of breaking news when scripts might be getting edited right up until airtime. Birkhead's treatment struck NBC's John F. Royal as wrong. He considered Pierre Comert an obstructionist who liked to keep NBC off-balance and "the real fountain head of that particular activity," referring to petty governmental interference with NBC's broadcasts. "If we are to exchange programs with [France] we must have the right to send program [illegible] and artists or speakers without censorship. *No other country imposes such conditions,*" Royal declared testily. He threatened Alfred H. Morton, Bate's supervisor, that "unless we get some satisfactory explanation of whether or not [the PTT and French government] are going to censor any programs out of France, we will cancel further programs out of that country."[52] Morton dutifully instructed Bate to look into the "evidence of rather strict censorship on the part of certain foreign ministries, particularly PT&T [*sic*] and Foreign Affairs." He asked Bate to pay a call on the head of the information and press service of the foreign ministry to determine "the attitude of the French" toward allowing U.S. journalists to speak freely on the air.[53]

As he had after the "Barthou incident," the diplomatic Bate tried to smooth ruffled feathers at Radio City and to defuse intercultural tension. "Dear Doc," he wrote in the first of two letters to Morton after his meeting with Comert, "I do not anticipate that 'furriners' will be asked to submit to any such close scrutiny [in the future]." Bate gently reminded Morton that contrary to Royal's claim, the BBC was known to censor from time to time but had faithfully kept its commitments to NBC when special event broadcasts occurred. "Don't worry about the French censorship," Bate wrote. "We both know what it is—and that it cannot be eliminated entirely. NBC has [Comert's and the PTT's] confidence, and at the end it was arranged so that May Birkhead left copies of her talks—at the time she broadcast."[54] Bate appeared to accept that he could no more end the PTT's bureaucratic officiousness than he could prevent John F. Royal's temper outbursts. He could only manage these forces with the aim of ensuring to the best of his ability that the PTT would not try to block NBC journalists outright if a major story was breaking.

"There Is a Front Page of the Air"

At CBS, European manager César Saerchinger also struggled with the PTT in clarifying expectations and finding workable solutions in the domain of news reporting. The veteran reporter held strong views about broadcasting and national difference. "Of all the broadcasting organizations in Europe," Saerchinger began, "Great Britain's is the most conscientious, Germany's the most efficient, Italy's the most ambitious. What shall we say of France's? The most casual? The most haphazard? It certainly is both of these, but at the same time the most amiable. Englishmen regard their radio as a great social force—religious, social, artistic, educational. The French, certainly, have no such ambitions about this latest contraption of the amusement world."[55] Saerchinger's idiosyncratic observations of French broadcasting underscored the ways in which the contrasting techno-aesthetic registers of U.S.–French broadcasting could create difficulties when U.S. broadcasters found themselves on the PTT's turf attempting to maneuver at the pace and in the manner customary to the major U.S. networks. The PTT's demonstrated need to "know whys and wherefores," as Fred Bate put it, and French radio's procedures of deliberate speed as a mode of ensuring information control could stall news reporting.

In an era when the networks were competing aggressively with print journalism for the freshest news, obstacles to meeting air deadlines created stress. Reports needed to be on time and plentiful. NBC's European manager, Max Jordan, recalled a nerve-wracking speech delivered to him by executive John W. Elwood: "There is a front-page of the air," Elwood barked, "and we need headlines on it twenty-four hours a day. Go and get some!"[56] "'Exclusivity' had [also] become a fetish by then," Saerchinger remembered, "a broadcast, however important or interesting, was only half a trick if it was not exclusive."[57] In mid-October 1931, some months after NBC's transatlantic successes at the Colonial Exposition, Prime Minister Pierre Laval agreed to a radio interview (through an interpreter) with CBS in Paris. Thirty minutes before the interview, Saerchinger found himself navigating "the human anthill" at the entrance of the Ministry of the Interior searching for the PTT technicians responsible for engineering the program. "At last I spied a French radio man; apparently there would be a broadcast, but he didn't know when. Time was nothing to him; a speech by the Premier would be taken when it happened, like a shower of rain. American broadcasting was run differently; they would 'take' the Prime Minister at thirty seconds after half-past six, or not at all [in French broadcasting, by contrast] everything happened in the nick of time or

just after. '*Comme toujours*,' coolly remarked a Frenchman standing near-by."
To Saerchinger's immense relief, the PTT pulled off the interview, but only
by forcing deliberate speed to become madcap haste. As Saerchinger knew,
a segment that arrived "just after" in commercial radio was not only a blown
segment, it could also mean an advertiser who could not be billed.[58]

Saerchinger attempted another exclusive report with the prime minister
aboard the French liner *Île de France* while Laval was sailing to New York for
a diplomatic visit. Saerchinger had great difficulty, however, reconciling the
different professional cultures and communication styles between himself
and the French radio crew on the boat.

> These optimistic Frenchmen were sure their radiotelephone equipment could
> transmit the proposed broadcast to New York when we were within a day of
> the American shore. But they forgot to mention that their "microphone" was
> just an adapted telephone mouthpiece. Laval was ready to talk—to greet the
> American people as a "messenger of peace," come to help "ward off the dangers
> which menace civilization." We set the broadcast for ten o'clock at night, ship's
> time, and started to make tests. Up in the wireless room, I shouted into the
> mouthpiece, trying to get myself heard by the American engineers: "this is the
> *Île de France* calling WABC, New York." "Hello WABC, hello W2XE, hello WLA
> and the rest!" No answer. They put on all their "juice"; so did I. Finally I had
> none left; I was too hoarse to talk. It was heartbreak. Morse messages came in
> to say New York couldn't hear us. I gave it up.[59]

The broadcaster's frustration with the crew's blithe assurances and the
inadequate state of the actual equipment reflected a pattern of deadline-
busting disconnections that marked the exciting and often rewarding, but
also ragged, cultural and technical interfaces of interwar U.S.–French radio.
In some cases, no amount of "juice," it seemed, could surmount the barrier
of different expectations, inclinations, and tools available that conspired to
keep French and U.S. radio slightly out of phase with each other.

"The Hour Came and Passed"

Concerns about censorship rose to the fore when France went through violent
political convulsions and U.S. journalists attempted to report on the events.
On the fateful night of February 6, 1934, French right- and left-leaning political groups and the police clashed in the streets of Paris. Fifteen deaths and
injuries to fifteen hundred persons resulted, which forced the dissolution
of the General Assembly.[60] César Saerchinger convinced Percy Philip of the
New York Times, who had seen the street fighting, to deliver an eyewitness
account via shortwave back to New York. "The great advantage was that

Philip had already got permission from the Quai d'Orsay for a similar talk he was making for Great Britain; he was a highly respected and trusted man," Saerchinger wrote. But when the two arrived at the PTT studios, the engineers on duty refused to budge without written permission from their superiors, who in the wake of the political chaos were nowhere to be found. "We remonstrated, talked, argued," recalled Saerchinger, "millions of listeners were waiting in America, and the programs of a hundred stations would be upset. Nothing moved them; they tried telephoning to somebody—but it didn't sound convincing. The hour came and passed—no lines." When Saerchinger confronted the foreign minister's foreign press liaison the next day, the official denied he had known that it was CBS and the *New York Times* calling from the studio. It did not console Saerchinger that the PTT had also squelched domestic news reports of the riots.[61]

NBC experienced better luck getting an early report out of Paris during the disturbances by avoiding the gatekeepers at the PTT studios entirely. Max Jordan teamed up with Edgar Mowrer of the *Chicago Daily News* to gather information from the streets: "We set forth in [Mowrer's] car," Jordan remembered,

> one of the few still functioning in the huge city. The streets were crowded with an angry mob. To avoid flying stones, and perhaps bullets, we stuck pretty close to the floor of the car while our heads bobbed up and down at the windows like marionettes in a Punch-and-Judy show. . . . Edgar and I saw a good deal on that exciting ride, and we were able to give American listeners "an earful." It was a report from the scene, more colorful perhaps than any written account of that day, in a broadcast delivered by candlelight. Electricity had been shut off, and Paris Americans were sitting around at the Ritz in the glow of what served their ancestors in times before kerosene and Mr. Edison.[62]

In a workaround to avoid the uncertainty of PTT clearance and also a power outage that might have affected a conventional transmission, Jordan used a telephone in the lobby of the Ritz to report the story to London for a radio circuit flash to New York. The tendencies of informal information control through obstruction and outright censorship during the 1934 riots impeded but did not deter U.S. broadcasters, who engineered strategies and solutions to pass reports through a tangle of technological, cultural, and political impediments to reach U.S. listeners.[63]

"Real Competition" and the News of War

The competencies in international broadcasting that Bate, Jordan, Saerchinger, and numerous others attained from the early to mid-1930s grew in-

Fred Bate (L) and Edward R. Murrow (R) furnished dramatic accounts of the Battle of Britain to millions of U.S. radio listeners.

creasingly significant as the European political crisis worsened. On March 12, 1937, Bate received a radiogram reporting a major personnel change at CBS. The aging Saerchinger had been released. His rumored replacement was a CBS director who had formerly worked for the Rockefeller Foundation. "If true," wrote John F. Royal, he "will provide you real competition [STOP]. He has traveled extensively in Europe [STOP]. Best of luck with your new adversary."[64] It seemed Edward R. Murrow was on his way to London.

The 1938 *Anschluss* and the Munich Pact both drew world attention to the precarious political dynamics in Europe and the strength of German Nazism. International broadcasters put the human and technical systems they had created to the test of intensive coverage of unfolding events. That year transformed Fred Bate and Edward R. Murrow into recognized stars of transatlantic broadcasting. Prior to the Munich crisis, Bate worked chiefly behind the scenes as a producer, mostly leaving the on-air reporting to members of the press corps. Suddenly, however, Bate was on call in the BBC studios. During the Munich crisis, he began broadcasting an average of six times daily to the United States. After Germany invaded France, Bate worked entirely from London. When the Battle of Britain began in summer 1940, "the key men" in that city reporting to the United States via radio, according to NBC's John MacVane, "were Ed Murrow and Fred Bate." NBC continued to like the chances of their fifty-two-year-old veteran against the thirty-year-old Murrow.[65]

Edward R. Murrow personified the nightly drama of the Battle of Britain for U.S. radio listeners. He is easy to picture standing on the roof of the BBC's Broadcasting House, cigarette in hand (cupped in deference to the blackouts, perhaps), delivering a mesmerizing report to listeners thousands of miles away. Murrow worked in the company of others on that rooftop, of course, including BBC and network technicians, and also Fred Bate, who broadcast extensively for NBC during the Blitz. The two broadcasters benefited mutually from a personal and professional camaraderie. Their families grew close under the wartime conditions. In addition to filing their individual reports, Bate and Murrow sometimes collaborated, for example, pool-reporting from a London air-raid shelter.[66]

Murrow arrived in London with little experience in the job assigned to him, but with extensive preparation in supporting areas. Unlike Bate, Murrow had a college degree and professional training as a writer and speaker. Surviving recordings of the two announcers' London broadcasts provide a contrast between the charismatic style and sonorous voice of Murrow and Bate's flat, higher-pitched delivery. Nor could Bate write with the equivalent rhetorical power of his CBS counterpart. Whereas Bate provided clear and competent reporting, Murrow's unique combination of skills elevated his reports to gripping theater.[67]

"A Terrific Pounding"

If Bate could not compete with Murrow's on-air talents, he surely matched his younger counterpart in dedication and output, performing dangerous, exhausting tasks on behalf of NBC. John F. Royal recognized the mounting physical and psychological toll on Bate. Royal worried that living in a war zone, absorbing the stress of nightly bombing barrages, and coordinating, producing, and delivering daily news reports was pushing Bate and a skeletal staff of two to the brink of exhaustion. "He has been taking a terrific pounding," Royal reported to NBC vice president Niles Trammell, noting that CBS had pulled William Shirer out of Berlin to save him from the grinding pace of daily reporting. Trammell ignored Royal's hint that Bate needed reinforcements. The network stuck with its ace.[68]

Late one night in early December 1940, as Bate prepared a script in the NBC offices adjacent to Broadcasting House, a descending German parachute bomb struck a building across the street and detonated. Deadly shrapnel exploded in every direction. Debris from the damaged building burst through the windows of the NBC office, sending shards of glass everywhere. In the chaotic aftermath, Bate was found wandering in the street. Bleeding and in shock, he clutched his script for the nightly broadcast. The heavy sweater he wore to ward off the winter chill had partially protected him. One observer reported that after the explosion the garment looked "like a sieve." Bate recalled the moment of the bomb's impact "like all of London pouring through the window."[69]

He suffered wounds to his ear, face, and arm, and tendon damage to both hands. After hospitalization in London, he traveled to New York for continued treatment and rehabilitation.[70] His brush with death added to his celebrity. Sensing a publicity opportunity, John F. Royal asked Orrin Dunlap, radio editor at the *New York Times*, to commission an article.[71] The paper obliged with "Reporting under Fire," in which Bate described the scene in London and the bombing. He joked that the biggest challenge for a journalist reporting the Battle of Britain was not the threat of bodily harm but the threat of the BBC censors. "Tall, gray-haired, well-dressed," the correspondent wrote, Bate "looked during the interview as if he were going to step out into the Piccadilly or Park Lane of the old days." Restored to health, Bate returned briefly to London. NBC shortly recalled him to New York, however, to direct the network's International Division, which handled all foreign shortwave services. His years as a transatlantic broadcast pioneer were over.[72]

In less than a decade, international broadcasts had evolved from experiments subject to technical failure into a regular presence in the homes of millions who followed world events. The international news roundup became a taken-for-granted instrument of international broadcasting. Bate and colleagues in Europe and the United States could take pride in having persisted in the difficult and sometimes frustrating work of making transatlantic broadcasting viable. Even when political and techno-aesthetic differences in U.S.–French radio offered no guarantee of a smooth interface and New York did not have Paris, the networks pursued relationships that were as functional and productive as possible. Despite economic and political uncertainty, PTT officials sought to maintain transatlantic exchange as a principle of U.S.–French relations. The German military victory and partial occupation of France in spring 1940 created an unprecedented emergency for the French population. It forced a revolutionary transformation of transatlantic broadcast communications and U.S.–French radio. The circumstances of the war and the Occupation shifted the way that France listened to, and thought about, the United States and radio. Broadcasting would grow into an integral element of a massive Allied-directed multimedia campaign to liberate France.

3 Voices of the Occupation

U.S. Broadcasting to France during World War II

Late one evening in fall 1941, more than a year after Germany defeated and partially occupied France, a French widow in the unoccupied southern zone of the country wrote a letter that contained a desperate plea. "Monsieur," she began, "Last night, you said, 'We wish to remind you that *The French Hour* is very anxious to get your suggestions,' [but] it is we who are very anxious. It is we who anxiously wait for your daily program from America. And when I say *we*, I mean the millions of Frenchmen who listen to your broadcasts, and are at last able to relax—and breathe freely!" Her letter to NBC's International Division in New York enjoyed a second life when her words were read aloud in a shortwave broadcast back to France several weeks later. She wrote again by airmail, describing life in her village, interspersed with allusions to France's political debacle. "I talk to you because you speak to thousands of Frenchmen every evening; Frenchmen scattered in the four corners of a world which has shrunk terribly, but in which, nonetheless, we are shut off from each other by high thick walls." She wanted NBC and others in the United States to know that "You Americans are right to have faith in the French people; you do not count on us vainly any more than our trust in you is unjustified."[1]

It has largely escaped historical notice that during the German Occupation (1940–44), in addition to the broadcasts of the British Broadcasting Corporation (BBC), international shortwave broadcasters in the United States, such as NBC and, later, the U.S. government's Voice of America (VOA) supplied broadcast news, entertainment, and moral support to France. Until late 1942, when Germany totally occupied France, international announcers regularly read excerpts from listener letters smuggled out of the country or mailed and forwarded via neutral countries, such as Spain or Portugal, to New York and London. Though neither as widely heard nor as influential as the French-language programs of the BBC, which offered Charles de Gaulle and the Free French regular access to the microphone, daily broadcasts from the United States transformed the scope and significance of U.S.–French broadcasting.[2] Thousands of letters reached NBC in response to its French-language programs. Whether recirculating the voices of the Occupation via on-air letter reading, providing news and cultural diversions, or participating in the Allied campaign to liberate France, transatlantic broadcasting helped strengthen ties and create new ones between the United States and France.

The exhortation to NBC from France to "speak to us more" conveys the extraordinary importance of radio from the outside world during the Occupation. Radio listeners in the occupied and unoccupied zones repeatedly described the importance of BBC and U.S. broadcasts in their daily lives.[3] Mailbag segments featuring listener correspondence and news from France provided an emotional lift, but also a megaphone to salute fellow listeners, and sometimes to talk back to Vichy and German authorities. Personal letters added drama, humor, and sometimes pathos to international broadcasts. Their circulation via the radio created a virtual forum in which anonymous listener thoughts and sentiments commingled. Kate Lacey argues that the act of radio listening could, under certain historical conditions, transform the raw content of programs into material for a symbolic or physically actualized form of collective politics. Like writing, speaking, and reading, radio listening represented an activity, often taking place with others physically present that furnished information for deliberation. It also fueled a variant of what Jürgen Habermas called "interiority" wherein disaggregated listeners, in this model, joined together mentally as part of a critical public united by a desire for change.[4] Radio listening could offer disenchanted Occupation listeners a way to connect with Free French exiles in London and New York. It could afford a mechanism for conjuring an imagined free France, or the future possibilities of one, out of the air itself.

This chapter explores the evolution of U.S. international broadcasting to France between 1937, when daily transatlantic foreign-language programs began in earnest, through to the liberation of Paris in summer 1944. Source limitations confine the focus to NBC's services, but other U.S. broadcasters offered regular programs, too. The chapter analyzes how the escalating European political crisis, World War II, the Occupation, and the Allied campaign to liberate France affected French listening practices, as well as the forms, institutions, and strategies of U.S. and Allied broadcasts.[5] It contends that the war emergency not only transformed the nature of U.S.–French radio, but it radically extended the technological capacities and strategic conceptualization of the use of radio as an international and global medium. Transatlantic radio and the circumstances of the Occupation would draw the United States and France into a newfound but somewhat ambiguous proximity by the time of the Liberation.

U.S. French-Language Broadcasting Goes Live: NBC's *The French Hour*

In July 1937, NBC's new International Division began daily shortwave newscasts to Europe in six foreign languages. It also launched daily foreign-language feature programs, including *The French Hour*. "A changing world, constantly diminishing in size, has dictated an extension from the domestic to the international radio field," wrote Lenox Lohr, NBC chief. "Listening to programs from beyond oceans," he continued, "we have realized that America, too, has something to tell the world, and the duty to tell it."[6] In the context of the European political crisis, the euphemism of a "changing world" needed no elaboration: Violence, fascism, political instability, and propaganda attacks against democratic regimes had flipped RCA's vision of worldwide broadcast "community" upside down. U.S. broadcasters realized that if the United States went to war, they would likely lose control over shortwave broadcasting.[7] By investing in more foreign-language broadcasting, particularly news and information, the networks proactively committed to promoting democratic principles abroad. The new programs signaled to government officials that Washington could expect help from the networks in getting foreign policy messages circulated abroad without the need for aggressive intervention in private broadcasting. No one foresaw, however, how short-lived this arrangement would be, or how the fortunes of France, the United States, and broadcasting would converge in spring 1940 or how *The French Hour*'s overseas outreach would prefigure the government's massive shift into foreign-language broadcasting once the United States entered the war.[8]

In summer 1937, NBC hired Fernand Auberjonois, a Swiss journalist, to host *The French Hour* from New York. Auberjonois had print journalism experience in Europe and in the United States where he had lived since 1933. "We have [chosen] a person who is completely at home in the language he uses on the air, but who, also, is completely in the American psychological climate," explained International Division head John W. Elwood. "He must understand the countries he is talking to; He must also understand the United States." Though not screened for his politics, Auberjonois understood that

Number of International Broadcasts on NBC Networks

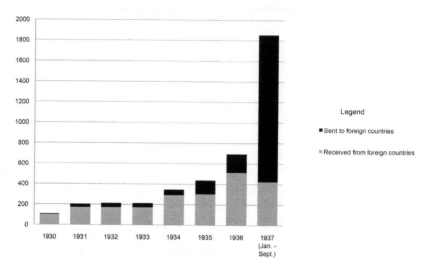

The 1937 launch of NBC's International Division underscored the commitment of U.S. broadcasters to international/global outreach. (NBC Collection, Library of Congress)

he would speak in the neutral cadences of the network and must respect the "American psychological climate," which in the late 1930s had continuing isolationist qualities.[9]

The French Hour consisted of fifteen minutes of news followed by music and cultural features. Raymond Gram Swing contributed occasional commentaries. Auberjonois moderated discussions on literature and the arts and presented "Messages to France," featuring personal greetings from French and U.S. celebrities, journalists, and other public figures.[10] At the end of the hour, Auberjonois invited listeners to share news and he read letters aloud over the air. Letters also gave NBC some indication of reception quality, as well as who was listening where.[11] In the first year and a half of the program, letters began trickling in from across the Francophone world, but few came from metropolitan France.[12] As an experiment, Auberjonois swapped out classical music for vernacular U.S. music. Responses soared. "Even from France, cards were flooding in asking only and always for 'mountaineers [*sic*] and spirituals,'" Auberjonois recalled. By spring 1939, the daily French-language newscasts and *The French Hour* reportedly commanded a solid audience. NBC International Division executive Guy Hickok boasted, "We receive here nearly a thousand letters a month in French, telling us that reception is excellent" and further that "A great deal of mail comes from Paris listeners."[13]

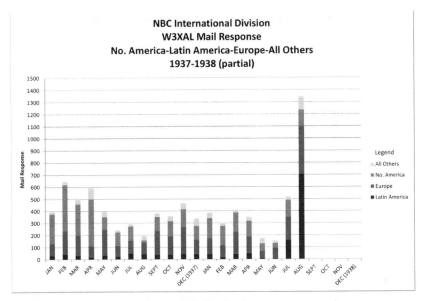

NBC's summer 1937 expansion to daily foreign-language news and programs services to France and elsewhere prompted a surge of listener correspondence. (NBC Collection, Library of Congress)

Interwar French listeners discovered *The French Hour* as they did other transatlantic programs through radio listings, word of mouth, and exploring the airwaves. Rebecca Scales notes that interwar French radio listings were not comprehensive, but most publications carried at least some information about U.S. shows. In Marseille, readers of *Le Dimanche Illustré* had the luxury of a detailed weekly schedule of programs coming from the United States. Listeners dialed in NBC's WNBI and WRCA for news and *The French Hour*. At other hours, they might hear popular entertainment (minus the commercials) courtesy of NBC's Red network. French radio listings also included special U.S. programs, such as performances from New York's Metropolitan Opera or celebrity news from Broadway and Hollywood.[14]

The troubles with news reporting on the PTT described in the previous chapter pushed French listeners toward international alternatives. A notorious case of the unreliability of the PTT came on September 12, 1938, when Adolf Hitler spoke via radio at the close of the annual Nuremberg rally. The U.S. networks arranged a live shortwave feed of Hitler's speech back to the United States followed by an English translation. In France, however, the PTT refused to carry the speech live. Officials promised listeners a broadcast of an authoritative French-language translation shortly after the speech ended. Unfortunately, the promised translation got delayed late into the evening, so much so that many disgruntled PTT listeners gave up and retired for the night, never knowing what the Führer had said that day. Compounding the irritation of PTT listeners, it became public knowledge that members of the French cabinet, tipped off to the availability of international feeds of the speech, abandoned the PTT for foreign stations themselves. During the Occupation, Allied intelligence agents would discover that the Nuremberg incident from years before remained a sore point for some French listeners, who mentioned it bitterly as an illustration of the PTT's failure to inform and keep the trust of the French public.[15]

Several weeks later, NBC's Max Jordan sent the first news of the Munich Pact to the United States via shortwave. An alert announcer in the International Division picked up the incoming news flash on a monitor and translated it into French on the spot, relaying the scoop back across the Atlantic. In the following weeks, letters came into New York thanking NBC for its international coverage, including one letter from France that declared, "I heard your announcement forty-nine minutes before any European station announced it." The establishment of high-quality and reliable international news reporting plus a talented multilingual staff in NBC's International Division (and other networks) gave U.S. broadcasters more features to attract French and international listeners than ever before.[16]

Radio Goes to War

The period from early September 1939 when France declared war against Germany, to early May 1940 when Germany invaded France, constituted the *Drôle de Guerre*, or Phony War. No shots were fired, but attacks on France via the airwaves grew heated. German propagandists bullied the French, mocked their leaders, impugned England's motives toward France, and invited the French to side with the Nazis.[17] Powerful transmitters targeted the waiting French troops massed along the Franco-German frontier. Soldiers listened to Paul Ferdonnet, a right-wing French journalist, who had defected to the Germans. Identified by the French government as the "Traitor of Stuttgart," Ferdonnet claimed that the French would be dying only to protect Britain's wealth and strategic interests, an assertion made by pacifist and Communist interests as well. Playing to the French Far Right, Ferdonnet warned of an imminent fifth column (that is, Communist) uprising inside France. "[T]he skill was unmistakable," notes Asa Briggs. "Information, propaganda and direct appeals were adroitly interspersed with recorded songs by Tino Rossi and Lucienne Boyer." Worried French officials monitored these broadcasts and combed soldiers' letters for evidence of eroding convictions but could neither corroborate nor rule out entirely the possibility of radio propaganda's damaging effects.[18]

France's Phony War airwaves contained other insidious messages in the form of "black propaganda." Whereas "white propaganda" referred to persuasive communication from an openly identified source, "black propaganda" referred to clandestine communication. It often involved deliberately misidentified providers of information. Misleading information could be used to manipulate, sow confusion, and drive wedges into the enemy's ranks. Using transmitters on unauthorized frequencies to disguise their point of origin, these German radio programs pretended to be the work of underground patriots in France. Radio Humanité (Radio Humanity), named for the Communist newspaper suppressed by the French government, slyly masqueraded as the voice of renegade French Communists. Using revolutionary slogans and attacks on capitalist greed and collusion, the station played to mainstream fears (sowed by Far Right nationalists as well) that France's true enemy was not Germany, but Communism. La Voix de la Paix (The Voice of Peace) attacked the government of Édouard Daladier as bellicose and incompetent. Dissembling black propaganda emissions like these picked up currents of popular disaffection and diabolically enlarged and distorted them in hopes of weakening France's resolve to resist a true enemy preparing its attack.[19]

On May 10, 1940, the German army achieved what was thought impossible by skirting the fortified Franco-German border and attacking France by way of the Low Countries and the Ardennes. Surprised, overwhelmed, and swiftly outflanked, France surrendered. The armistice of June 22, 1940, dissolved the French constitution and partitioned the country into occupied and unoccupied zones. Germany controlled Paris, the northern interior and frontier, and a zone extending the length of France's Atlantic Coast, which placed two-thirds of the French population under military control. From Vichy, octogenarian and World War I hero Marshal Philippe Pétain represented France and oversaw the population residing in the unoccupied southern zone.[20] Violent repression came next. As Julian Jackson describes, tens of thousands of political dissidents (Communists, Freemasons) died and six hundred fifty thousand Frenchmen were forced into labor camps. An estimated seventy-five thousand French Jews were exterminated at Auschwitz, and an additional sixty thousand persons went to concentration camps. An estimated thirty to thirty-five thousand French resisters also were killed, along with thousands of innocent men, women, and children. Some of these crimes proceeded with Vichy's direct collaboration, including deportations to death camps. The Milice française (French militia) suppressed the Resistance and performed reprisal killings and state-sanctioned murder. The destruction of the French economy, rationing, and widespread hunger compounded France's misery.[21]

Scholars agree in hindsight that the direct impact of radio propaganda on French morale or the will to resist Germany was probably negligible. German military tactics, daring, and execution rather than depleted French morale probably decided the outcome. Contemporaries were less certain, however, about the root causes of the defeat, and German, French, British, and U.S. intelligence agents all believed to various degrees that French listeners had fallen prey to radio manipulation. Faith in the power of mass communication and radio propaganda also influenced how the United States and its allies pursued their strategy to fight World War II, including techniques of communicating with the French population.[22]

In the aftermath of the defeat, many stations in the north of France ceased broadcasting. Some closed voluntarily, others were sabotaged, and still others fell into the hands of the Germans.[23] After a brief interruption, national broadcasting resumed in the occupied zone. The French government nominally controlled Radio-Paris, the former PTT station, but it served the propaganda purposes of the German occupiers and French collaborators. In most respects, however, there was a semblance of normality at the station. Many technicians, staff, and talent remained on the job. Major French stars and celebrities also appeared on Radio-Paris. A large audience continued to listen to Radio-Paris, perhaps because 70 percent of its daily content was entertaining music.[24]

The Vichy government established a radio authority that supervised public and private stations in the unoccupied southern zone.[25] Although not nearly as popular as Radio-Paris, or easy to hear across France, Radio-Vichy, as it became known, served the national government's hall-of-mirrors propaganda campaign. Its programs enshrined themes of "work, family, and country," which were central to the Vichy's conservative nationalist agenda. Radio-Vichy provided a platform for Marshal Pétain to burnish his image as a national treasure and a paternal savior of France. Radio-Vichy also extended the exclusionary idea of a French national family that could not abide Communists, Freemasons, or Jews.[26]

On September 6, 1940, the French-language service of the BBC presented *Les français parlent aux français* ("The French Speak to the French"), a daily thirty-minute program. French personalities and journalists, such as Pierre Bourdan, Jean Marin, and Maurice Schumann, presented news reports, commentaries, and droll entertainment.[27] In addition to fifteen minutes of news, the program offered such varied segments as historical and political reports, roundtable discussions, and music—including banned French military tunes, popular *chansons*, and satirical compositions such as Jean Oberlé's *Radio-Paris ment* ("Radio-Paris Lies"), a song for children (and adults) set to the melody of *La Cucaracha*. The mischievous adaptation circulated widely. One intelligence report found that it surfaced as a chant at a playground in the city of Tarbes in southwestern France.[28] The irreverent hosts transformed Vichy's clunky national revolutionary slogan "work, family, country" into a sarcastic jab: "work nowhere to be found, family scattered, country humiliated."[29]

The BBC provided war news that Radio-Paris and Radio-Vichy deliberately distorted or suppressed. It furnished airtime to Charles de Gaulle and his surrogates to champion the Free French movement on the program *Honneur et patrie* (Honor and Country), also hosted by Maurice Schumann. The BBC's "The French Speak to the French" monitored and corrected the misinformation broadcast in France. One of the first lessons the BBC imparted was that that the Germans and collaborationists controlled Radio-Paris like a marionette.[30] Broadcasters attacked the station for encouraging and abetting the repression of French citizens and for lying to the public.[31] Pétain's radio addresses received polite but pointed criticism.[32] The BBC encouraged listeners to ignore the platitudes of the Pétain government and examine the regime's practices. They were told that France was itself a "land of the pogrom, a land of shame," as a result of Vichy's assistance in the Paris roundup and deportation of Jews to Auschwitz in July 1942.[33]

Like NBC's *The French Hour*, the BBC's French-language service included a *Courrier de France* (Mail from France) segment that invited listeners to send news for possible excerpted broadcast over the air. Correspondents thanked the BBC for the messages of hope contained in other listener letters. "We live in a kind of moral chaos and cannot see our way through the world of lies and—worse than lies—half-truths, in which we move," reflected a listener in Lyon. "It is a marvel to me that in spite of this there should be so many stout hearts and loyal minds who maintain that truth is worth fighting for at all costs."[34] Listeners cheered when a bold letter writer lambasted the Occupation authorities: "I envy you so much to be able to tell those swine the truth about themselves," wrote a fan from St. Julien, who confessed he tingled with delight when a French correspondent's "expressions of disgust with Vichy" got a mass airing on the radio.[35] Because the names of correspondents were redacted, but not their regional locations, it became a sport among some listeners to guess who in their town or city might be writing secretly to the BBC. "In the past week," wrote a Bayonne listener, "everyone has been trying to pierce the incognito of the person who has written from here."[36]

By February 1942, estimated radio set ownership in metropolitan France numbered 5.26 million, with the highest concentrations in Paris, along the

northern coast, in urban industrial centers, and in provincial cities such as
Bordeaux. A postwar survey found that 90 percent of adult males during
the Occupation reported having access to a radio. Four out of five radio sets
in France had "all-wave" capability, and U.S. shortwave programs could be
heard reliably in Paris.[37] Further south, however, transatlantic shortwave
reception became more problematic. "While many people try to get the U.S.
broadcasts, few have sets good enough to hear them," reported an informant
in Cannes. Demand to hear international broadcasts drove up the costs of
radio sets. A high-quality unit could fetch up to 1,700 French francs in Paris,
or about a month's wages for the average worker. Journalist Janet Flanner
discovered that even as Parisians relinquished their possessions to buy food
and soap because of chronic shortages, their shortwave radios remained "the
last household objects of value" that they would sell.[38]

In the French provinces, high-quality manufactured sets were harder to
obtain, and homemade radios constituted an estimated one-quarter of all
sets in use. Many people built sets from kits or patronized radio repair shops,
which performed the labor and furnished replacement parts. The know-how
to build and maintain a working set was distributed across the population
thanks to military service, amateur radio clubs, and PTT regional associations. Bartering foodstuffs in exchange for parts and vacuum tubes or for
repair services from a *petit artisan* helped listeners in the provinces maintain
access to international broadcasts. Such coordinated and cooperative efforts
meant that by 1942 shortwave transmissions could be received "among even
the poorer and more remote sections" of France with a good quality set.[39]

Jamming and Cross Listeners

Occupation and Vichy authorities grasped the threat that international broadcasting posed to their authority.[40] On October 9, 1940, the German military
began electronic jamming of the BBC and other international signals. Jamming could not stop international transmissions, but it could create an almost
intolerable racket that could deter uncommitted listeners. Listeners learned
to recoil quickly should jamming cause deafening bursts of noise, howls,
or crackles from the radio speaker. Listening to jammed signals required
such "intense effort," that often "people were 'worn out' by the end of the
program."[41] "Look here," exploded one frustrated listener in the course of a
letter asking the BBC for more powerful transmissions, "do you intend with
your inadequate waves to leave us to rot away peacefully in our little corner,
drugged by Vichy propaganda? . . . you must not abandon us!"[42] BBC engineers attempted to elude jamming by hopping from frequency to frequency,

Zones of German Occupation, 1940. (Map courtesy of Justin Jocque)

but that afforded only a temporary solution since jamming signals could also be switched. In the final analysis, jamming could not consistently prevent a determined listener from receiving international broadcasts.[43]

On October 28, 1940, Occupation authorities barred listening in public to "British stations, and in general, all stations delivering anti-government propaganda." The order reflected fears about the programs from providers other than the BBC, which included U.S. shortwave broadcasts. The punishment for publicly engaging in so-called "black listening" was a fine of up to 100 francs and up to six months in jail. The following year, a new law banned listening anywhere to critical international providers. General Otto von Stülpnagel, who oversaw the German-occupied zone, threatened stern measures to stop clandestine listening, including forced labor and even the death penalty.

In the majority of prosecuted cases, available evidence suggested that the punishment usually consisted of "a fine and fifteen days imprisonment."[44]

General François Darlan, a Vichy supporter, warned that overzealous enforcement of the listening ban might drive a curious but otherwise quiescent population toward de Gaulle and the Free French. In the contested Alsace region, authorities waged an intensive campaign against black listening. They confiscated equipment, imprisoned offenders, and sentenced some to a year's hard labor. Elsewhere, enforcement appeared haphazard or even lax. "Gendarmes at Aix-en-Provence, for instance, in reprimanding a Frenchman who had been denounced for black listening not only performed their task with many apologies," read one report, "but even suggested that, if he should listen next evening he should close his windows." Unbowed by the intimidation, a listener told the BBC, "We shall take precautions, but we shall continue. What should we do without your news?"[45]

Since the advent of broadcasting, French listeners had consumed national and international radio, but after the events of 1938 and throughout the Occupation, "cross listening" or "eavesdropping" as intelligence officials called avid international listening, became a preoccupation. Speculating on French audience patronage of the avowed propagandists at Radio-Paris and Radio-Vichy, Asa Briggs writes, "People listened not only to what was 'projected' deliberately at them, but also 'to what was projected at somebody else.'" Audiences listened for reliable news of the world, but also to gain insight into the silent thoughts of others whose political loyalties might be inscrutable. The "high thick walls" separating French people from one another might conceivably be scaled through such critical listening exercises.[46]

Jean Guéhenno, a Parisian teacher, writer, and *résistant,* fit the profile of a cross listener. He followed radio news from Belgrade, Berlin, Budapest, London, and New York, as well as from Radio-Paris and Radio-Vichy. He counted himself among the select few who heard Charles de Gaulle's *appel du 18 juin 1940* (the Appeal of June 18, 1940), the call to resist the armistice with Germany that de Gaulle issued from London via the BBC.[47] As a cross listener, Guéhenno first heard the terms of the armistice reported on German radio. In spring 1941, he chuckled into his diary after exiled French broadcasters on the BBC encouraged listeners to mark the letter V for victory on walls, stones, and other public edifices as a sign of resistance, and many audaciously responded.[48]

Cross listening to the BBC, U.S. shortwave, and numerous other providers afforded Guéhenno enough reliable information to pick apart lies and propaganda messages in French newspapers and on the air. "Whoever would analyze the Vichy and Paris press this morning (and also the radio bulletins),"

Guéhenno wrote privately, "would assuredly have plenty of fine examples of misappropriation, distortion, omission, and lies that make up what in the prison of Europe one calls news."[49] Pétain's broadcasts made Guéhenno dyspeptic: "the same pathetic tripe *(gnangnaneries)*—familial, artisanal, religious, folkloric—they really abuse folklore at Vichy—flowing interminably like a trickle of dirty water."[50] Though he hid his colorful reactions in the pages of his diary, Guéhenno's cross listening gave him a sense of mission within the "prison house" he and many others occupied between 1940 and 1944.

Walking the Line: *The French Hour* and NBC's Neutrality Policy

To the surprise of NBC officials, transatlantic mail continued arriving at *The French Hour* even after the fall of France. "With much pleasure we listen to your French hour," wrote one Parisian in 1940, "which informs us better than our own what is going on in old Europe."[51] From Gascony, a listener praised Raymond Gram Swing's commentaries: "Your [translated] adaptation is excellent." Yet another thanked the International Division for bringing news of resistance activities, such as a political assassination in October 1941: "It was through [NBC] that I heard that the German Lieutenant Colonel Holz had been executed by two French patriots at Place St. Pierre at 8 a.m. in Nantes," wrote a listener.[52] Another wrote to *The French Hour* to condemn the anti-British propaganda diffused via French national radio. In an act of citizen radio journalism, the correspondent listed a rundown of crimes perpetrated by German authorities and opportunistic French citizens: "The Germans are stealing our butter from Charente, from Normandy, wheat from the Beauce, cattle from the Franche-Comté, sugar from the North, and furthermore they come to 'buy' stuff in the free zone. . . . And what about . . . hoarding by French merchants, who whisper in your ear that they can sell a liter of oil for twenty-nine francs?" The writer added, "We are hungry and thirsty for the truth!" Having reported his own news, the correspondent politely requested that his letter be forwarded to London to the attention of the BBC.[53]

U.S. commercial broadcasters like NBC avoided taking partisan positions as a matter of standard procedure and policy.[54] "The Declaration of Neutrality obviously makes it necessary for our program staff to carefully edit any material we broadcast or rebroadcast to foreign nations," wrote NBC's O. B. Hanson in response to the German invasion of Poland in September 1939. As a subsidiary of RCA and an affiliate of General Electric, NBC feared any action that might ruffle its international business partners, foreign broadcast officials, U.S. advertisers, or pro-German or isolationist listeners.[55]

Inside the International Division, however, where numerous European expatriates worked, the start of the war and the Occupation created a tense atmosphere that grew almost unbearable for Fernand Auberjonois. News from France could be reported, and listener letters could be read, but NBC expected *The French Hour* to maintain a balanced tone, despite the host's privately critical view of U.S. isolationism and strong antifascist beliefs. Auberjonois became embroiled in a conflict involving the spouse of a major advertiser, who for reasons unknown had "an unbounded admiration" for Marshal Pétain. "She suggested to the President of [NBC] that he put out a personal message on our shortwave to the head of what remained of the French state to let him know that all of America approved of his politics," Auberjonois recalled. To his great shock, the network agreed. Incensed by NBC's willingness to pander to a valued client in violation of its own rules, Auberjonois threatened to resign. The network refused to budge. At this point, NBC's resourceful vice president, John F. Royal, privately told Auberjonois that he had a solution in mind, and sent the angry announcer home. Auberjonois snuck back, however. From another studio, he listened to a monitor speaker of the outbound transmission as it became engulfed in interference. Royal had instructed engineers at RCA's shortwave facility to sabotage the signal. Back in the broadcast booth at Radio City everything sounded fine. Royal gambled that if anyone in France inquired about the transmission, NBC could explain that while happy to have appeased the request it could not control the atmospheric conditions that might have affected the broadcast on its way to France. Auberjonois quietly returned to work.[56]

NBC chief Lenox Lohr's pledge that the network intended to uphold its "duty" in times of international strife included offering NBC's shortwave facilities to U.S. government officials and the White House when needed. If President Franklin D. Roosevelt wanted to speak to France directly, NBC and other carriers could justify carrying the broadcast as the act of a neutral carrier furnishing a news story. U.S. networks broadcast the president's inauguration internationally in 1933 and 1937, including foreign-language translations. When Roosevelt delivered a major address about the possibility of the United States going to war in spring 1941, the international listening audience, including France, numbered an estimated twenty million persons, though some, like Jean Guéhenno, complained of shortwave jamming.[57]

Political events kept testing NBC's official policies of neutrality, however. When Marshal Pétain condoned Germany's appropriation of military bases in French-mandated Syria on French radio, Roosevelt fired back with help from shortwave. On May 15, 1941, the president delivered a speech expressly directed to the French people.[58] NBC prepared an immediate French translation and dedicated ten hours of its European shortwave services that day to airing a thirty-minute special, which it ran each hour. Auberjonois read the translated speech expressing the president's grave concern about evidence of active collaboration between Germany and Vichy, which appeared to violate the limits set by the Franco-German armistice.

NBC's Roosevelt broadcast marathon marked the beginning of what appeared to be a shift in policy at the network. That day Auberjonois made no effort to project a neutral attitude toward the Vichy government. After delivering news reports between cycles of the speech, he read passages of letters from *The French Hour*'s mailbag, which he prefaced by saying, "This is what Frenchmen in France think of the Vichy government and of the occupying Nazi Army." He also interviewed the French ambassador to Germany, Fernand de Brion, on the program, bluntly asking "if he represented the French people or Berlin, and if he was not a Fifth Columnist before the war."[59] Later that summer, when Occupation authorities banned public celebration of Bastille Day claiming they feared civil disorder, NBC produced a compensatory on-air celebration via shortwave. The network "celebrated [the holiday] for them," wrote journalist Earl Sparling, "with the kind of patriotic music they would not be hearing along their own boulevards, and with messages from Charles Boyer, Eva Le Gallienne, Col. William J. Donovan, and a stirring tone poem by Fernand Auberjonois, head of the NBC French Section." Such partisan gestures by NBC did not go unnoticed in France. One PTT Vichy loyalist angrily interrupted the start of a transatlantic news feed by an NBC reporter to declare in English: "There will be no transmission from Vichy tonight!"[60]

Reading letters from occupied and unoccupied France on the air entailed potential risks for the correspondent. It remained conceivable that authorities or Vichyites might identify and try to punish a correspondent. *The French Hour* took precautions to protect privacy. Auberjonois instructed the NBC staff handling the mail and translating the letters into English to delete names and any personal references that might reveal too much about the correspondent. In spring 1941, unbeknownst to Auberjonois, an ambitious junior publicist walked off with a freshly translated letter that had not been redacted. The resulting press release declared, "From the letters received in New York it is evident that many Frenchmen are listening to the program in spite of the Gestapo." The release included considerable personal information and the actual name of the correspondent. An incensed Auberjonois contacted the heads of the division.[61] "While this is a very good story from a news standpoint," agreed one executive, "from a national standpoint there are certain phrases that are not discreet." John F. Royal rebuked the publicist

for poor judgment: "I think we are guilty of a grave breach of ethics when
we circulate for publication such a letter," he declared. Royal also colorfully
excoriated the French correspondent for sharing personal information in
the letter: "With all the clues she gives to her identity, it would be child's
play for the sees-all, knows-all Gestapo to put the finger on this woman. . . .
Any third-grade detective from the Missing Persons Bureau could locate
this woman in twenty-four hours." The publicist retained his job but was
instructed never to circulate the contents of any letters outside the division
without first seeking permission. No harm is known to have come to "this
woman," as Royal called her, who also was spared Royal's invective.[62]

To the benefit of historians, the correspondence received by the BBC's
French-language radio programs survived the war, but the letters received
at NBC's *The French Hour* and other U.S. providers are not known to have
been so lucky. Tallies of letters received were sometimes compiled in International Division reports, and fragments of specific letters would be quoted
in memoranda, but these are the only known traces of the letters known to
have survived. A notable exception is a series of letters sent to NBC in fall
1941 from the widow in rural southern France mentioned at the start of the
chapter. Auberjonois selected her first letter dated September 5, 1941, from
the weekly mail and read parts or all of it over the air. The listener heard her
words on the air, which prompted a response written in diaristic installments
dated September 28, October 3, and October 4, 1941. Writing repeatedly to
international broadcasters was a practice common to correspondents to the
BBC, too. The letters to NBC contained reflections on politics ("Evil is sweeping over the world like a hurricane"), food and clothing shortages ("we count
our slices of bread and butter"), apologies about bad typing ("Last night I
forgot one of my fingers under the bread knife"), and affectionate references
to "Arthur," her shortwave radio. The correspondent never denounced the
Vichy government openly, except in one sly instance. She reported asking
a village schoolboy what he had done on the first day of classes, to which
he replied, "We were taught to sing '*Marshall Pétain, Savior of France*.'" She
then added sarcastically, "He had, however, bought a really beautiful eraser."
Throughout her writing, the correspondent often used the collective plural
("we") to share a sense of others in her village, but it also could have been a
reference to all French people enduring the Occupation to the best of their
abilities.[63]

Executives at NBC's International Division found the letters so powerful
that they commissioned an elegantly printed pamphlet, *France Speaks to
America*, which included the letters in the original French alongside English
translations. The pamphlet included an unsigned preface that began with a

{LA FRANCE PARLE A L'AMERIQUE}

{FRANCE SPEAKS TO AMERICA}

*vres pour vous dire quel bien vous nous faites, pourtant j'ose vous
écrire. Je n'ai rien de plus à vous dire que vos autres correspon-
dants. Il semble d'ailleurs à vous entendre que vous sachiez infi-
niment mieux que nous tout ce qui se passe ici, ce qui s'y pense,
souffre, espère, étouffe.*

*Je vous écris d'un village que vous aimeriez. Il est pauvre
mais magnifique. Sa population est de cent soixante âmes. Et
quand je rencontre les gens du village, ceux qui, il y a peu de
temps encore, me disaient: "Qu'est-ce qu'ils disent à Londres?"
interrogent: "Et alors, comme ça, qu'est-ce qu'ils vous disent en
Amérique?"*

*C'est vous, Américains, qui avez raison de faire crédit au
peuple français; vous ne comptez pas plus vainement sur lui
qu'inutilement il espérait en vous.*

*Sachez bien que vos actes nous émeuvent, croyez que nous
nous sentons avec vous étrangement unis et parfaitement
solidaires.*

*J'étais à Marseille, l'hiver passé, quand vous avez envoyé
des nourritures pour les enfants de France. J'étais au printemps
dans un village qui bénéficia de 21 jours de pain blanc. On disait
"le pain américain" comme l'on dit "l'heure allemande." Et ces
mots prenaient une grande signification. Manger le pain américain c'était bien, et les plus simples le percevaient, accepter à
l'heure la plus démunie l'aide du meilleur des amis.*

{6}

you a word nonetheless. Besides, you seem to know much better than we what is going on here; what we think, hope, suffer
and hide.

You would love this little village from which I am writing
you. It is poor but magnificent, with 160 inhabitants. I am
lucky enough to have a radio on which I can get your broadcasts,
and the people around here now ask me: "Well, what are they
saying in America?" instead of: "What is London telling
you?" as they used to.

You Americans are right to have faith in the French people;
you do not count on us vainly any more than our trust in you is
unjustified.

Believe me, we are moved by what you are doing, and we
feel a complete solidarity between your country and ours.

I was in Marseille last winter when you sent food for our
children. Last spring, I stayed in one of our villages which had
twenty-one days of white bread. People spoke of "American
bread" as they did of "German time." And this phrase became
charged with its own special meaning. It was a good thing to eat
American bread (the simplest among us could see that), and
accept during these hard days a gift from the best of our friends.

And now I am at my village, unchanged in centuries, with
its old castles, its fortified churches, its rivers lined with poplars,
and its barren moors. This is a land of wheat and vines—real

{7}

NBC compiled the 1941 correspondence of a female listener in Southern France
into the pamphlet, *France Speaks to America.*

question: "What do the French people think of America today, now, in the
fall of 1941?" An answer came several lines later: "It is more than a message
from an unknown listener to a broadcaster; it is the voice of oppressed France
speaking to America. For this reason, we think you will read it with your
heart as well as your mind." The target audience for the pamphlet would appear to have been Francophiles in the United States, French expatriates and
exiles, French diplomats, U.S. politicians, and possibly even the Federal Communications Commission (FCC). The preface mentioned the uncertainty
of those wondering about how ordinary French people regarded France's
"capitulation" to Germany. "We had underestimated their courage, their will
to make themselves heard," the preface added.[64] In addition to documenting
the resistant spirit of one listener, the pamphlet also registered the impact of
NBC's overseas broadcasts on the civilian population of France.

On December 14, 1941, one week after the surprise Japanese attack on Pearl
Harbor that drew the United States into the war, John W. Elwood sent a copy
of *France Speaks to America* to John M. Begg, an assistant chief in the State

Department's Division of Cultural Relations. "[I]t seems to me," Elwood wrote in a cover note, "now that we are at war, that the letter has especial meaning, not only for the immediate future, but in planning for the years to come."[65] Begg expressed "great interest" in the pamphlet. He promised to share it with "other interested officers in the Department." Elwood's gesture suggested he hoped to demonstrate the strategic power of international broadcasting to connect with foreign populations. It also is likely he shared the pamphlet to demonstrate NBC's goodwill and desire to serve as an (independent) ally of the U.S. government. The peacetime barrier formally dividing U.S. international broadcasters from the federal government had given way, however, and a new era had begun.

Enter the "Yankee Doodle" Network

On June 8, 1942, Jean Guéhenno discovered that the U.S. government was coming to Europe by air: "Henceforth twice a day, London is relaying a bulletin of the most hopelessly naive, but fearlessly confident American news."[66] The program's velocity ruffled Guéhenno, however: "It begins with a swing genre musical theme, a sort of *bamboula nègre*," he wrote in his diary. "The news follows at breakneck speed. . . . German towns fall; Japanese ships are swallowed up; planes, tanks, American vessels populate the air, the land and the sea. It seems that the actual pace of the war has changed; it is comforting for a moment, and then we are engulfed by the feeling of the idiocy at the core of what has become of us."[67] In its style, pace, and syncopated music theme, the Voice of America network (VOA) embodied the power, abundance, and speed of the U.S. broadcast techno-aesthetic. As encouraging as an uptick in "the pace of the war" might be for Occupied France, something about the VOA's packaging of war news into up-tempo reports left at least one French listener feeling skeptical about these cheerful U.S. radio announcers and all the more impatient with France's unhappy circumstances.

The launch of the VOA to serve international audiences, and the Armed Forces Radio Service to serve U.S. military personnel, established the U.S. government as a new force in international broadcast communication and media production.[68] The Communications Act of 1934 gave the U.S. president authority to direct the uses of communications to serve "national defense and security."[69] The formation of the VOA followed several years of preliminary discussion involving the executive branch; government agencies, such as the U.S. State Department and the FCC; private broadcasters; and Congress.[70] In summer 1938, one year after NBC premiered *The French Hour*, the Roosevelt administration's interdepartmental committee on shortwave (headed by FCC commissioner Frank R. McNinch) and the International Communications group at the State Department's Division of Cultural Relations formalized plans for a government-directed radio service.[71]

In July 1941, President Roosevelt established the Office of the Coordinator of Information (COI), headed by Col. William J. Donovan. The COI operated under the aegis of the Office of Emergency Management (OEM). When the United States entered the war, the COI split in two, with Robert E. Sherwood heading the Foreign Information Service (FIS), which oversaw "white propaganda" shortwave broadcasting and Donovan leading the Office of Strategic Services (OSS), which participated in strategic communications, including clandestine radio work, or "black propaganda." The FIS began broadcasting to Europe in January 1942, and the inaugural broadcast of what became the Voice of America network occurred on February 24, 1942.[72] In June, Roosevelt's executive order 9182 placed the journalist Elmer Davis in charge of the Office of War Information (OWI), which took charge of the VOA. Percy Winner, a former network radio executive, handled VOA broadcasting to France.[73]

The OWI leased the prime hours of the day from private shortwave providers for reaching European listeners. The VOA produced the content but relied heavily on the technical expertise of professional broadcasters to help produce and deliver programs. By March 1942, the VOA furnished more than twenty bulletins or programs in French each day. Many U.S. network technicians and producers transferred temporarily to the OWI as part of their military service. In this manner, private broadcasters represented an integral part of the human and technical infrastructure now at the disposal of the U.S. government.[74]

OWI policy directed that any important message intended for France be broadcast in English, German, and Italian to keep jammers busy and to promote the greatest chance of reception by the multilingual population residing in the country. The OWI standardized content across the language services so that the message delivered was identical and simple so as not to confuse listeners or undermine U.S. authority.[75] Although BBC and U.S. intelligence reported positive responses to the VOA, some listeners found the programs boastful and long-winded. "They give far too long descriptions of what the production will be and how ready the country will be in the future. The French want to hear what is happening now," wrote an impatient resident of Nîmes in June 1942. Another VOA listener agreed that the "commentators [*sic*] are usually too lengthy." The informant suggested adopting shorter bulletins and commentaries because "People do not have the patience to listen longer."[76] Reports indicated that some listeners preferred the programs of U.S. private networks that used to be available during prime listening hours. François Navarre found network programs more interesting because they possessed "an individual tone" that the VOA's regimentation quashed.[77] Albert Guigui, secretary of the CGT (France's leading communist trade union) reported that he found "the American broadcasts remarkably well adapted to the French spirit," adding that he preferred the commercial network programs from New York to VOA shows.[78] The fact that more than a few people in occupied France complained of being bored by the VOA spoke volumes about the difference in program philosophy and technical skills between private networks and the productions of the U.S. government. It also attested to the strain and edginess of living in an unfree society.[79]

"To Bring the Broadcaster to the Front Lines"

In November 1942, Allied forces landed in North Africa along with radio specialists attached to the Overseas Branch of the OWI. The Psychological Warfare Branch (PWB) functioned in partnership with the OWI under the command of the Supreme Headquarters Allied Expeditionary Force (SHAEF), headed by U.S. General Dwight D. Eisenhower. In a year's time, more than one thousand participants created a staggering multimedia endeavor (print, photograph, cinema, broadcast) in North Africa to help SHAEF liberate France and Europe. The OWI/PWB ranks included British, U.S., and French civilian and military personnel, including a number of former U.S. broadcasters, among them Captain Fernand Auberjonois, who had volunteered for the army and received training in advanced psychological warfare techniques.[80]

The PWB's broadcasts supplied news of Free French activities along with information about Allied military plans that were intended to smooth the way for France's liberation and the establishment of a new French government.[81] The PWB gathered intelligence, monitored Allied and enemy airwaves, produced and aired broadcasts, and built and operated fixed and mobile transmission systems through its radio division. Its propaganda shops produced millions of leaflets, including program guides to OWI and VOA broadcasts, which were airdropped over French territory.[82]

Working with Free French authorities in Algiers, the PWB cobbled together a network of nine broadcasting stations across Algeria and Tunisia.[83] On February 3, 1943, the Free French under General Henri Giraud inaugurated Radio-France. It broadcast from Algiers on a medium-wave signal to metropolitan France and the Maghreb. Radio-France attacked the Vichy government, championed de Gaulle, and called on listeners to support the Free French and the Allied troops in liberating France. U.S.-erected transmitters and technical assistance supported the endeavors of Radio-France, which created occasional awkward moments when Radio-France ignored OWI directives on scripts, news, and commentaries and "broadcast whatever it pleased" instead.[84]

The degraded quality of life in France under the Occupation, dissatisfaction with Vichy's corrupt and ineffectual leadership, and the people's widespread desire for change were known quantities to the PWB. French attitudes toward the United States and England confounded easy assessment, however. Strategists fretted about how U.S. troops would be greeted when they arrived in France. The OWI/PWB radio campaign assumed that in addition to news and information, French listeners needed careful preparation for the arrival of the troops. PWB officials believed that the psychological effects of war, military defeat, and the Occupation had generated widespread skepticism toward the broadcast medium itself, which had been subject to ceaseless manipulation for so many years.[85]

Allied intelligence analysts agreed that years of propaganda exposure had left many occupied listeners reluctant to trust anything they heard over the airwaves, including news from their ostensible allies. "You must know that this propaganda is assuming enormous proportions," a correspondent told British intelligence. "*You* [monitoring the airwaves from England] hear the radio, but you cannot see the posters plastered everywhere, the inscriptions, the 'stickers,' the scattered leaflets."[86] An intelligence agent in Toulouse wrote, "The Frenchman has become distrustful. So many promises have been made him. All these vibrated in the same chord—patriotism, sacrifice, liberty, and heroism—and by dint of overmuch vibration the chord has ceased to vibrate altogether. No further promise, no man, no idea can now make him budge." Allied broadcasters noted repeated listener requests for a "maximum of truth, facts, and figures." Broadcasters were bluntly told, "News must be served without sauce." The chief of U.S. Naval Intelligence, C. H. Coggins, warned the OWI to proceed cautiously in its unprecedented operation "to bring the broadcaster to the front lines." Misapplied communication could be dismissed as propaganda. The French population, he declared, "wants to get all the facts of the present war," he wrote, "and *wants to do the thinking itself.*" Careless embellishment or overkill by OWI and PWB broadcasters could erode rather than strengthen trust in the intentions of the advancing Allies.[87]

"Enthusiastic, Apoplectic and Breathless Modes of Delivery"

In summer 1943, the PWB began the "preliberation phase" of its "long-range program" for French-language broadcasting, which supplemented conventional broadcast transmissions from North Africa, England, and the United States, with bulletins furnished by mobile broadcast trucks capable of hailing occupiers and occupied alike when the troops crossed into France. PWB messages aimed at assuring "future whole-hearted cooperation with the Allies," by stressing Franco-American friendship; establishing the credibility of the United States; countering any impulse that France "abandon the democratic way of life"; and quashing Axis propaganda impugning U.S. motives for taking the fight to Germany.[88]

OWI strategists hoped to bolster trust in the Allies and deepen distaste for the Germans without overselling the virtues of the United States and Great Britain. They also wanted to avoid stepping on the toes of the Free French, whose communications set the critical tone adopted toward Vichy. Notwithstanding the many spirited letters and resistant sentiments collected in Occupied France, U.S. intelligence looked patronizingly on the average French citizen, who was portrayed as vulnerable, unreliable, and needing special handling. With no trace of irony, officials warned broadcasters that French listeners must not feel condescended to. Wrote one analyst, "If the desire of victory in France is of unchangeable strength and consistency, the belief in victory has its ups and downs. France will remain, until the day of liberation, like a patient straining with his being toward healthy." The perception of a sick or damaged polity is one that would carry into future plans and programs to rejuvenate France after the war.[89]

The OWI had accumulated extensive intelligence from French listeners about their radio likes and dislikes that warned them of how under certain circumstances the U.S. techno-aesthetic could rub the average French listener the wrong way. A training bulletin for field broadcasters explained that to persuade a French audience, the U.S. broadcaster must resist "enthusiastic, apoplectic and breathless modes of delivery." The bulletin added that while an exuberant and excited approach might suit the occasion for U.S. listeners, "The French audience is particularly sensitive to understatement; the French feel that Americans have a tendency to overemphasize rather than understate. They have been encouraged to believe this by some of our broadcasts on the shortwave." Failure to temper emotion also could be dangerous for listeners because it might incite "premature moves, uprising, revolts against the authorities right at the start. . . . Civil strife is a definite menace. Appeals to unity must be made. This is one more reason why a calm approach is in order." Broadcasters habituated to the hucksterism of U.S. commercial radio would have to adjust for an audience believed allergic to slick propagandists: "There is no room in the unit for 'announcers,' for people who, because they are used to selling soap, talk with soap in their mouth," the bulletin declared sternly.[90]

Recent historical events also represented a potential landmine that broadcasters needed to avoid, or at least treat very carefully for fear of triggering negative associations. OWI officials directed PWB broadcasters to be politically sensitive in view of the awkward circumstances of the return of U.S. soldiers to France for the first time since World War I. "Avoid the 'Lafayette we are here' theme," admonished the training bulletin, referring to the melodramatic phrase reportedly uttered by an aide to U.S. General John J. Pershing on the Fourth of July 1917 in Paris.[91] Treatment of the Allied advance had to be respectfully counterbalanced "by playing up the French angle and any part French forces play in this war." Irwin Wall describes a culture of "antipathy" and distrust at the highest levels of the U.S. government for both Vichy and the Free French, which percolated through the ranks of the armed forces. The PWB perspectives toward the occupied population ranged from anxiety and condescension to empathic concern and confidence that France would rise up when the situation demanded.[92]

By the first quarter of 1944, intelligence reports suggested that as expectation of liberation grew, the public attitudes that so concerned the OWI were improving in France. "The despair and apathy prevailing in France during the first three years after the Armistice are no longer conditions of the French psychology," boasted Wallace Carroll, deputy director of Area One of the Overseas Bureau of the OWI. "The attitude has now grown into one of an awakened spirit, vigorously demonstrated by a newly discovered self-confidence and by a self-respect reminiscent of prewar France."[93] Along with the optimistic assessment, the memorandum contained sobering news. "As a corollary to the above, the French people have grown increasingly suspicious and apprehensive of Allied policy and intentions. This is particularly reflected in the declining interest in the BBC broadcasts." Although thirst for war news among the French seemed unquenchable, reports suggested that French listeners were greeting other programs with "discontent and boredom," chiefly because of "1. Suspicion of purely propaganda material, which can be checked by the listeners; 2. Anxiety over the Anglo-American delays on the military front; 3. Adverse reactions to indiscreet broadcasts." The memorandum remained vague on the nature of the third category, and data on attitudes toward the VOA were not forthcoming, but the report reiterated a core finding: "Being extremely skeptical and trained to regard propaganda with utmost suspicion, the French audience insists on hearing the truth in the news."[94] A further interpretation could be that the time for talk had passed. Occupied listeners wanted action.

The French Speak to the French, Again

"The liberation of French broadcasting [was] one of the most striking events of the insurrection," recalled French journalist and *résistant* Pierre Crénesse of the events of summer 1944. In 1938, at age nineteen, Crénesse debuted as a cub reporter at commercial station Radio-Cité, where he trained with the pioneering broadcaster Jean Guignebert. In 1940, Radio-Cité closed. Guignebert and Crénesse separated, but they later reconnected through the French Resistance's *Comité de la libération de la radio*, run by Guignebert.[95] The group surreptitiously built a studio in Paris on the rue de Grenelle, and laid plans for a takeover of the airwaves by the Free French. With help from composer and radio producer Pierre Schaeffer, the group secretly compiled banned recordings of patriotic French songs, clandestine poetry, and protest literature for broadcast once the insurrection began.[96]

On August 20, 1944, with the Allies converging on Paris, Radiodiffusion de la nation française (French National Broadcasting) came to life. That evening, Jean Guignebert gave the microphone to his protégé, Pierre Crénesse, who addressed an invisible audience:

> The microphone of French National Broadcasting was baptized tonight in the course of these historical moments. It was baptized in a climate of truth, because this microphone will never lie, as you were lied to by what you have heard in Paris for the last four years. We will keep in close contact with you . . . we will tell you what is happening in the capital, will announce the arrival of the main body of the army, will tell you that Paris is free.[97]

As Crénesse later wrote, "Paris had regained its voice, still weak, which mingled with the noise of the gun. But the world pricked up its ears: London and New York, Moscow and Algiers were counting the beats of our heart, were hearing the voice of the reborn French nation, its spasms and hiccoughs, as it delivered itself from lying and the silence of destruction."[98]

In the delirious days that followed, Free French broadcasters collected statements from Resistance leaders and described scenes in Paris. Pierre Crénesse darted around the city, calling in reports from telephone booths. PWB and U.S. network journalists arrived with the military. They coordinated communications with the Resistance and produced reports of their own, including some from the rue de Grenelle studio, which appeared to be no secret

Pierre Crénesse (at right with microphone) reported on General Charles de Gaulle's triumphant procession through Paris on August 26, 1944. (Courtesy Inathèque de France)

to anyone. NBC reporter John MacVane found it to be "crowded with British and American broadcasters." In their midst was a PWB broadcaster named Simon J. Copans, who had landed at Normandy and would establish himself as a beloved fixture of jazz radio in France. "We seized the opportunity to make several recordings of cheering crowds and happy Frenchmen," Copans recalled. Other PWB operatives, Captain Fernand Auberjonois among them, pooled recordings with *Radiodiffusion de la nation française*, as well as the BBC, U.S. networks, and the U.S. broadcasting station in Europe.[99] Finally, on August 26, French radio called Parisians into the streets to witness an extraordinary spectacle: the dramatic arrival of Charles de Gaulle in Paris. As de Gaulle toured the City of Light, a photographer documenting the event caught Crénesse in the procession, microphone in hand, capturing ambient sound of a historic occasion.[100]

International broadcasting during the Occupation helped serve a divided population in a state of crisis. The producers of French-language international programs in New York and London provided news and other programs that enabled listeners to reflect upon their circumstances, share their thoughts with others on the air in some cases, and privately and collectively imagine

a free future. Broadcasting helped sustain a radio nation comprised of occupied listeners searching for a semblance of a unified society in the face of
military occupation, partitioning, and authoritarian government. By writing
letters and conveying messages to the BBC, U.S. networks, and the VOA, and
hearing the words of ordinary French people—as well as Charles de Gaulle
and the articulate and entertaining spokespersons of the Free French movement in exile in London and New York—French listeners found a space in
which to counter the ugly everyday tenor of the Occupation.

The request to "speak to us more" that reached the United States and
NBC's *The French Hour* in fall 1941 marked a dramatic shift in the importance of U.S.–French broadcasting. With the liberation of France, the two
allies found themselves in a state of complex, and somewhat disorienting,
interdependence, the likes of which had not previously existed. U.S.–French
radio embodied the complexity. As the leaders of France and the United
States considered the needs of their respective societies and laid new plans,
transatlantic broadcasting took on a heightened role. It would serve as a nexus
for the repair of postwar French infrastructure, new forms of outreach to
the United States, and also, as a controversial field of U.S.–French Cold War
geopolitics.

PART II

Shaping a U.S.–French Radio Imaginary, 1945–74

4 Served on a Platter

How French Radio Cracked the U.S. Airwaves

In summer 1949, five years after the impromptu "baptism" of post-Occupation French broadcasting on the rue de Grenelle, Pierre Crénesse accepted an international "Oscar" of radio from *Variety*, the leading U.S. media and entertainment magazine. Crénesse and Radiodiffusion française (RDF; French national broadcasting) had recently launched five acclaimed new radio series in the United States. The programs aired weekly on some two hundred U.S. stations from coast to coast. The award testimonial sounded a familiar refrain for people familiar with U.S.–French broadcast encounters to date: "One of the biggest obstacles in the way of international exchanges has been the great difference between the techniques and the conceptions of radio in the United States and radio in other countries." Pierre Crénesse, the citation continued, "has shown himself to be one of the rare radiomen competent in this business of microphones-across-the-oceans, and demonstrated a rare talent for providing American stations with French programs that have the rhythm of American radio, without sacrificing either the cultural context or their national flavor."[1] *Variety* implied that the techno-aesthetic divide separating French and U.S. broadcasting appeared bridged at last.

The five series had a complicated pedigree that blended transatlantic cultural production with Cold War geopolitics. Produced in English by a team of French and U.S. nationals in Paris and New York, some of whom were on the payroll of the U.S. government, the series reflected a peculiar amalgamation of U.S.–French broadcasting. The national sounds came from France, yet they were not exactly of French make. The happy meeting of French "national culture" and U.S. "rhythm" that defined their mass aesthetic appeal reflected the complex circulatory and transnational operations of the mediated geopolitics of the Cold War. In design, execution, and distribution, the programs manifested a politically tinged inventory of representations of France for U.S. consumption that served U.S.–French political interests in specific ways.

When World War II ended, the U.S. Congress directed the Voice of America (VOA) to direct its energy to promoting U.S. interests abroad and countering the threat of global communism. The State Department absorbed many of the key strategic activities of the Office of War Information (OWI) and Psychological Warfare Branch (PWB), which included operating the VOA. The VOA has garnered extensive historical study for its uses around the world, its impact in the affairs of U.S. allies and foes alike, and its contentious political reception at home. The history of other U.S. government–backed operations within the radio systems of foreign powers is less well known, however. The State Department Office of Information and Educational Exchange (OIE), whose members included former OWI and PWB officers, assisted in the reconstruction of postwar French broadcasting, which included aiding an RDF unit known as the French Broadcast System in North America (FBS).[2]

This chapter analyzes the little-known history of the FBS in Paris and New York as an offshoot of the RDF and the impact of its export programs on U.S. broadcasting. The FBS accomplished what French broadcasting had been unable to accomplish previously: It produced and distributed English- and some French-language programs to scores of commercial, not-for-profit, and educational U.S. stations. The distributions began in 1946 and continued into the early 1970s.[3] Several FBS series also aired in France. This chapter follows the establishment of the RDF's first permanent news bureau in New York, which helped coordinate FBS operations. It assesses the effects of the 1948–51 European Recovery Program (the Marshall Plan) on the development of postwar U.S.–French broadcasting. The creation of the FBS and its success in the United States raises important concerns about the visible and invisible presence of U.S. power in French affairs. It sheds light on France's struggle to manage its postwar affairs and pursue its interests in association with a potentially domineering ally. Finally, it reveals the unexpected leverage points that transatlantic broadcasting afforded France, and the unforeseen implications for both the United States and France as they pursued a particular broadcast partnership during the Cold War era.

We Want Troush!

Three months after the liberation of Paris, the strategic mission of the OWI in France appeared to be accomplished. The massive Allied campaign begun in 1942 that used fixed transmitter and mobile radio technology to communicate with the occupied population in French had produced the desired ends: France was free and restoring its democratic institutions. Wallace Carroll, OWI deputy director of Overseas Operations, issued a statement on future policy that warned of the risk of entanglement in French affairs: "The OWI must exercise spartan resolution in keeping itself as an organization, as well as its individual personnel, apart from French internal politics."[4] The OWI must not abuse its power, he argued. France must be left to assert its rightful sovereignty. And yet war damage and sabotage in the final days of the Occupation had left France with a broadcast communications system "reduced to close to nothingness." Only about five to seven high-wattage transmitters operated reliably across the country (down from more than two dozen prior to 1940). Their combined output reached only about half of metropolitan France. Charles de Gaulle's provisional government needed rapid improvements to inform citizens and assert its authority. France required updated and expanded communications of all kinds for its future economic growth. To other U.S. policymakers, furnishing assistance in France's rebuilding process seemed pragmatic and not political in the least.[5] Carroll's warning of the dangers of entanglement went unheeded.[6]

In June 1945, the OWI and the United States Information Service (USIS), predecessor of the United States Information Agency (USIA), built the Roosevelt Studios, not far from the Champs-Élysées in Paris. The building that housed the new studios belonged to the RDF, which had courtesy access to the U.S. facility. In exchange for office space for VOA broadcasters, the U.S. government contributed coal for heat, cleaning services, and a sizable record library for shared RDF and VOA use. The everyday routines of radio, such as booking studio time, setting up equipment, writing and translating scripts, directing, recording, and engineering broadcasts brought together French and U.S. nationals. Some of these producers, talent, and technicians would join the FBS in 1946.

E. N. "Ned" Brandt, a U.S. FBS employee, recalled how all the producers angled to work with one engineer in particular, René Trughet, known to all as "Troush." Trughet specialized in sound-on-disc transcription recording, a means of creating a studio recording for instant reuse. Producing a broadcast-quality result required a deft touch. "That was new technology at that time [and] very few Frenchmen, particularly, knew how to use [it]," Brandt remembered, "Trughet was one. Everybody wanted 'Troush' to transcribe their stuff." In its first year, RDF personnel spent an average of seventy hours a week in the Roosevelt Studios producing programs for the French national system.[7]

Like many U.S. nationals tied to radio in Paris, Ned Brandt moved across a permeable membrane separating the RDF's French Broadcasting System and the U.S. State Department. Although some FBS employees were footloose U.S. expatriates and students with interests outside government work, others were ex-OWI, U.S. Army intelligence officers, and even Office of Strategic Services (OSS) employees (the forerunner of the Central Intelligence Agency). During the war, Brandt worked as an army intelligence officer at Le Havre and then for United Press International (UPI) in Detroit. In 1947, he returned to France for a job that fell through. He turned to magazine writing and landed a gig as a book critic for the FBS. Two years later, he became a press attaché at the U.S. Embassy promoting the Marshall Plan but continued to moonlight as an FBS scriptwriter. Asked to specify the relationship between the FBS and the U.S. State Department, Brandt would respond only: "I was working for both, one at a time." Robert Carrier, another U.S. citizen and FBS announcer, also worked for U.S. intelligence services during the war and then in Paris for the OSS.[8] The FBS existed in a liminal state somewhere between the RDF, which formally oversaw its operations, and the State Department, which supplied a number of the members of its U.S. staff.

The Pragmatics of Courtesy

After the Liberation, U.S.–French broadcast ties developed as a series of low-profile friendly arrangements with mutually beneficial characteristics. By December 1944, VOA transmitters operating in New York, Algiers, and London relayed French broadcasting's national evening news program, *Ce soir en France* (France Tonight). The relay transformed a faint signal incapable of reaching all of France into one that allowed it "to blanket most of Europe, the Mediterranean region and Middle East." It is unclear whether the relayed programs included any mention of the VOA's role. The State Department considered the arrangement a restricted topic, which leaves open the possibility that French listeners might not have known how the RDF program reached their homes or the extent to which the RDF program depended on a U.S. transmission system.[9]

The VOA relay remained in place during an era of political contention in France over U.S.–French relations and U.S. power and influence abroad. Richard F. Kuisel points out that high politics should not be mistaken for public opinion. Polls suggested that the French generally felt favorable about the United States. Pro-U.S. French politicians, however, faced accusations of being subservient to the will of the United States. Outspoken critics on the French Left questioned the motives of U.S. foreign aid, and numerous activists and intellectuals criticized the United States as an imperial force.[10] Certainly the subject of the VOA transmitting U.S. programs from outside the border into France divided public opinion. Opposition arose in coming years over the U.S. plan to activate a transmitter in Tangier, for example.[11] The VOA gladly relayed *Ce soir en France* because it mostly presented the United States in a favorable light. The series blended U.S. and French news stories, presented features on U.S.–French historical milestones, and ran biographical profiles of U.S. writers (John Dos Passos, Theodore Dreiser), along with ethnic and popular male African American musicians (George Gershwin, Rudolph Dunbar, and Duke Ellington). Including U.S. cultural figures known for their social criticism and sympathies with the political Left, as well as the inclusion of ethnic and racial minorities, shows how RDF producers managed a pro-U.S. editorial stance by channeling mild criticism of U.S. society through the words and life experiences of U.S. citizens themselves. Such gestures acquainted listeners with voices of difference and diversity in U.S. culture while sending a powerful ideological message about the freedoms of speech and opinion U.S. citizens enjoyed to criticize their compatriots. Likewise, demonstrating the apparent openness, tolerance, and ethno-racial diversity in U.S. arts and culture helped deflate criticism of economic and racial segregation in the United States. These ideological frameworks of U.S. inclusiveness resembled those employed by the OWI in its victory campaigns against fascism and racism during World War II, which got a second life with the State Department as the Cold War took shape.[12]

On August 31, 1945, with such informal arrangements operating between U.S. and French government broadcasting, President Harry S Truman abolished the OWI and the Office of Inter-American Affairs (OIA) and assigned their work to an interim international agency. As Truman explained, however, "some of our foreign information operations will continue to be necessary." The president promised that this work would not compete with private enterprise or interfere with the sovereign communications of other countries: "Rather it will endeavor to see to it that other peoples receive a full and fair picture of American life and of the aims and policies of the United States government." On January 1, 1946, the State Department's Office of International Information and Cultural Affairs opened, changing its name the following year to the Office of Information and Educational Exchange (OIE). Forty percent of the OIE's annual budget went to the International Broadcasting Division (IBD), which handled the VOA, including subsidizing VOA broadcasts to France and supporting VOA program preparation of the kind going on at the Roosevelt Studios.[13]

In November 1945, RDF and State Department officials reached another informal understanding that opened French domestic airwaves to U.S. government programs. The negotiating parties avoided an official diplomatic agreement because such formalities drew scrutiny and could have invited embarrassing public opposition. Under the new pact, the VOA would continue its nightly relay of the RDF's *France Tonight* if in return the RDF would pick up a shortwave VOA program on its national network. French law prohibited nongovernment broadcasting and broadcasting by a foreign power on French soil. A relay did not technically constitute a broadcast, however, and the loophole allowed the RDF to add the VOA's propaganda program, *Ici New York* (This Is New York), to its daily national schedule. As in the case of the British Broadcasting Corporation's (BBC's) terrestrial relay of VOA programs to France during the Occupation, a ground relay of a transatlantic shortwave program made it vastly easier to hear. The decision embedded U.S. government broadcasting within the fold of the RDF.[14]

A National Radio Service Is (Re)Born

As Philip Nord argues, the "conservative, state-centered modernization" project of France's Fourth Republic (1946–58) extended to radio.[15] On March 23, 1945, the provisional government under Charles de Gaulle dissolved the vestiges of France's interwar public-private radio arrangement. It annulled all private claims to broadcasting and made radio a public monopoly. The new RDF had much in common with its interwar and Vichy-era national predecessors. It operated as an extension of the state. Despite the efforts of Jean Guignebert and the *Comité de la Libération de la Radio* to promote a public service alternative modeled after the BBC, de Gaulle had refused and his decision stuck. The RDF continued under the Ministry of Information, with a supplementary budget and a government-appointed head.[16]

Disenfranchised private broadcasters and others who dreamed of a public system protected from state interference expressed dismay at what amounted to a "political setup—run by government appointees" in which broadcast journalists received advisories from state ministers. The innovators of the interwar era who had developed the medium's possibilities, including independent news on commercial stations, "were left to 'educate' and 'entertain,'" in Hélène Eck's words, while the state controlled broadcast news.[17] Eck notes that French writers and intellectuals, such as Jean Cocteau, André Gide, and Colette, registered their disappointment and disgust by boycotting the new French radio system.[18]

A Manhattan Foothold

In summer 1945, France took a decisive step advancing U.S.–French transatlantic broadcasting. Paul Gilson, French journalist, writer, and poet, with experience at Radio Luxembourg, arrived in New York to establish the Correspondent Services of the RDF in the United States. From temporary quarters at the French consulate, Gilson covered the newly formed United Nations and produced commentaries for U.S. stations seeking a "French point of view." He recruited Roger de Goupillières, one of Paris's premier producers, to assist in day-to-day operations and to cover news from Washington, D.C. They used the facilities of the VOA in New York to broadcast reports to Paris.[19]

Westbound programs from Paris to North America remained sparse, however. Those with all-wave equipment could tune to daily thirty-minute shortwave programs in French and English. The broadcasts from Paris included news, editorials, feature stories, and a French-language lesson. But such programs made little to no impact on the consciousness of the average U.S. listener, who, unlike listeners in most other parts of the world, ignored shortwave and listened virtually exclusively to AM radio (FM was not yet a popular option).[20]

In 1946, the RDF appointed Robert Lange, a French national, to find solutions for getting French-produced broadcasts onto U.S. airwaves. The French Broadcasting System in North America (FBS) joined Paul Gilson's French Broadcasting in North America (FBNA). The FBNA served the French national audience with breaking stories, interviews, political roundups, and special-event coverage. Lange's job as FBS chief was to make deals and act as a distributor of English-language programs made in France.[21] Before the war, Lange worked in journalism. He acted as editor-in-chief of *La République*, a radical socialist newspaper. He also founded *Freedom*, an English-language internationalist quarterly in Paris. A de Gaulle supporter, Lange fled to London in 1940 and moved on to New York, where he worked for the VOA during the Occupation.[22]

"To rebuild the respect of America" for France, Lange proposed a two-way program exchange in which music, drama, and cultural radio series produced by the FBS would be swapped for U.S.-produced material. Lange crisscrossed the United States, courting radio executives, station managers, and the National Association of Broadcasters (NAB), the influential trade organization whose members included a significant number of independent stations unaffiliated with the major networks that sought more and better content. Lange suggested two possible distribution modes of FBS-produced material. The first borrowed from an arrangement the BBC currently used, in which U.S. client stations received direct shortwave feeds from abroad that were relayed live or recorded for later use. The second offered an alternative to the technical coordination issues and uneven sound associated with shortwave broadcasts. Lange proposed a "wax net," which in industry parlance meant a distribution of prerecorded programs on disc for use by participating U.S. stations at a time of their own choosing.[23]

Sound-on-disc transcription recordings emerged internationally before World War II and offered a flexible means of capturing and reproducing sound. Unlike phonograph records, which required a multistep manufacturing process to reach a playable form, transcription discs could be created with special studio equipment and played back instantly. They lacked the durability of phonograph records but could be reused sparingly. As early as the late 1920s, U.S. radio stations used transcriptions to create multiple copies of a program that could be distributed to other stations. The use of transcriptions on U.S. radio remained selective, however, because federal regulators encouraged live over canned music, and, as Alex Russo has argued, commercial networks had built their identity on the premise of featuring live material. Special circumstances during World War II allowed the Armed Forces Radio Network (AFRN) to use V-Discs, mass-produced transcriptions of popular U.S. radio programs to entertain U.S. service personnel.[24]

The FBS proposed a modified arrangement in which transcription masters would be made in Paris, shipped to the United States, and mass-produced as 33^1/$_3$ rpm disc copies distributed across North America. A platter distribution

The FBS platter series allowed listeners across the United States to hear the latest French popular music, among other offerings.

system offered technical consistency, ease of use, and flexibility to FBS partners. Stations could subscribe to any platter series they wanted and schedule episodes without being reliant on a shortwave feed at a prescribed time. According to the musical entertainment publication *Billboard*, "wax nets" represented a minor trend in postwar U.S. broadcasting. Platters appealed to programmers and advertisers interested in reaching niche audiences ignored or overlooked by commercial networks, whether non-English-dominant listeners in cities or border areas, or, in this case, Francophiles.[25] The broadcast of prerecorded musical performances raised potential legal and policy questions partly because of U.S. networks' aforementioned commitment to original, live programming, but also because of pressure from the American Federation of Musicians, which fought the use of records to protect studio orchestra jobs for union members.[26]

On April 27, 1946, *Billboard* announced, "France is getting ready to resell itself to the peoples of the world through its overseas broadcasting service." The story reported that Lange had 145 stations committed to the platter distribution, including NBC's WEAF and WQXR in New York City. "The programs from France will be prepared by a group of forty American radio men in Paris," explained the *New York Times*, "and will include news commentaries, fashion, and shows." Another story mentioned the involvement of "ex-U.S. Army men" in Paris, neglecting the detail that these workers had close and continuing ties to the State Department. If journalists saw irony in France's "overseas broadcasting service" being composed chiefly of U.S. nationals, they reserved comment.[27]

In January 1947, broadcast journalist Pierre Crénesse arrived from Paris to augment the staff of the RDF's New York bureau. The office staff grew to eleven and the bureau moved out of the consulate and into private offices at 501 Madison Avenue.[28] There were encouraging signs of growth in France. Three networks (Chaîne Nationale, Chaîne Parisienne, and Paris-Inter) and forty-one medium-wave transmitters now served metropolitan France. The RDF also operated ground-wave and shortwave transmitters serving Brazzaville, Tunis, and Algiers. The system employed four thousand people. The economics underpinning the growth were precarious, however. The system was in debt to the equivalent of US $30 million, cutbacks to services were imminent, and there even were rumors that the government might legalize commercial broadcasting again.[29]

On April 1, 1947, the FBS rolled out prototypes of the proposed U.S. transcription programs. U.S. program directors recruited to help advise the FBS did not like what they heard. "Unhappily, [the early programs] were not for the most part up to American standards of broadcasting due to a lack of experienced help in the know-how of American techniques," reported Pierre

Crénesse. Evidently the "ex-U.S. Army men" and their RDF counterparts had not mastered the production skills required of mainstream U.S. programs. To attend to this techno-aesthetic issue, the RDF brought to Paris Edward Gruskin, U.S. producer of the nationally popular *Vick and Sade* radio comedy series. He worked on upgrading the productions coming out of the Roosevelt Studios to the techno-aesthetics of mainstream U.S. broadcasting.[30]

As the FBS contemplated programming options, political developments shaped the future of U.S.–French relations and transatlantic broadcasting. In spring 1947, France's coalition government expelled the members of the French Communist Party (PCF), which formed an opposition party. The remaining coalition faced added antagonism from the *Rassemblement du peuple français* (RPF), a far-right nationalist party championed by Charles de Gaulle from the political sidelines. (De Gaulle had resigned as head of the provisional government in January 1946.) In 1948, the RPF demanded that the government investigate fiscal discrepancies found in national audits of the government covering the previous two years.[31] The audits revealed lax accounting practices and questionable spending by government officials on luxury automobile pools, vacations, and purchases of wine, liquor, and lingerie. A scandal erupted as France's polarized factions seized on the revelations in an effort to discredit their political opponents.[32]

The repercussions of the scandal reached all the way to the New York bureau and the staff of the FBS. Available details are scant, but FBS chief Robert Lange and two RDF producers were accused of financial misconduct. *Variety* wrote about "shenanigans of some of the execs" at the FBS, and another newspaper reported "funds misuse." Worried that the crisis threatened the future of the bureau and the FBS exchange proposal, Wladimir Porché, the new director general of the RDF, personally investigated. He removed Lange, disciplined staffers, and promoted Pierre Crénesse to head both the news bureau and the FBS.[33]

"A Garden Does Not Live without Currents of Air"

Twenty-nine-year-old Crénesse had been called "the most popular radio commentator" in France. His celebrity credentials included making the cover of the splashy *Semaine radiophonique* (Radio Weekly) in 1946. One admiring female colleague compared him to dancer Fred Astaire for his slim build, suave air, and slightly protuberant ears. More substantively, Crénesse's familiarity with commercial media from his years at Radio-Cité made him an excellent candidate to introduce French programs to U.S. listeners.[34] Crénesse convened a fresh advisory committee of U.S. radio program directors. These helpers came from independent stations in major metropolitan areas and shared a commitment to internationalizing U.S. broadcasting. Ted Cott of WNEW, a New York NBC affiliate, chaired the group. He had apprenticed under Seymour Siegel (also on the committee) at WNYC, New York's flagship nonprofit municipal broadcaster. Other advisers were Eugene H. King, WCOP Boston; Bernard Musnik, WLW Cincinnati; Arnold Hartley, WOV NY; and Arthur Ford, WNEW New York.[35]

Crénesse's zeal for expanding French radio in the United States and his centrist politics appealed to the U.S. State Department. After the Liberation, Crénesse broke with his mentor, Jean Guignebert, the left-leaning radio activist who challenged de Gaulle's vision of French radio and lost his job because of it. "Pierre was a journalist. He was not a political man," recalled his widow, Miriam Crénesse. Douglas H. Schneider, Paris section chief of the USIS, responded favorably to the young broadcaster's centrism. "Crénesse is very friendly toward us," Schneider wrote in a confidential State Department memorandum after the two met in January 1948. Alluding to the coalition opposing the PCF and the RPF, Schneider added, "Crénesse is, I believe, '*Troisième Force*' [Third Force] in politics. . . . He certainly expresses strong

Pierre Crénesse (second from right) directed the New York operations of the French Broadcasting System (note the turntable capable of playing the 16" transcription disks used for the platter series). (Courtesy Inathèque de France)

anti-communist feelings." Like Wladimir Porché, who remained head of the RDF for eight years despite numerous changes of French governments, Crénesse believed (rightly or wrongly) that one could practice the art of broadcasting without succumbing to the influence of political ideology.[36]

Crénesse took charge of French broadcasting in New York amid acute economic and political instability in France. The French treasury was siphoning off radio set license fees to cover other bills, and the Foreign Ministry offered only limited support to the RDF's international shortwave operations. (The U.S. government was quietly paying for the RDF New York bureau's shortwave transmissions back to Paris.) "The year 1948 is dominated by the theme of destitution [*misère*]," moaned one RDF official, "and is dominated entirely by the budget problem." The RDF cut staff and services, slashed national broadcasting hours, and temporarily reduced almost all of its shortwave services to the United States. Daily broadcasts to the United States plummeted from two hours to a mere fifteen minutes.[37]

Disappointed that France should scale back its international outreach, U.S. listener Stanley Worris declared, "Adequate programming for the United States and Canada is an absolute essential for a comprehensive short-wave schedule."[38] With no power to set economic policy, Porché paraphrased Voltaire's *Candide* to defend international broadcast funding: "If someone should say, 'Cultivate all the corners of your garden before growing flowers elsewhere,' we would reply, 'every culture needs exchange and revival. A garden does not live without currents of air.' Such is the true meaning of international radio. We cannot refuse the hospitality of others, nor close our doors to those who so generously open theirs."[39] Despite Porché's eloquence, French radio in the United States could not exist on air. It needed substantial resources that the French government did not have, or would not give, to create a meaningful presence on U.S. airwaves.

Dollars for the Dial: The Marshall Plan and French Broadcasting

The political spasms in France that propelled Pierre Crénesse to the head of the New York bureau had further ramifications for the future of U.S.–French radio. Having expelled the PCF from its ranks, the French coalition government formally aligned with the United States. Massive infusions of foreign aid followed. Signed into law by the U.S. Congress on April 3, 1948, the European Recovery Plan (i.e., the Marshall Plan, 1948–51) stimulated France's economy and increased public spending options. It pumped $12.5 billion into Europe.

Because it represented the keystone of continental Western Europe in the eyes of anticommunist strategists, France received the largest allotment of financial support ($2.9 billion). Through its French Mission, the Economic Cooperation Administration (ECA) released aid in the form of "counterpart funds" to support French development projects, such as boosting international travel and tourism and building up French broadcasting.[40] In 1949, the FBS New York bureau annual operating expenses totaled $114,800. Supplemented with Marshall Plan aid in 1950, the figure increased 29 percent.[41] Counterpart funds supported an RDF production team's cross-country trip to record news stories about the United States, equipment upgrades at the Roosevelt Studios, Edward Gruskin's consulting fees, and Ned Brandt's salary with the FBS. In these and other ways, counterpart funds directly affected U.S.–French operations at the Roosevelt Studios, including some of the production costs of the FBS platter series.[42]

The U.S.–French political alignment and passage of the Marshall Plan removed the obstacles to the FBS platter launch. Because so many stations interested in French programs were noncommercial, educational, and nonprofit, the RDF decided to furnish the platter series free of charge to stations. In spring and summer 1948, after a second wave of programs tested well with audiences, the national launch commenced. *Five Centuries of French Music* presented French orchestral, choir, and solo classical performances; *Songs of France* emphasized folk cultural traditions and their music; *Gai Paris Music Hall* featured popular music curated by the producers of the RDF program *Hot Club de France*; *French in the Air* presented language lessons in a humorous vein with a professor, his assistant, and a slow-witted pupil; and *Bonjour Mesdames* (Hello, Ladies) explored French fashion and lifestyle topics.[43]

"An Exceptionally Strong and Interested Audience"

Less than a year into the launch, one or more stations in each of the fortyeight states—along with Alaska, Hawaii, the Virgin Islands, Japan, and the Republic of Panama—ran one or more of the series. *Gai Paris Music Hall* and *Five Centuries of French Music* reached more than 220 stations.[44] The results of an anonymous peer review of sixty-one U.S. program directors published in *RPM*, a broadcast trade magazine, named the FBS the "international organization supplying the best program material" in U.S. broadcasting. *RPM* praised the FBS "For bringing the spirit and culture of France without propaganda and without political frills [and] for letting us know that the French people like us and vice versa."[45]

Accolades from stations receiving the platter distribution arrived from across the country. "I would like to congratulate you on the fine programs you have been sending to WJWL and assure you that they are being well received by our listeners," wrote a program director from Delaware. "It is our pleasure to air programs of such high caliber over our station." Another wrote, "[W]e consider the records received from you among the finest available.... Many of our listeners tell us that they make a great point of listening particularly to the *Masterpieces of France* [*sic*]." A third program director mentioned "many favorable comments" from listeners in reference to *Paris Star Time* and *Masterworks from France*. WDET in Detroit reported "a large audience" for the FBS series, as did KAAA in Red Wing, Minnesota, which shared the news that *Gai Paris Music Hall* and *Masterworks from France* "have built an exceptionally strong and interested audience."[46]

By 1950, the national distribution had increased to three hundred commercial and noncommercial stations, with Crénesse pursuing further subscribers and special projects. In 1952, one hundred NBC affiliates from Bangor, Maine, to Birmingham, Alabama, picked up *Stars from Paris*, a repackaged version of *Paris Star Time* with room for commercial insertions.[47] "Mail and station response to the program has been excellent," wrote an NBC program supervisor. "Our management [in New York], too, is most enthused and delighted with *Stars from Paris*. Talent appearing on this program is always of the best caliber."[48] News of the positive reception of the platter series even reached France, where one Parisian journalist wondered half-seriously why France appeared to reserve its best radio programs for foreigners.[49]

The FBS production formula combining what *Variety* called the "rhythm of U.S. radio" with French "cultural context" and "national flavor" had required extensive cross-national testing and tweaking. Crénesse modestly attributed much of the success of the series to his advisers in U.S. broadcasting. "It has taken us years to adapt to the American standard," he told an audience of U.S. radio executives, "but we have finally been able to achieve it, thanks to the advice of our Consultant Committee of Program Directors.... we have proved that French producers can create fine entertainment for the American public." As a sign of appreciation, Crénesse successfully recommended advisory committee chair Ted Cott for the French Legion of Honor.[50]

The Power of Piaf

Managing the FBS platter distribution represented only part of Crénesse's work for French broadcasting. He broadcast biweekly U.S. newscasts from New York to France. He also tried to obtain short sustaining programs from

U.S. stations that could air in France. In April 1949, to publicize the platter series, the FBS formed a virtual International Goodwill Network (IGN) of U.S. stations carrying French programs. Participating stations were invited to produce five- to ten-minute messages translated into French on any theme they wished. Crénesse suggested that stations prepare interviews with U.S. citizens from various walks of life. The resulting material of good quality would be distributed in France on Paris-Inter, which also carried several of the FBS series.[51] Evidence indicates that only a limited number of FBS subscribers answered the call. Not all had adequate staff or resources to respond to such a request. Other countries, including Great Britain and the Netherlands, were offering, or considering offering, free programs to U.S. stations, too, which caused the NAB radio trade lobby to complain that foreigners were competing unfairly with domestic radio producers. Some in the radio industry even lamely asserted that foreign suppliers ought to pay to be heard in the United States. To blunt such potential criticism of the IGN, Crénesse saw a strategic value in presenting the platter series as an international exchange rather than a one-way distribution.[52]

The FBS platter series and IGN exchange program, such as it existed, comprised elements of the Cold War calculus shaping postwar U.S.–French

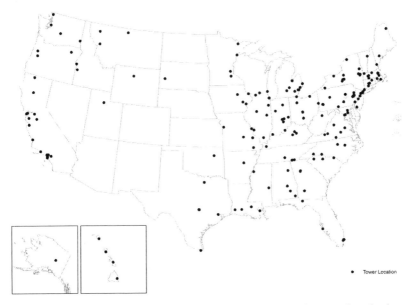

In 1949, the International Goodwill Network spanned more than two hundred U.S. stations from coast to coast. (Map courtesy of Justin Jocque, Henry Duhaime, Elena Lamping)

broadcasting as a form of mediated geopolitics. The French government did not have the communications armature to operate a governmental propaganda machine on the scale of the VOA or other major world powers. Through the mechanism of the FBS, however, and the VOA's shared services, the French government succeeded in reaching U.S. listeners with its preferred cultural messages. When Crénesse urged IGN affiliates to interview ordinary U.S. citizens for French listeners back home, he acted in a double role as broadcast journalist in the United States gathering *vox populi* and as a government employee shaping international broadcasting to strengthen the state. Just as the VOA campaigned on behalf of the U.S. democratic system, the RDF used the FBS and U.S.–French radio to radiate French cultural influence abroad. Speaking to U.S. radio colleagues in 1950, Crénesse explained that:

> It is impossible for the New York office of RDF to cover items of local interest throughout the States, to show how Americans live in small towns, in rural districts, to contrast living in Washington, D.C., with life in the state of Washington. Yet, we wanted the people of France to understand that the *imperialism* of the Middle-Western farmer is only a struggle against inclement elements, and that the *spirit of conquest* of the Detroit worker is only a desire to secure pension benefits for his old age.[53]

Crénesse explained IGN exchange as a pragmatic response to limited resources for newsgathering. The IGN recruited member stations to work as journalists themselves, gathering testimony from U.S. farmers and River Rouge autoworkers. The pragmatic rationale for this "exchange" was steeped in Cold War politics, however, as Crénesse's speech also made clear. Accusations of the "imperialism" of U.S. agricultural combines and the "spirit of conquest" of mass-industrial global manufacturing reflected the words of critics on the French Left particularly, who saw France capitulating to U.S. capitalist power and losing its moral compass. Some in France viewed news of the U.S.–French radio exchange, not without reason, as political propaganda. "If Mr. Crénesse wants to establish direct contact among peoples," wrote *Radio-Liberté*, the French communist newspaper, "he should let American workers and farmers know that French dock workers in Saint-Nazaire and La Pallice persist in braving police violence and misery rather than unload American weapons of death." The reference to French strikers refusing to unload U.S. ships believed to be bearing armaments destined for the French colonial war in Indochina underscored frustration over U.S.–French policy and its impact on struggles for political self-determination. The editorialist expressed anger at the censorship and ideological manipulation of the mass media in both France and the United States. It is unclear whether the writer or the French public believed Crénesse spoke regularly on U.S. radio. (He did not.) Critics knew enough, however, about the RDF's behavior in France to be somewhat suspicious about the uses of French radio as a propaganda instrument abroad. In this editorialist's estimation, U.S.–French radio was not being used to challenge official views, ask searching questions, or stimulate deeper political awareness among the U.S. public about France and foreign affairs.[54]

Attacks on censorship and ideological biases in French broadcasting, and personal criticism of Crénesse as a mouthpiece for the French state, Uncle Sam, or both, clashed with the broadcaster's self-image as a professional journalist who happened to be in the employ of the French state. Though he produced his reports for the RDF in the same studios and transmitted over the same equipment as the VOA, Crénesse did not consider the VOA's French-language services and the RDF's news broadcasts to France as interchangeable.[55] He also resented the officious diplomats at the French consulate who hovered at the edges of the RDF's New York operations. In spring 1952, Crénesse wrote to Wladimir Porché seeking clarity on the institutional and editorial autonomy of the New York bureau relative to the French consulate. Crénesse complained of pressure from Roger Seydoux, French consul general in New York. "Over the course of several conversations," wrote Crénesse,

> He told me that his desire was to expose American radio stations to the political point of view of France. I replied to him that this was very difficult, that stations offer us their hospitality, that my role, with my musical and cultural programs, was to open the door to other activities, giving the people the habit of a favorable disposition [*goût de penser*] toward France, that the National Orchestra and Edith Piaf would play this role better than academic dissertations on efforts in Indochina or in Tunisia, that in the end I would not wreck the position of the RDF which has a potential audience of forty million listeners and has obtained this prize because it presents French culture without political propaganda.[56]

Porché's response, if any, is not known to have survived. Views of the preferred content of the FBS platter service had never approached that of "academic dissertations," and the well-known position of the gatekeepers of access to the U.S. airwaves from NBC's Fred Bate to the postwar era made the threat of French public affairs programs supplanting French music unlikely. Crénesse's passionate defense of the platter series as a cultural rather than an ideological project may be a sign that by the early 1950s, he felt the strain of the inconsistencies of working as a journalist for a public broadcast system committed to state information control. Defending the power of Piaf and of French music as pure and apart from the manipulative games of cultural

Pierre Crénesse championed the singer, Édith Piaf (shown here delivering a 1949
Christmas radio greeting) as among France's most persuasive arguments for
relevance to American listeners. (Courtesy Inathèque de France)

politics may seem naive in retrospect, and even a bit self-serving, but it appeared heartfelt. Crénesse's insights into U.S. broadcasting, which Seydoux,
his adversary, clearly lacked, made him fiercely protective of the gains the
FBS had achieved. The liberties of artist and musicians could be trusted to
communicate truths about France and French culture rather more than other
forms of French broadcasting.

Seeds of Change in U.S. Broadcasting

Subsidized programs from France did more than burnish France's postwar
image; they nourished a latent revolution slowly transforming U.S. broadcasting. After World War II, the number of licensed AM (amplitude modulation)
stations in the United States jumped 25 percent and then doubled to more
than a thousand stations by 1950. Between 1946 and 1948, FM (frequency

modulation) licensees also soared from 456 to 1,020. The addition of so many new stations, coupled with commercial broadcasting's preoccupation with developing television, left radio ripe for reimagining. Scores of colleges, universities, and nonprofit organizations began broadcasting on AM and low- and medium-power FM. Such stations often welcomed new ideas and new sounds, which made them popular with listeners, often young and educated, seeking alternatives to orthodox commercial fare. Radio reformers such as the members of the FBS advisory committee represented a vanguard willing to develop partnerships between international providers and nonprofit educational radio stations. They recognized that unfilled airtime and a quest for cheap or sustaining programming reflected a demand that they and French national broadcasting could help meet.[57]

When Pierre Crénesse first arrived in New York, he began attending the conferences of a small organization calling itself the National Association of Educational Broadcasters (NAEB). "Who was NAEB?" joked Harry S. Skornia, a Big Ten university communications and journalism professor. "Some thought it was a bunch of young, not very heavy-weight (academically) idealists from the cow colleges."[58] Skornia, an NAEB pioneer, was no hayseed from the provinces, however. He held a doctorate in French literature and consulted in the creation of the West German broadcasting system. Early NAEB members included program directors and managers from some of the most innovative nonprofit stations in the country, including WNYC in New York and KPFA in Berkeley. For the next quarter-century, the NAEB, French broadcasting, and other international partners enlarged the spectrum of programs on U.S. airwaves. Their labor and imaginative solutions to resource scarcity and limited technological power helped prepare the soil from which modern educational public broadcasting grew.[59]

The institutional origins of the NAEB stretched to the educational radio activist organizations of the 1920s and 1930s, which argued that broadcasting needed to serve more than commercial interests. Educators and reformers insisted that the public airwaves should be utilized to engage humanistic concerns and to help listeners understand themselves and the world.[60] In 1925, the Association of College and University Broadcasting Stations, "Believing that radio is in its very nature *one of the most important factors in our national and international welfare*," requested federal support for nonprofit educational broadcasting. It was rebuffed.[61] In the early 1930s, the National Committee on Education by Radio (NCER) fought against the commercial radio lobby to conserve broadcast spectrum space for federal educational projects. The NCER and others battled fiercely, but they could not sway Congress or the industry to support their viewpoint. Regulators considered advertiser-supported major networks as best equipped to serve the "public interest, necessity, and convenience" of the listener/consumer. As a result, those stations committed to educational, cultural, and community-oriented programming were relegated to the margins of U.S. broadcasting for decades.[62]

The postwar expansion of licensing for nonprofit educational stations created opportunities for expanding program choice on U.S. radio, but it also produced a U.S. variant of the techno-aesthetic of scarcity that had hobbled interwar French national broadcasting. Nonprofit educational stations operated on slender budgets and often lacked sufficient resources to retain adequate professional staff to produce original programming of suitable quality. Although the NAEB offered an institutional structure, it lacked funding for programming and networking services.

Hub and Spoke

Radio program exchanges represented a cooperative notion from broadcasting's early days that inspired a postwar innovation. In 1949, WNYC began experimentally sharing programs recorded on magnetic reel-to-reel tape with its NAEB partners. In 1951, major grants from the Ford Foundation and the W. K. Kellogg Foundation allowed the NAEB to begin regularly and economically delivering programs to cash- and content-strapped nonprofit educational stations. The system centered on a state-of-the-art duplicating device that could simultaneously produce eleven broadcast-quality copies of a master tape. The duplicating machine made it possible for the NAEB to copy professionally produced foreign and domestic programs that could be cheaply distributed through the mail to affiliates. Member stations broadcast the programs and mailed the tapes back to the NAEB, to be forwarded to the next scheduled user. Whether named because of its hub-and-spoke distribution concept or its low-tech postal distribution methods, the "bicycle network" linked French broadcasting to U.S. educational stations to a new extent.[63]

In spring 1953, WNYC's Seymour Siegel, head of the bicycle network project, teamed with Crénesse to distribute the first of more than one hundred taped dramatic, musical, and cultural programs produced in Paris by Radiodiffusion-télévision française (RTF).[64] From New York to San Francisco, listeners were treated to the *Great Plays Festival*, featuring classic French drama by the Comédie Française. They heard performances of classical dramas in French from Molière, Corneille, Hugo, and Rostand. Modern works by Giraudoux, Pagnol, and Cocteau also circulated. "Actually, there's a fair-sized audience for this kind of fare," noted a commentator in *Variety*, who praised the French-language initiative as a "sock offering" that would be useful to expatriate native speakers and French-language students.[65]

By the mid-1950s, in addition to the five FBS platter series, waves of taped programs produced for French- and English-speaking audiences crossed the Atlantic to become available to more than seventy-five NAEB member stations. These distributions continued steadily until 1974, when the French government dissolved the Office de radiodiffusion-télévision française (ORTF), its public broadcast monopoly. Funding from the Broadcasting Foundation of America (BFA), a Rockefeller Foundation project "to nurture an international conversation" between U.S. and foreign broadcasters, helped sustain the transatlantic distribution work.[66] U.S. stations participating in the bicycle network could receive up to four major musical series annually and several dramatic series consisting of thirteen half-hour episodes. In all, NAEB affiliates could obtain up to four hours of French programming per week.[67]

The range of cultural programs demonstrated the colossal output of French broadcasting as it benefited from postwar economic prosperity. The diversity of topics was unavailable to the U.S. audience through any other electronic medium, including cinema. The programs covered the lives of great French poets and actors. They celebrated monuments (*Seeing Paris*), women (*Great Women of France*), pioneering scientists (*They Showed the Way*), and explorers (*France Was There*). French regions, rivers, and mountains got their due, as did legendary French floods. French radio's exports included features on esoteric modern music, such as dodecaphonism (twelve-tone composition), explorations of celebrated modernist composer Pierre Schaeffer's *musique concrète*, and also scientific and philosophical talks, profiles of French authors, and even the delights of hiking in Yugoslavia.[68] In an ironic inversion of the techno-aesthetic paradigms of U.S. and French broadcasting, France now provided abundant programs, but of unimpeachably high quality, to the resource-scarce and deliberately paced listening communities of the NAEB and BFA bicycle networks.

As much as the bounty of French radio filled holes in the culture of U.S. broadcasting, it also perpetuated gaps and silences that became ingrained in the transatlantic stream of U.S.–French cultural politics of which radio was a component. Rather than supporting an experimental enlargement of French broadcast conventions, the distributions of the 1950s into the 1960s reflected the tendency of French broadcasting to shy away from sensitive topics, such as French colonial history and the struggles over decolonization. Cultural presentations detached from politics became the foundations from which U.S. radio listeners came to recognize and think about France and French society.

In 1955, however, Henri Noguères, a socialist activist, journalist, and historian, helped establish Europe N° 1, a commercial *périphérique* broadcasting independently into France from the Saarland. Europe N° 1 embraced active news reporting and investigated stories that the RTF suppressed, such as the French government's use of torture against rebel nationalists in Algeria. The station also would provide independent coverage of the political turmoil in France of May 1968.[69] In 1956, Noguères wrote and hosted *France and North Africa,* six thirty-minute programs for the RTF, which traveled the U.S. bicycle network in translated form. The timely series appeared in the midst of the as-yet-unnamed battle over Algerian independence that would retrospectively be named the Algerian War (1954–62).[70] Noguères's series titles were "History of the People of North Africa," "Algeria," "The Birth of the Algerian Personality," "Tunisia, from Protectorate to Independence," "Morocco, from Protectorate to Independence," and "Conclusion."[71] For those in the United States fortunate enough to hear it, the series engaged a set of topics rarely circulated on French radio in the United States. In 1957–58, the RTF unveiled a second Noguères production, *The French Story*: "A series of 39 episodes retracing, in a manner accessible to the U.S. public, the history of the French people and the principal historical events of the history of France from Gaul to 1914."[72] The series touched on France's colonial history but left off at the start of World War I. Noguères's contributions stand out as exceptional among the conventional repertory of representations of France contained in export programs to the United States. The topics broke from the conservative and Eurocentric field of vision that typified RTF-distributed content to the United States.[73]

The FBS platter series and the bicycle network permitted French radio programming to gain a sustained national hearing in the United States for the first time. These initiatives created a vibrant and lasting French broadcast presence on U.S. airwaves from the late 1940s through the 1960s. The stimulus of the Marshall Plan and the leadership of Pierre Crénesse enabled French music and cultural programs to reach hundreds of U.S. stations in many of the nation's largest cities as well as scores of college and university towns. When the Marshall Plan ended, the foundation-supported initiatives of the NAEB and BFA helped the RTF furnish original content on reel-to-reel magnetic tape to nonprofit educational broadcasters struggling to survive. Even the humblest 250-watt or closed-circuit radio station in Binghamton, New York, or New Albany, Ohio, had access to commercial-free, professionally produced classical and popular music, drama, and cultural content from France, along with high-wattage NAEB member stations in Detroit, Chicago, New York, and San Francisco, which utilized their participation in the bicycle network to reach a significant metropolitan audience. In 1964, the NAEB reorganized into the National Educational Radio Network (NERN); by 1966, NERN affiliates across the United States numbered 150 and shared 1,895 programs, including many French offerings. The Public Broadcasting Act of 1967 established the Corporation for Public Broadcasting and a "public" (as opposed to simply educational) mission for U.S. broadcasting. In 1970, the CPB, in consultation with the NAEB, formed a Radio Advisory Council that established National Public Radio (NPR), which grew into a vibrant and thriving alternative to commercial broadcasting.[74]

The next chapter takes a closer look at one of the most popular of the FBS platter series that ran across the United States for almost two decades. *Bonjour Mesdames* (Hello, Ladies) was the first weekly transatlantic women's radio talk show in history. It engaged the perennial U.S. fascination with French women: their fashion, their style, and their lives in postwar Paris. The series also explored the powerful pull that France exerted on U.S. men and women who traveled to France after World War II to live, work, and study. Returning to the complicated entanglements of technology, politics, and culture that defined U.S.–French broadcasting, the chapter studies how *Bonjour Mesdames* enlisted radio to explore changes in gender and sexual politics and women's and men's places during the Cold War.

5 The Air of Paris

Women's Talk Radio, Gender,
and the Art of Self-Fashioning

In summer 1948, two Anglo-American women sat in the Roosevelt Studios talking like the best of friends. "It seems to me that Paris can be all things to all women," remarked Bonnie Cashin, a rising star in U.S. fashion, "and I think every little inch of it will be of interest to American women."[1] She directed her comments to Marjorie Dunton, host of the talk program *Bonjour Mesdames* (Hello, Ladies), and to radio listeners across the United States:

> [You] just walk the wonderful little streets of Paris. And the little rue du Bac, where all the little antique shops are, and that wonderful little street where you live, what is it, the rue de Varenne? And your windows overlooking the monk's garden, and the wonderful little trees, and the animals? I think [listeners would] love to hear all about that. . . . And the Montparnasse section, and the wonderful little cafés, where poets get up and recite their poetry at night. I think all of that they'd love to hear. I think you should tell them to bring a lot of good comfortable shoes, though, they'll need that. The cobblestones are a problem![2]

Cashin's virtual walking tour with an aside about sensible footwear captures the breezy tone of the first U.S.–French weekly talk radio program in history. The series used conversation about fashion, style, and personal development as a means of connecting the lives of U.S. and French women during the Cold War.

Between 1948 and 1964, the French Broadcasting System in North America (FBS) every week produced two fifteen-minute episodes of *Bonjour Mesdames* that shipped on vinyl discs to hundreds of U.S. broadcasters in cities, such as Chicago, Detroit, New York, Los Angeles, Philadelphia, and San Francisco, and to college and university towns. The program lavished attention on

French fashion, glamour, and luxury goods and celebrated French craft and artisanship.[3] It solicited listener queries to build segments on style, fashion, international travel, study abroad, and life and work in France. The program's emphasis on friendship, consumerism, and cultural exchange furthered the agenda of the Marshall Plan and U.S.–French diplomatic relations. Enlisting themes of transnational gender solidarity, it hailed French and U.S. women as allies, whose joint commitment to repairing the damage of the war and the Occupation would help make Paris once again a city that could be "all things to all women."[4]

This chapter argues that *Bonjour Mesdames* warrants critical attention as a transatlantic radio genre experiment and as an ideological artifact of the mediated geopolitics of the Cold War. *Bonjour Mesdames* contributed specifically to discourses of gender and sexual politics linking France and the United States. The series focused on commonalities and complementary differences between U.S. and French people. U.S.–French social and cultural differences arose as topics of polite curiosity, however, rather than issues to analyze. The broadcasts celebrated postwar creative enterprise and touted cultural and educational exchange and tourism to France.[5] They ignored international events, news, and politics. Persons holding critical opinions of any dimension of U.S.–French relations did not appear on the program. In these respects, *Bonjour Mesdames* appeared a quintessentially conservative and ideological product of Marshall Plan–era radio statecraft sponsored by the U.S. and French governments.

What complicates such an interpretation, however, are the complex ways in which the program's content and the voices appearing on it linked the recovery of postwar France to U.S. and French women's changing lives in the postwar world. Created by Marjorie Dunton, an Anglo-American former Paris fashion designer, *Bonjour Mesdames* fostered a gendered forum for U.S. and French women's voices that had never existed on the radio. The series considered the personal and professional lives of French women across the lifespan and described related opportunities that U.S. listeners could pursue for themselves in France. By taking women's lives and aspirations seriously and encouraging listeners both female and male to seek experiences beyond the borders of the United States, the series engaged popular discourses of postwar nationalism, gender, sexuality, and men and women's places. Hailing U.S. women as agents of change in U.S.–French relations through consumption choices and international travel, the series pressed against what Joanne Meyerowitz has called "the stereotype of postwar [U.S.] women as quiescent, docile, and domestic."[6] It shaped U.S. Francophilia as a gendered pursuit in aesthetic self-reflexivity in which learning about French culture and style enabled U.S. women to realize their personal potential, and also to strike a blow for the advance of French women. *Bonjour Mesdames* also made unexpected room for unconventionally gendered U.S. and French men. Their regular appearances on the program as guests and announcers and their voices and stories extended the range of possibilities and meanings for self-transformation among listeners who imagined becoming someone new or different in France.[7]

Equating the pursuit of style, fashion, and commodity consumerism with identity formation raises numerous historical and theoretical problems. In many respects, *Bonjour Mesdames* appeared to be constructing what feminist critics have called the "modern girl," an icon of depoliticized feminine empowerment realized through the mastery of style, elegance, and consumerism.[8] According to Ann Laura Stoler, the glorification of high fashion and style as a cosmopolitan credential is also implicated in transnational "relations of empire" predicated on economic and cultural exploitation of invisible or unacknowledged others. Ironically, in equating women's progress with matters of personal style and fashion sense, *Bonjour Mesdames* legitimized an industry whose power to influence international standards of feminine beauty as European and racially white excluded entire categories of French and U.S. women. It invited an unacknowledged complicity between French and U.S. purveyors and pursuers of style and the imperial, colonial history of France.[9] The notion of style as a cultural competency came at a cost to unseen and unrecognized women (and men) subjected to the exploitative effects of mass consumerism, cultural appropriation, and neocolonialism.[10]

Such a critique cannot entirely account, however, for the varied content of the series and the scope of its interests and concerns that extended beyond bourgeois consumer practices. The author discovered surviving recordings of the series from the late 1940s to the early 1960s that make it possible to explore such textures in depth, and to incorporate techniques of critical listening not otherwise possible. *Bonjour Mesdames* offers the historian a chance to hear French and U.S. women and men in conversation with each other at a turning point in postwar U.S.–French relations.[11]

"Gender Damage"

Bonjour Mesdames brought U.S. listeners into intimate proximity to French women in the aftermath of a traumatic conflict that exacted a high toll on the populations of both the United States and France. Total war mobilization in the United States destabilized women's lives and created personal, familial, and professional stresses, even as some women gained work skills and seized experiences particular to wartime. In France, argues Mary Louise Roberts, the war and the Occupation inflicted "gender damage" on the French population. Casualties numbered in the hundreds of thousands, including soldiers killed in action and imprisoned in POW and forced-labor camps. Tens of thousands of resisters died. There were others, however, including politicians, generals, privateers, and Occupation collaborators, whose behavior stained the reputation of France and of French men. French women were implicated in France's unfortunate circumstances, too, in ways that linked the politics of gender, sexuality, and women's place with the health of the nation. Occupation-era propaganda harped on France's alleged weaknesses, and Marshal Pétain's national revival program called for a return to conservative male and female gender roles, which further inflamed perceptions of a gender problem in French culture.[12]

Roberts demonstrates that the period between D-Day and the Liberation compounded French women's gendered troubles when they came into contact with U.S. soldiers fighting their way through civilian areas. As described in chapter 3, mass-circulated U.S. military materials portrayed French men and women in a fragile state. Military and civilian publications portrayed French women as passive victims needing "rescue" by U.S. troops. Roberts shows how military and civilian discourse harmfully sexualized and denigrated French women and contributed to incidences of sexual misconduct toward French women by U.S. servicemen. As part of the political purge after the Liberation, an estimated ten to thirty thousand French women were denounced for alleged intimate relationships with German occupiers and their French allies. An enraged populace subjected some of those accused of compromising their virtue and their national loyalty to public head shaving, physical and sexual abuse, and state prosecution.[13]

As recounted in chapter 3, U.S. officials considered France's defeat and military occupation as psychologically and culturally damaging to the entire population, and *Bonjour Mesdames* can be understood in part as an exercise in gender and societal repair broadly construed. By the logic of the series, French women working in creative endeavors, designing the fashions, modeling the clothing, and promoting the brands were not only shaping the international world of fashion and style, they were engaged in therapeutic work that advanced their personal fortunes but also helped repair a gender-damaged society.[14] *Bonjour Mesdames* celebrated women as emblems of resilience, competence, and enterprise. The gender repair project had salutary implications, but paradoxically it could not be called psychologically emancipating in any broad sense. In attempting to rehabilitate a powerful, time-honored, and forward-looking notion of modern French womanhood, the series too often idealized women as embodiments of a virtuous and unbowed Republic with implicit racial and gendered characteristics that imposed high demands on women of postwar France to demonstrate their worth to the world and to their gender.

The decision to develop a women's talk program for the FBS platter series proved an effective transnational communications strategy because of the genre's familiarity on U.S.–French airwaves. During the 1920s and 1930s, daytime "farm-home" and "home service" programs for a domestic female audience appeared throughout the United States. A related genre of women's shows appeared on daytime French radio. Female hosts addressed gendered concerns such as childrearing, beauty, health, and home economics. In the mode of the women's pages of newspapers and magazines, daytime programs dispensed advice and often invited listener correspondence as a way to personalize programs. In the United States, the format often incorporated informal conversation between a regular host or hosts and visiting "neighbors" and guests. Richard Butsch identifies a "domestication strategy" within such gendered conventions that shaped radio as a family-friendly domestic appliance tailored to particular gendered applications.[15]

Numerous scholars agree with contemporary critics who viewed the women's talk/advice genre as a manipulated forum that provided a means for outside "experts" to influence bourgeois consumer decisions and police normative female behavior to the exclusion of substantive political topics concerning women as a social group. Other critics, however, have found redeeming features in a genre in which female voices and experiences prevailed and shaped a sphere of gendered talk that had substantive meaning for participants.[16] Kate Lacey found progressive gender politics in women's radio during the Weimar Republic, though the genre would ultimately swerve toward more conventional reinforcement of women's place among domestic concerns. The "domestication strategy" prevailed in Great Britain and Australia too. In interwar France, independent and PTT stations furnished conventional women's advice, beauty, and gendered advice programs. As Joelle Neulander has shown, only one weekly program on Radio-Cité, the *Women's Forum*, allowed women to speak on substantive issues of the day, however.[17]

During the 1930s, U.S. networks supplied occasional shortwave talks by U.S. women to the BBC and other overseas partners. NBC also experimented with a magazine-format program, *The Women's Page*, which it beamed to Central and South America. French fashion and style, however, so dominated the women's pages of U.S. newspapers and periodicals that U.S. networks could not ignore it. Paris spring fashion bulletins became a staple of international news broadcasting.[18] Briefly before the war, Paris Mondial (formerly the Poste Coloniale) also broadcast a short-lived *French Mailbag: Life in Paris* feature in English to the United States. Prior to *Bonjour Mesdames*, however, no international broadcast series linked U.S. and French women (and some men) in such a particular way for such an extended period of years.

The *Bonjour Mesdames* Ensemble

Marjorie Dunton represented the creative force behind *Bonjour Mesdames*, which she wrote and produced. Her life mirrored a guiding principle of the series, namely that embracing Parisian life and realizing personal potential were intertwined. Dunton grew up modestly in a provincial town east of Toronto, Ontario. She quit school in her teens to support her family as a bookkeeper. She married and in the late 1920s made her way to France. She took over a Paris dressmaker shop and began designing her own sportswear, dresses, and accessories, notably leather bags and gloves. Dunton presented her fashions internationally and had clients in Canada and the United States. During the Occupation she remained in France, but she lost her home and her business. After the Liberation, she turned to fashion journalism.[19]

Dunton developed her first international radio program, *This Is Paris*, for the Mutual Broadcasting System after the war ended. It focused on leading European designers, such as Cristóbal Balenciaga, Lucien Lelong, Elsa Schiaparelli, and Edward Molyneux. The French national tourist office and the *Chambre syndicale de la haute couture*, a trade organization for French high fashion, backed the show. Dunton wore a signature turban and "long and loudly colored fingernails," and her rich, energetic voice communicated an excitement for fashion that worked well on the radio. In 1947, Dunton became artistic director of the FBS in Paris. She served as a contributing correspondent during the pilot phase of *Bonjour Mesdames* and then moved to permanent host and producer.[20]

Each episode of *Bonjour Mesdames* started with a signature theme. Two piccolos played a syncopated melody in harmony over softly strummed guitar. As the music faded, a male announcer declared, "*Bonjour, Mesdames!* Hello, ladies, from Paris." He welcomed listeners to "your program, meant to answer your requests from America." And each week he posed the question "What can we do to bring Paris to you?" Three responses would be selected from the letters sent to the FBS office in New York to plan the weekly show. A typical episode consisted of answers to two listener questions followed by an interview with a French or U.S. studio guest. The program invited a mix of French and U.S. fashion luminaries, entrepreneurs, singers, chefs, hairstylists,

Marjorie Dunton hosted *Bonjour Mesdames* with flair and insights derived from her career as a fashion designer in Paris. Photo circa 1937.

magazine editors, models, dancers, actors, students, musicians, and writers. Most, though not all, French guests resided in Paris.[21]

Two female cohosts assisted Dunton on the show in its early years. Pamela Wilde, a U.S. national, was born in Los Angeles and raised in Paris. The daughter of a Hollywood film executive, she studied ballet and worked as an actress in addition to her radio work.[22] Berthe Steinberg spoke English with an accent suggesting that she might have grown up in Germany, or possibly Alsace-Lorraine. Robert "Rex" Regent, Scott Beach, Ben Smith, and Robert Carrier—all native English speakers with North American accents—handled announcing duties.

With the exception of an occasional ad-libbed *"n'est-ce pas," "oui,"* and *"non," Bonjour Mesdames* ran entirely in English. French-speaking guests on the show spoke English well enough to follow their cues from scripts. FBS staff coached some guests beforehand on pronunciation.[23] Because of its English-only format, *Bonjour Mesdames* presented France as a foreign country with a rich culture, but without a language of its own. French-accented English shaped the audience's perception of native French people.

The monolingual Anglocentrism erroneously supported the belief of many U.S. tourists that French people responded favorably to being addressed in English.

The program's conversational quality gave the appearance of informality, but Dunton scripted the interview segments with guests in advance. Preparation and efficiency were critical because each fourteen- to fifteen-minute episode was recorded live to transcription disc in a continuous take. A cut transcription, like a phonograph record, was permanent. It could not be edited or remixed. The production pace, materials, and engineering costs meant that a recording session would be interrupted midstream only for a serious flub or mechanical problem. As a result, the occasional stammer, cough, or ad-libbed deviation from the script could become part of the broadcast version. The transcription recorded in Paris would be transferred to a durable master disc and flown to a Manhattan record-pressing plant, from which hundreds of $33^1/_3$ rpm sixteen-inch vinyl records were stamped and mailed to U.S. stations.[24]

Who Listened?

Correspondence selected for broadcast indicates that *Bonjour Mesdames* enjoyed a core audience of educated middle- and upper-middle-income listeners. *Bonjour Mesdames* aired in major metropolitan areas, which made the potential audience for this and other FBS platter series considerable. Correspondence also arrived from smaller cities in New England, Virginia, and Florida, as well as from college and university towns in the Midwest.[25] Correspondents fell into several general categories: educated, affluent women, some of whom had visited or resided in France before the war; female professionals in creative fields; and college-age and slightly older single women seeking travel, study-abroad opportunities, professional training, and European adventure.[26]

In name and by design, *Bonjour Mesdames* catered to females, but males participated in the program both on and off the air. Letters from female listeners were broadcast as a rule, although the discussion occasionally turned to the male companions of listeners. There is reason to believe that some men listened to the program with their female partners, and that male professionals in the fashion and art worlds in the United States, as well as male listeners interested broadly in Paris and style, might have followed the program.

Bonjour Mesdames expressly addressed wealthy older female listeners with the means and leisure time to vacation and shop in Paris. A New York listener asked Marjorie Dunton whether personal buyers, such as Helen Scott, who advertised her services in the *New Yorker* magazine before the war, still welcomed queries from prospective clients seeking luxury goods from Paris. Dunton reported that Scott had retired, but that her partner, Marjorie Booth, had taken over the business. A short primer on how to shop at Paris boutiques followed, with a recommendation that U.S. women stock up on perfume and gloves (far cheaper than at home). Booth advised listeners to retain a *vendeuse* or "saleswoman" to perform a formal introduction if they hoped to get inside any major fashion house. Even if such consumption advice only applied to wealthy shoppers, the average listener could enjoy a vicarious fantasy of conquering Paris as an informed consumer.[27]

Scarcity and Its Virtues

In its early seasons, when economic conditions in France remained poor, *Bonjour Mesdames* ran segments exploring how Parisian women coped with everyday concerns after the war, especially continued shortages. Not only did Marjorie Dunton lose her home and her business as a result of the war and the Occupation, but her marriage broke up. As a consequence, she had first-hand knowledge of the "much lower standard of living" prevailing in postwar France than during the 1930s. She talked about her personal experience to generate listener appreciation of France's struggles. Dunton mentioned the acute Paris housing shortage and admitted that she felt lucky to have a small apartment to herself. She described the rationing of coal, butter, electricity, and gasoline that left many French taxis inoperable because their tanks were empty by the end of the day. "We've had no milk since 1939," Dunton exclaimed. To illustrate the impact of rationing on meal preparation, she explained that the standard monthly allotment of butter (slightly over half a pound) "serves one Sunday morning breakfast with waffles!" She mentioned other changes since the war. "I have no servants now," Dunton confided. "I haven't a car either. I have fewer clothes." Some listeners might have rolled their eyes at the thought of equating hard times with an absence of hired help, but managing on two sticks of butter for an entire month, and struggling to find taxis running when you lacked a car, established a contrast between the relative economic security of the average *Bonjour Mesdames* listener and the average Parisian. Dunton's anecdotes about waffles and fewer clothes conveyed the war's lingering effects in a way that standard recitations of statistics could not.[28]

Dunton hastened to reassure her well-heeled listeners planning excursions to Paris that a dearth of servants and taxicabs did not alone signal the imminent collapse of French civilization. "I'm still rich enough to share the marvelous artistic and cultural life of Paris," she reported cheerfully. "And I can still manage to eat well." Dunton suggested that if U.S. visitors were flexible and set aside their expectations of abundant comforts, and if they walked (minding the cobblestones) instead of relying on abundant high-speed taxis, they would assuredly find the high quality of life associated with prewar Paris.[29]

Dunton underscored the point that whatever hardships the French continued to face, the city famed for luxury goods and services had reopened for business. "Stores are full again of beautiful merchandise," she announced (even if few French people could afford what they sold). "Everything you can dream of . . . Paris is still a woman's paradise." The images of ration coupons and French children without milk clashed with those of opulent French department stores and designer shops filled with "beautiful merchandise." These remarks implied that France could be restored to wholeness again, through generous and empathic consumption by U.S. visitors, whose collective tourism and shopping could assist in a broader economic and cultural recovery of France.[30]

Listeners expressed interest not only in the glamorous side of French life, but also in the stories of average French women. As Marie Whiteside of New York wrote, "all we hear about French women [on the program] only concerns career girls, scientists, or famous actresses. There are certainly right here in America thousands of women who have no other title than wife and mother. Well, they are the ones who interest me." *Bonjour Mesdames* responded to this criticism by interviewing Geneviève Hervey, a French woman who had recently arrived in Paris from Algeria. Seeking permanent living arrangements amid the housing shortage, Mrs. Hervey lived temporarily in a cheap hotel with her husband and an eighteen-month-old baby, whose bassinette was kept in the bathtub. To supplement her partner's nominal income and to contend with rising food prices, Mrs. Hervey planned to go to work herself. She had formed a babysitting cooperative with friends to allow affordable nights out in Paris. The segment offered an accessible reference point for listeners to appreciate France as both a "women's paradise," and a bricks-and-mortar city composed of people of all socioeconomic classes trying to put their lives in order.[31]

Mrs. Hervey said that she planned to enter the workforce to support a growing family, but most French women on *Bonjour Mesdames* worked to fulfill creative professional pursuits. When a listener from Waterbury, Connecticut, wrote to say that she had heard that "French women don't hold executive positions," Ginette Spanier, the *directrice* of Pierre Balmain, a leading fashion house, refuted the claim. Cohost Pamela Wilde introduced Spanier as a leader in a competitive field and an author of a recent memoir: "And here she is, looking terribly chic in her sleek black suit. Balmain's, isn't it, Ginette? . . . With a little pleated chiffon blouse, and a string of pearls, and her hair combed back off her face. But Ginette, we want to know about your career." Endorsements of fashion brands served as part of the rationale for the series from the perspective of French broadcasting, and Spanier also had a book to sell. She identified, however, a substantive change she had observed brought by the war and Occupation that affected all French women. "Before the war, there was still a sort of Victorian feeling about women working. Before the war, it was unheard of for a doctor's wife, like I am, to earn her living in *business* [emphasizes word as if it were an epithet]. But now, life has gotten so terribly expensive in France that all of the French women have got to get doing work."[32] Conditions of economic necessity could force young mothers like Geneviève Hervey into the labor force, but they also could support socially acceptable conditions for women like Spanier to pursue her occupational ambition. Modernity challenged conventional gender roles and might unsettle patriarchal authority by a conservative's estimate, but the story Spanier told was of necessity transforming possibilities for women in ways to allow them to circumvent Victorian constraint on married women of means who chose to work.

Spanier would never be mistaken either for an average French female worker hustling to make ends meet after the war or a sociologist. Between dropping names of designers and sharing anecdotes about selling mink coats to celebrity customers like Marlene Dietrich, Spanier was no typical Parisian. Women in domestic service or working as seamstresses behind the scenes at Balmain remained invisible with Spanier's modern narrative about work and career. She insisted, however, that despite heading a prestigious French fashion house, she related to the challenges facing working women. "Everybody thinks that I slither into work in the afternoon, and I want to prove that it isn't true. And I want to prove that [my life] has also had its downs as well as its ups," Spanier declared of her memoir. "I [still] have to get up in the morning."[33] The claim that the war and Occupation had obliterated a lingering "Victorian feeling" that frowned on middle- and upper-income French women going to work established a positive theme equating women's progress with personal and societal progress.

"Make Those Dreams Come True"

College-age and older single women wanting to visit, study, work, and live in France formed the second major listener cohort of *Bonjour Mesdames*.

Queries from "young career girls" prompted segments on how one might land a job as a French air hostess, gain employment in cabarets and theaters, become a fashion designer or a model, learn about bookbinding, and take up jobs in publishing or broadcasting. *Bonjour Mesdames* also promoted U.S. women in the arts through short interviews with U.S. singers and performers debuting in Paris.[34] The series presented international living as an exhilarating challenge for U.S. women that could be managed through preparation, self-reliance, and self-discipline. To emphasize the point, an aspiring U.S. fashion writer confessed to listeners that it was "tough sledding to find work in Paris" at first because she had arrived in Paris without knowing a word of French. "I don't recommend it as a procedure," she warned.[35] The advice qualified the claim that France would be "all things to all women" without effort. Adaptation, resilience, and a willingness to accept the inevitability of setbacks were valuable skills prospective U.S. visitors to France would want to cultivate as they prepared for visits of long duration.

Many younger listeners wrote the show asking for advice on surviving in Paris on a budget. When a listener wondered whether she could survive in Paris on $100 a month, she received an affirmative reply from Catherine Wheeler, a U.S. expatriate, who explained that she lived on two dollars a day in a hotel next to the Ritz with a roommate and a shared bath down the hall. "You need lots of nylons and low-heeled shoes," Wheeler reported. "Bring Nescafé, tea, soap flakes. All the rest is easy to find over here now." With that, program announcer Rex Regent chimed in solicitously, "We hope you'll get in touch with us as soon as you arrive and we'll do everything we can to make those dreams [about Paris] come true."[36] The neighborliness of a classic U.S. women's domestic talk show echoed again when cohost Berthe Steinberg invited an anxious would-be visitor to "come to see me at the French Broadcasting System here on the Champs-Élysées. I'll be delighted to be your guide and help you discover Paris."[37] We do not know whether any listeners actually accepted these invitations. They suggested the show's efforts to combine the intimacy of a U.S. women's talk program, tourist-friendly appeals, and the cultural diplomatic aims of the Marshall Plan, in which the spirit of Peoria and Paris would symbolically occupy common ground.[38]

With partial underwriting from the U.S. State Department, it is not surprising that *Bonjour Mesdames* became a platform for talking about the Fulbright international exchange program established by the U.S. Congress after World War II. Whitney Walton notes that France had "a special allure for women more than men" as an international exchange destination, which made the series a potential recruitment tool for the new program. The topic of single women traveling abroad would need to be treated gingerly, however, in the face of conservative postwar gender and sexual politics in which women's place and young women's personal freedom remained contentious topics in the United States. Suspicion of France and French people remained another potential obstacle in promoting educational exchange as a form of cultural growth. Harvey A. Levenstein argues that many twentieth-century U.S. travelers to France (civilians no less than soldiers) viewed French culture as licentious. Cultural phobias about different continental standards of morality and sexual behavior abroad might undermine U.S. support for study-abroad programs, particularly if they involved young women. As Walton shows, the State Department worked to allay unnecessarily alarmist thinking about sex and student safety among students and prospective parents of students considering overseas exchange program.[39]

Airing on college and university campuses across the United States and in major cities, *Bonjour Mesdames* repeatedly debunked the caricature of French women as weak or morally lax by presenting the stories of resilient and accomplished French women. The program strongly supported the desire of many U.S. students to have international living experiences by either working or studying abroad. The series rejected trends in conservative sectors of U.S. and French culture to demean women, impede their efforts at higher education and professional advancement, or interfere with their pursuit of personal liberties.

Letters to the series not used for broadcast are not known to have survived, and so it is difficult to establish the editorial philosophy of the program about letters that asked questions that the show chose not to answer. Listeners appear to have been fully supported to ask personal and professional questions about France, but Marjorie Dunton shied away from exploring the private lives of French people. Rituals of dating, courtship, marriage, and divorce received little attention, as did the topic of sex. Dunton's personal life included divorce and remarriage, but such topics were evidently not an area she deemed appropriate for her radio program. By contrast, U.S. and French women's glossy magazines, a growing postwar medium, willingly juxtaposed U.S. and French women's affective concerns.[40] Kitty Campbell from Philadelphia managed to pique Marjorie Dunton's curiosity about personal topics, however, when she wrote asking "Whether everyone in France is being psychoanalyzed like they are in America?" Dunton invited Dr. Anya Paillard, a Jungian psychoanalyst, to respond. Dr. Paillard responded to the question in the negative, but averred that the French demonstrated significant interest in Freudian and Jungian techniques.

"Marjorie, love is the greatest problem," Paillard began. "And not only from the sex point of view, but love as the greatest relationship in life. After that comes solitude, the greatest suffering of man, and then religious problems. So many people find themselves lost and without a spiritual ideal. You'd be surprised how many [in France] are without hope." Asked to share a "problem story" from her practice, Paillard obliged with the discussion of a female client who divorced her philandering husband and then remarried him, only to discover the cheating behavior repeated as he "more and more sought outside [sexual] interests" while refusing a second divorce. With Jungian analysis, however, Paillard reported that the client discovered she had "an immense mother complex," which, once revealed, allowed her to reconcile with her husband and preserve the marriage.[41] "That's a really nice story," responded Dunton mildly as the segment gave way to cheerful string music. The patient's apparent self-blame because she had a "mother complex" implies that she flexed in order to reconcile to her husband's behavior, but in a manner that left conservative acceptance of male straying unchallenged.

The program tiptoed around the subject of U.S.–French friendship, platonic or otherwise. Jean Colbert, a U.S. college student, visited the studios toward the end of a three-month sojourn in Paris. She announced that she had perfected her French by striking up conversations with strangers and traveling alone as often as possible on buses and trains. The volunteered remark received no follow-up question, as if to suggest the series' prim attitude toward personal and intimate matters for the most part, but also its curious reluctance to explore U.S.–French interpersonal communication at the root of cultural exchange programs. Alluding to the experience of being a young single person in France, Colbert declared, "I think part of the enjoyment of the trip to Paris will be making the mistakes, and doing some things wrong, and some things right and figuring things out for [yourself]." A slightly more forthcoming treatment of cross-cultural friendship and intimacy came from Michel Sciama, a French college student, who spoke of "a very happy year" of international exchange spent at Kenyon College in Ohio. Asked by Pamela Wilde to contrast French and U.S. educational systems and youth cultures, Sciama obliged: "When we come out of our high school, our *lycée*, we know nothing but facts, you know?" [He laughs.] "The American high school boy has plenty of good times. [While in *lycée*] we had none. . . . When we're young we had no dates, no dances. Of course, later on [and here he pauses for effect] we catch up!" [Sciama chuckles mischievously, as does Pamela Wilde.][42]

"I Think That's Fashion News. Isn't it, Françoise?"

French and U.S. fashion models visited the Roosevelt Studios as guests of the series to discuss current styles and their industry careers. As a promotional vehicle for Paris as a glamour capital, it would have been counterproductive for the program to reflect critically on the ways that commercial fashion had historically objectified, exoticized, and sexualized women in service of what critics call a "feminine beauty system." Under circumstances when the show focused on models, the conceptual intermingling of fashion, glamour, and sexuality in the world of fashion modeling demanded careful treatment, lest *Bonjour Mesdames* present the fashion world and France in anything less than a flattering light.[43]

On one such occasion, a letter from a Mrs. John Burr of New York prompted a visit from Françoise de la Fuente, a high-end Parisian model. Robert Carrier introduced the segment: "Mrs. Burr has seen so many pictures of lovely girls modeling Paris fashions in French magazines that she wants to know all about them." Cohost Pamela Wilde picked up the cue:

> PW: Françoise de la Fuente, Pierre Balmain's pride and joy, and one of Paris's most glamorous girls, has come here today to tell us about herself. She *is* lovely, isn't she, Bob?
> RC: She's beautiful, Pam. Tall, dark, and . . . [appreciative pause] . . . and terrific!

Although only the briefest of interchanges, the moment illustrates a pattern that scholars of sexual discourse often observe. As Beth Montemurro and her coauthors explain, "There are taboos about women openly discussing their own sexual behavior, sexual desire, or sexual problems in large part because sex talk is masculinized."[44] A scenario of women commenting on one another's sex appeal might be confusing or offensive to some listeners. This cultural convention may clarify why Wilde found it necessary to bring Carrier back into the segment when normally the announcer would be silent after the introduction of the visitor. Wilde needed Carrier to perform the "man's work" of assessing the beautifully attired but invisible model as a sexual object. His description was economical, but the pause to eyeball her and the enthusiastic response told the audience all it needed to know about the sexual dimension of her appearance. For Wilde or another female cast member to have ratified the sexualized glamour of the model would be difficult (culturally speaking) and possibly offensive to the sensibilities of listeners, even as it would be disingenuous to deny the power of high fashion to deliver erotic and artistic effects.

Once de la Fuente's sex appeal was established, Marjorie Dunton began the interview. She riveted her attention on de la Fuente's outfit and described it in fastidious detail, speaking increasingly rapidly as the interview progressed, mostly ignoring the model's attempts to establish herself as a human presence on the program:

MD: Françoise is wearing a black tailored suit, and this suit is piped with, it's
   sort of a satin cord, isn't it, Françoise? And the buttons are in natural amber,
   is that right? And the skirt is very, very slim, and I think that's fashion news.
   Isn't it, Françoise? And tell me, what's that you have on your lapel there?

FDLF [IN A THICK ACCENT]: That's a big gold bee.

MD [APPRECIATIVELY]: A great big gold bumblebee, isn't it?

FDLF: Um-hum.

MD [RAPIDLY]: And that darling little off-the-face Sayre hat in mole, felt, and
   chiffon. And it matches your Cartier, what, are these pearls or . . . ?

FDLF: Opalines.

MD [ENCHANTED]: Opalines!

FDLF [WITH A PAUSE THAT SUGGESTS SHE'S STRUCK A POSE]: And . . . the
   gloves!

MD [ENRAPT]: . . . And the gloves to match! Yes. And those gloves are [pause
   as if she inspects them, then triumphantly] carded! Let me see, and your
   umbrella there . . . Well, that's an amazing umbrella!

FDLF: It's an umbrella with a big [unintelligible] to put the gloves in it.[45]

The introduction of the "lovely" model, Dunton's fascination with the mi-
nutiae of her Balmain outfit, and the unintentional comic relief of de la
Fuente struggling to communicate in English made for entertaining radio.
It also represented an intriguing case of how a female-centered program
made the desirable features of the model known to the listener in a way that
acknowledged, but also channeled, sexual desire down conventionally appropriate heteronormative cultural tracks. Dunton's technical ogling of the
Balmain-clad model was a reasonably safe (albeit artificial) way to present
radio fashion news while contending with a model in the flesh.

Bonjour Mesdames found ways to connect the spirit of haute couture to
the vernacular style of everyday French women of all social classes that could
be extended to listeners as well. In an interview with the editor-in-chief of
Marie-Claire, the women's fashion weekly, listeners learned that contrary to
popular myths about Parisians, only a tiny percentage of women patronized
designer shops. Instead, they "have their own little dress makers or even make
their clothes themselves," relying on patterns published and mass-distributed
by *Marie-Claire* and others catering to middle-income and working French
women.[46] The segment promoted the magazine, which some listeners, like
the aforementioned Mrs. Burr, read closely. It also placed the ordinary French
woman making her own clothes on a continuum with the wealthy patron of
the enormously expensive and labor-intensive products of Paris's celebrated
designers. The segment defined French fashion as a broadly distributed creative labor practice that was widely accessible to women. French fashion

thrived because of its roots in traditions of skilled female labor, personal style, and ingenuity, but also its cultural and historical role in binding the various strata of French society together.

The theme of self-fashioning as a French national practice worth of emulation by *Bonjour Mesdames* listeners related to the French fashion industry's response to postwar international economic and cultural competition. The House of Heim was famous for sportswear, such as the *atome*, a revolutionary two-piece women's bathing suit that created a brief stir before the bikini eclipsed it. On a visit to the Roosevelt Studios, Jacques Heim conceded that the war and Occupation had enabled the U.S. fashion industry to advance its international reputation relative to France. Heim explained, however, that the nature of business on the two sides of the Atlantic remained technically and aesthetically utterly different. His discussion of differences in designing fashion (a technology of a sort) fell coincidentally within the techno-aesthetic cluster of scarcity, quality, and deliberate speed. "The French designer is always an individual," Heim declared. "We have the constant genius of the fabric manufacturers and the accessory designers to draw on [whereas] the U.S. designer has to consider the big industrial field that is mass production. She must produce a best seller. The dress must be fairly easy to reproduce. She must think of the thousands of women who will buy this dress. . . . Over here the idea is what counts. We give way to our creative fantasy. We experiment, often at a loss, but it's part of our tradition." Heim concluded, "The American designer will be better equipped if she passes through the two poles of the fashion world. . . . Paris as a free creation center and the United States as an industrial adaptation center."[47] Conceding nothing to the U.S. "big industrial field" of abundance, speed, and technological power, Heim suggested a utopian future of complementary differences in U.S.–French fashion could be achieved with "creation" and "adaptation" at its heart that made room for a U.S. advance in the international arena without direct cost or compromises to the French fashion tradition.

"A Dior Skirt's a Tricky Thing to Play With"

Periodically, Dunton shared her own creative expertise with listeners who needed help from a fashion insider. A letter "from a young law student" who wished to remain anonymous inspired a memorable episode that linked young listeners to the transnational processes of self-fashioning that defined the stylistically astute Parisian. "This young lady is fully conscious of the importance of being well dressed, but like many others, she has to do it on a limited budget. She's particularly worried about a full-skirted suit she bought last year. Miss X. says everybody's talking about the slim silhouette in Paris and the long and short of it is, how can she bring her skirt into this year's look?" Berthe Steinberg quipped: "My last season's skirt makes me look like Mae West," to which Dunton briskly replied. "Suppose we make this a roundtable discussion on 'how to bring last year's skirt into the new 1948 fall and winter line,' hmm?" Dunton, Steinberg, and Wilde then tackled the fashion emergency as a makeover challenge.[48]

MD [TO BERTHE STEINBERG]: You say your skirt is too full. First of all, how is it cut?

BS: Well, it's gored, Marjorie, and it starts getting full from the hips down.

MD: Well, then I think your problem is easy. Now, let me tell you how Jean Dessès would handle this skirt. First, he'd simply take in the gores, creating a stem line to the knees, and then from the knees down he'd let the gores break into a gentle umbrella movement.

PW: Hmm. That sounds very nice.

BS [POLITELY]: Yes, well, that would be all right, but I'm not very tall, you know.

MD: Then, Berthe, perhaps the new Pierre Balmain line, would be, well I think it would be just the thing for you! Now Pierre would pencil line the gores in the front, and in the back, too, until he came to the knees. Then, at the back of the knee, Berthe, he'd let the gores break into walking fullness.

PW: That sounds nice!

MD: It is, too. And personally I like the way Balmain gives us the new slim silhouette without, well, you know, without resorting to the hobble.

BS: Oh, I do, too!

PW: Marjorie, tell me, what to do with mine? It's a Dior and it has yards and yards of—I suppose you'd call it a bias cut. I really can't figure it out!

MD: Oh, Pam, you know, a Dior skirt's a tricky thing to play with, and anyway if you're a Dior fan you can go on wearing it this season. You know that Dior is the one and only designer who hasn't favored the narrow skirt, and besides, you're the tall and Narcissus-like type and you can get away with it.

PW [TRAILS OFF DOUBTFULLY]: Yes, but uh . . .

MD: Well, quite frankly, Pam, I'd either leave it alone or I'd have the skirt completely taken apart and remade.

Shop talk (not to be mistaken for shopping talk) about how to update a garment coupled with Dunton's understanding of the techniques of leading French designers combined the domestic U.S. women's talk show genre with informed comments on Paris high fashion. Addressing the anonymous law student, Dunton said: "I hope you've been able to get an idea for that skirt of yours. But if you're tall and thin, don't worry too much about your full skirt. Shorten it to the new length, which is between 13 to 15 inches from the floor, and let it swish about in the continued Dior manner."[49] The segment turned a U.S. student's insecurity about style into a hands-on discussion about taking charge of clothing design. The shop talk transformed the mysterious theme of style into a dialogue that brought U.S. listeners a step closer to the techniques and marquee names of 1950s French fashion, which it also burnished in the process.

Our Hearts Were Young and Gay: The Unconventional Men of *Bonjour Mesdames*

Male guests and announcers expanded the range of voices celebrating the vitality of Paris. The series demonstrated that U.S. men often pursued experiences, education, adventure, and alternatives to conventional lives in France in ways similar to those of women. Marjorie Dunton welcomed male chefs, restaurateurs, hairdressers, opera students, actors, dressmakers, and fashion designers as guests. An episode titled "The Struggles and Successes of Young Men in Post-War France," implied that Paris could be more than a "women's paradise."[50] *Bonjour Mesdames* suggested that Paris could also be a haven for men who loved European culture, sophistication, and style. It could accommodate men craving the experience of personal liberty, nonconformity, and a sense of community and safety to express their differences that might not have been available at home. For more than a few men, the attractions of Paris included opportunities to express gender unconventionality and pursue same-sex encounters.[51]

When Bonnie Cashin advised Marjorie Dunton to recommend Montparnasse to first-time Paris visitors, the destination would been an obvious one to listeners at all familiar with historical and contemporary France. Nineteenth- and twentieth-century French literature and poetry, painting, drama, photography, and later, cinema, contributed to Paris's reputation as a center of daring artistic expression, glittery nightlife, and pleasurable pursuits, which included a reputation for sexual freedom.[52] Montparnasse had long stood at the center of Parisian nightlife. F. Scott Fitzgerald, Ernest Hemingway, Gertrude Stein, and numerous others glamorized the area already known to be frequented by French and European artists, intellectuals, writers, models, radicals, and adventurers of all description. In the post–World War II period, Montparnasse still welcomed bohemians, rebels, immigrants, and unconventionally gendered and same-sex subcultures.[53]

Although homosexuality and criminality often were conflated in modern France as elsewhere, the law had historically shielded same-sex activity from legal persecution. The French Revolution abolished antisodomy laws, which placed France in a special category of demonstrated tolerance of homosexuality. Paris, like other major European cities, accepted homosexuals for the most part provided they conducted their affairs discreetly. Before the Occupation, the bars, nightspots, and public urinals of Montparnasse offered cruising grounds for homosexuals. In 1942, however, the Vichy regime set the age of same-sex sexual majority at twenty-one and criminalized "antinatural" sexual acts. Vichy's policies carried forward into the Fourth Republic, but enforcement remained lax. In the 1950s, although policing of homosexuals had increased, Paris remained a beacon for sexual and gender nonconformists, including U.S. homosexuals, bisexuals, and lesbians of various races and ethnicities.[54]

Repression of unconventionally gendered and homosexual men in the postwar United States contributed to the attraction of Paris.[55] As John D'Emilio and George Chauncey demonstrate, U.S. laws and customs stigmatized homosexuals to a far greater extent than in France or Germany. The homosexual taboo spanned almost every facet of U.S. public life from Hollywood and theatrical entertainments to professional life and politics. Antihomosexual sentiments in the United States reached a crescendo after the disruption of gender and family norms during the Great Depression and World War II. As Allan Bérubé argues, the sex- (and race-) segregated conditions of military service created large-scale opportunities for intimacies that had not existed previously. Changes in sexual culture in the 1950s contributed to a backlash against sexual minorities propped up by anxieties about Communism. In 1953, President Dwight D. Eisenhower banned gay people from holding government jobs because they were perceived as weak, susceptible to blackmail, and overall security threats. Congressional investigations purged many employees from the U.S. State Department on the basis of their sexual behavior. Bars and nightclubs frequented by homosexuals and lesbians after World War II suffered frequent forms of legal and police harassment that continued mostly unchecked until the Stonewall riots of 1969 helped ignite the U.S. gay-rights movement.[56]

The U.S. men drawn to *Bonjour Mesdames* took an unusual interest in women's lives, women's clothes, and bohemian Paris. Many lived in the City of Light because they enjoyed working in the arts and creative professions.[57] Dunton took pleasure in her male colleagues and sometimes chatted with them during the program, which created space for these unconventionally gendered men to present themselves to listeners. As professional announcers, these men mostly conformed to vocal conventions of male speakers in broadcasting. On occasion, however, they revealed a different side of themselves. In the mode of gender performativity described by Judith Butler, these men sometimes staged unconventionally gendered behavior in the form of vocal affectations or the use of colloquial expressions that communicated their difference, while never verbally disclosing the taboo subject of same-sex behavior often equated with unconventionally gendered men.[58]

Announcing for the show appears to have been a popular part-time job for these men while they pursued other creative interests in Paris, such as acting, education, cooking, music, and writing. Ben Smith, a U.S. national, perfected his announcing through voice lessons and rose to a high managerial rank in French broadcasting. Several others also developed full-time careers in professional media outside France. Scott Beach and Robert Carrier passed through the FBS before continuing to successful professional careers in the United States and England in acting and commercial broadcasting.[59]

Listeners wondering what drew these men to a women's fashion radio program could only speculate about their private lives on the basis of the sketchy biographical information they shared on the air. Staff at the Roosevelt Studios who spent time together outside work got to know each other's dispositions more directly, however. Ned Brandt recalled the announcer Robert Carrier as a "wild guy." Over the course of a long evening at a high-spirited party, Carrier used his persuasive charisma to convince the straight-laced Midwesterner to temporarily abandon his journalistic aspirations to enroll in art school. Carrier's interests included writing for women's fashion magazines, such as *Vogue* and *Harper's Bazaar*, cooking, and pursuing acting roles, which he had done since childhood. Fluent in French and German, he left the Office of Strategic Services (OSS) for wealth and fame as an internationally celebrated chef, restaurateur, and best-selling food writer and television host. Dubbed "London's gayest gourmet," and remembered as "theatrical, camp, and with a penchant for superlatives," Carrier retired to France, where he lived with his longtime companion, the writer Oliver Lawson-Dick.[60]

In the early 1950s, another U.S. citizen and *Bonjour Mesdames* announcer, Scott Beach, revealed an unconventionally gendered identity to Marjorie Dunton on the show. Describing what brought him from Portland, Oregon, to Paris, and what drove his passion for theater, music, and French life, Beach said coyly, "I suppose you might say I'm something of a Mulligan stew." He described his apartment as "a wee bit out of the ordinary. Oh, but I really don't know, unless you have preconceived notions about living room walls lined with silk velvet and a heating system such as Rube Goldberg might have invented." Beach confessed to Dunton, "I've gone completely French [lowering voice mock-conspiratorially] I even have a beret . . . and I wear it furtively." Beach left the show after completing a Fulbright fellowship in music and returned to the United States. He became a prominent actor, broadcaster, and "bon vivant" in San Francisco, and came out publicly as gay in 1978 after the tragic deaths of San Francisco Mayor George Moscone and Harvey Milk, the first openly gay man to be elected to public office in California. In some sense, however, Beach had already announced his pride in being different to the listeners of *Bonjour Mesdames* decades earlier by going "completely French."[61]

Only rarely, such as in the Beach interview, did the unconventional gender identities of the male cast members spill into the content of the segment. Dunton needed foils periodically during her responses to listener letters when no outside guest was present. In one episode, announcer Rex Regent and Dunton performed a comic role-play built around an imagined relationship between a spendthrift man and a lady partner who covets a very expensive Parisian indulgence. The routine developed from a listener letter read by Regent, asking for the latest news on fur coats from Paris. The letter writer "has a Persian lamb coat," explained Regent, "which she says is getting 'very tired and needs remodeling' and she's hunting for a new fur coat to commemorate a birthday that's coming up shortly. [Wry aside:] That's going to be hard on somebody . . . [more loudly] Marjorie, what is the fur situation in Paris this season?"

> MD [FULL OF VERVE]: Oh, rich and luxurious and wonderful, Rex! I think it's the most interesting season in furs since before the war! . . . I saw a press preview at Revillon yesterday that used up all my adjectives. To tell you the truth I started polishing my Aladdin's lamp then and there hoping for just one of those coats under my pillow.
>
> RR [TEASINGLY]: Uh-oh. Here we go, gentlemen!

Dunton chuckled and played along with the needling because it grew increasingly obvious that the segment consisted of excerpts from a press release most likely prepared for Dunton by the Revillon Frères furrier. As the description of furs and styles coming out of Paris began to grow interminable, Rex interrupted Dunton:

> RR [IN AN EXAGGERATED SINGSONG]: Oh, Marjorie, there are frantic signs coming from the [recording] engineer!
>
> MD [LAUGHS]: Well that means I have to hurry [spoken in a tone suggesting she'll do nothing of the kind].

Dunton returns to her script about fur in a tone of voice that makes no effort to disguise the fact that she's reading it verbatim. Rex interrupts a second time.

> RR [LIGHTLY PROTESTING]: Marjorie, if this is your idea of hurry!
>
> MD [WITH THEATRICAL EMPHASIS]: But just a minute, Rex! I simply *have* to tell Mrs. Gruskin that diamonds or other precious stones set in gold or platinum are worn on the left shoulder of your fur coat, and a sister clip is worn in the hair on the right side.

REX [INTERRUPTS SARDONICALLY]: . . . And a brother clip on father's wallet!
MD [LAUGHS IN MOCK EXASPERATION]: Oh, dear me!

As the segment teetered on the edge of self-parody, listeners may have wondered whether what they heard was on-air insubordination or a lampoon of the segment's blatantly commercial content. Regent's cheeky asides and retorts violated the conventionally subdued, gendered performance of an announcer. Likewise, Dunton's peculiar defiance of Regent through her resistance to his repeated interruptions (and the concerns of the engineer) put her in a curious oppositional relationship to conventions of polite, ladylike talk radio.

Bonjour Mesdames represented one of the more popular of the FBS platter series. It presented a transatlantic perspective on the role of U.S. and French women and men united in common purpose through style and self-fashioning during the Cold War. It presented French women as resilient heroes of their own lives, engaged in gender and societal repair through creative labor. *Bonjour Mesdames* explored traditional French style and connected its living history to aesthetic processes that cut across French society and bound it together. It supported the principle of student exchange, travel, and adventure to France for self-discovery, particularly for young women. The program also unobtrusively supported gender unconventionality among the male staff. Their on-air presences supported an incipient form of transnational gay sexual politics passing largely unnoticed in the mainstream media of the period, but the politics is evident when close listening techniques are applied. If repairing "gender damage" to French women had a conservative quality of restoring France to its prior glories, the fact that the series tolerated gender flexibility for both women and men suggests more progressive possibilities for gender repair and self-fashioning than the program's primary ideological function might suggest.

These themes had positive implications for renewing and deepening U.S.–French ties, though they tended to take for granted an exclusionary set of conditions of Franco-American affiliation. Reflecting the conservative institutional and ideological tendencies of government broadcasting, *Bonjour Mesdames* and other FBS programs promoted an economically, culturally, and racially coded celebration of Franco-French identity developed for a narrow constituency of imagined U.S. allies. The effect of an idealized metropolitan French female identity juxtaposed with a white, middle- to upper-middle-class idealized Francophile supported a paired geopolitical logic of its own that excluded much of the French and U.S. population. That logic arguably normalized modern relations of imperial coexistence between the United

States and France by ignoring the sociopolitical pressures building up in postwar France, particularly the stresses of decolonization, the Algerian War (1954–62), and the daunting challenges of rethinking the nature of modern French national identity.[62] It also discounted the multiethnic and multiracial population of the United States. Popular discourses of Paris as a cultural destination and as a catalyst of personal transformation subordinated the great majority of U.S. and French women. The series focused primary attention on pursuing beauty and urbanity, and ignored other kinds of concerns and issues that might also enrich the future of U.S.–French ties.

Master of the House

On June 27, 1964, Radiodiffusion-télévision française (RTF) reorganized as the Office de radiodiffusion-télévision française (ORTF). From a gleaming facility overlooking the Seine known as the *Maison de la radio*, literally "the House of Radio," the ORTF churned out massive quantities of content (still chiefly radio broadcasts) for domestic and international consumption. The monumental House of Radio testified to French broadcasting's growth in technological power and program abundance amid France's postwar prosperity. It also symbolized the concentration of state power and information control in the hands of Charles de Gaulle's government. Back in May 1958, as the French government readied to negotiate with rebel Algerian nationalists, an attempted military coup helped bring down the Fourth Republic. De Gaulle returned to power as president of the new Fifth Republic.[63] U.S. strategic concerns in Europe, North Africa, and the Middle East continued to pressure France to behave in accord with U.S. wishes, which provoked de Gaulle, who wanted to break free of U.S. hegemony and assert France's independent will. The strategic commitment to transatlantic exchange that bolstered the FBS culturally and politically began changing shape. France no longer needed or desired the kinds of boosts it had once received from the United States to conduct its broadcast operations. By the mid-1960s, exclusive of music, French broadcasting produced more than 250 English-language programs for export to twelve countries. English-language services represented the second-most-common foreign language used after Spanish and averaged almost two hundred hours of programming annually. At peak size, the ORTF operated five national radio and three television channels and cranked out twenty-six thousand hours of radio programming alone. Its staff topped sixteen thousand persons.[64]

After more than nineteen years in New York, Pierre Crénesse returned to Paris to finish his career. Before his departure in 1962, Crénesse's allies in U.S.

public broadcasting and the French government saluted his contributions to internationalizing broadcasting. In 1964, Marjorie Dunton retired from *Bonjour Mesdames*. Journalist Patricia Vossen started a new women's talk program, *Patricia in Paris*, for the ORTF. Though a skilled interviewer, Vossen could not match Dunton's infectious enthusiasm or passion for fashion and style. Without the urgency of post-Occupation cultural repair or the resources released by the Marshall Plan to sustain excellence, *Patricia in Paris* served as an entertaining but undistinguished program. It ran as an offshoot of an idea of postwar U.S.–French gender repair and therapeutic self-fashioning that had seemingly passed.

The final chapter of the book turns to U.S.–French radio in the late 1960s and early 1970s, and the consequences of the tight rule of French society and broadcasting by Charles de Gaulle upon French radio services to the United States. In May 1968, national political upheaval rocked France and catalyzed ORTF reforms that initiated the final major phase of U.S.–French radio prior to the 1974 breakup of French state broadcasting. The "events of May 1968" established a basis from which a new aesthetic and political sensibility reached the United States via U.S.–French broadcasting.

6 The Drama of Broadcast History after May 1968

[Setting: Paris, 1969]
SHE: You've brought me here to the Place de l'Odéon to talk about the theater?
HE: No.
SHE: To talk about the Latin Quarter?
HE: No.
SHE: Well, then, to talk about the barricades?
HE: Oh, do be serious, can't you?
SHE: Because, you know, I'm getting sick of all those horrible things like heads being chopped off and blood flowing from the guillotine.[1]

In late 1969, French broadcasting—the Office de radiodiffusion-télévision française (ORTF)—produced the latest episode of *De la Bastille à l'Arc de Triomphe* (From the Bastille to the Arch of Triumph). The English-language radio drama series followed two present-day characters witnessing events of the French Revolution and its aftermath. The program opened in the contemporary Latin Quarter with banter leading to a question about barricades, an admonishment to "be serious," and a complaint at "getting sick" of witnessing "horrible things . . . and blood flowing." In 1969, as the dialogue suggested, current events and the French revolutionary past were part of an interconnected conversation in politics and in the mass media. In the United States, too, where ORTF programs aired in major cities and on college and university campuses, many listeners were mindful of continuing protests and conflict over the meaning of U.S. national ideals and governing principles.[2]

The new U.S.–French radio dramas originated from a reorganized unit of the ORTF created in association with the French foreign ministry. The *Direction des affaires extérieures et de la coopération* (DAEC; Direction of

Foreign Affairs and Cooperation) focused chiefly on France's current and former overseas *départements* and territories (*départements d'outre-mer, territoires d'outre-mer*: DOM-TOM). In addition to shortwave broadcasting and program development, DAEC supplied technical training and production assistance to the DOM-TOM. It also prepared English-language radio programs on magnetic tape for the United States. The writers of DAEC's twenty-eight-minute historical dramas experimented with aesthetic techniques and storytelling devices such as flashbacks, humor, imagined historical dialogue, and swerves into ironic self-referential narration. Their methods brought a new sensibility and perspective to bear on the radio dramatization of French history for U.S. audiences. Shaking up convention, the programs made a modest but discernible challenge to the reverential quality of traditional ORTF output. They invited critical listener reflection about the media shaping of French historical memory.

This chapter explores the four-year lifespan of DAEC by analyzing selected scripts from several dramatic series. The chapter explores how dramatized treatments of French history brought events from French history into close proximity to the lives of contemporary listeners and the social changes and political concerns affecting France and the United States in the late 1960s and early 1970s. DAEC scriptwriters investigated the horrors of revolutionary violence, gently probed the trauma of the recent world war, found inspiration in unlikely French historical figures, and sometimes lampooned the tired genre of conventional history programs. The series introduced U.S. listeners to figures from the French past whose biographies were treated as relevant to contemporary societal issues in the United States and France.[3]

The experimental and slightly irreverent English-language dramas that DAEC produced offered a counterpoint to the prevailing tendencies of French broadcasting that Pierre Bourdieu famously dissected in *La Distinction* (published in English as *Distinction* in 1984). Using survey data of the leisure practices and attitudes of Parisians and provincial French people from 1963 and 1967–68, Bourdieu conceptualized a system of aesthetic taste production and social power in France. He singled out French broadcasting for legitimating status hierarchies in France by producing formally tasteful but elitist and exclusionary highbrow public culture. In a preface to the book's English-language edition, Bourdieu likened the work of the ORTF to U.S. public broadcasting and "educational television (Channel 13, WQXR, WGBH, etc.)."[4] After the postwar interplay between the (O)RTF and early U.S. nonprofit educational broadcasting described in previous chapters, it is interesting to contemplate how the DAEC dramas of the late 1960s and early 1970s reached toward audiences in the United States in part by pushing against the formulaic conventions of U.S.–French radio in provocative ways.[5]

Broadcasting and "the Events of May 1968"

In May 1968, a few blocks away from where the fictitious "He" and "She" spoke knowingly about violence and revolutionary upheaval in an episode of *De la Bastille à l'Arc de Triomphe*, demonstrators marched to the Sorbonne in solidarity with student protestors at the University of Nanterre, whose school had been shuttered in response to reform demands and whose student leaders had been threatened with harsh discipline. Events in the vicinity of the Sorbonne veered out of control and protestors clashed with French riot police; hundreds were arrested and many on both sides were injured. In the coming days, thousands of protestors, some behind makeshift barricades, confronted the authorities in what appeared to be the start of a modern-day revolution. Images of street fighting, shattered storefronts, and billowing tear gas circulated internationally. Throughout May, more protests, massive labor strikes, and marches of hundreds of thousands of demonstrators paralyzed France. The battle scenes in the Latin Quarter clashed with the idealized depictions of Parisian bohemianism and café culture cultivated by the French tourism industry and popularized in the United States and elsewhere through art, literature, photography, cinema, and, of course, radio.[6]

Experts offer different interpretations of the legacies of the "events of May 1968," but most agree that the unrest cannot be traced to a single cause, a bounded constituency, or a set of uniform demands. Protestors demanded greater liberty and called for educational, labor, and social reforms. They decried France's hierarchical, rigid society, its institutional sclerosis, cultural conservatism, and militarist foreign policy. Their actions forced the dissolution of the National Assembly at the end of May. President Charles de Gaulle scheduled national elections. The Gaullist party won these resoundingly in late June, but de Gaulle resigned the following spring. The upheaval subsided, leaving many of the institutions intact that demonstrators had hoped to see reformed.[7]

The ORTF drew the ire of protestors in May 1968 who viewed it as an embodiment of conservative statism and information manipulation. The law still required that all broadcast news coverage be subject to the approval of the information and finance ministries. Writer and journalist Paul Guimard remembered that the Algerian War (1954–62), sometimes called "the war without a name," had only a shadowy existence on French public airwaves. "We spoke of it like we talk about traffic accidents today: from time to time, a statistic emerged, that is, 'since the first of January 1955, there were so many attacks and so many victims,' etc. But we never exposed listeners to the fact that there was a rebellion for Algerian independence going on."[8] In 1956, the government instituted a prescreening rule on all broadcast news

reports to screen out content objectionable or threatening to the state. The
return of Charles de Gaulle to power during the "crisis of May 1958" afforded
no relief for journalists seeking to report freely. To the contrary, de Gaulle
systematically manipulated the broadcast media, which included denying
airtime to political opponents. In 1959, radio journalists called for financial
autonomy from the government and for an independent monitor to mediate
between the government and broadcasters in order to prevent biased news
reporting. Jean Chalaby notes that advocates of journalistic freedoms for
broadcasters drafted one dozen reform bills to limit ministerial meddling,
but none reached the General Assembly.[9] In 1964, the government declared
the ORTF a new, reformed body, but adjustments to its mission were cos-
metic, and the state's meddling and censorship persisted. "'Autonomous' in
principle," writes Thierry Lefebvre, "the ORTF remained nevertheless under
the control [*tutelle*] of political power."[10] In a stunning display of a lack of
public confidence, one 1964 poll indicated that more than 90 percent of the
French public *disbelieved* the news presented by French broadcasting.[11]

Frustration over government interference in the work of print and electronic
journalists prompted Opération Jéricho, a series of protest marches outside the
ORTF in 1968. (Musée de Radio France)

When the protests in the vicinity of the Sorbonne turned violent, ORTF reporters attempting to cover the story were yanked from the field, leaving the *radios périphériques*, RTL, and Europe N° 1 to cover breaking events. Some twelve thousand ORTF personnel went on strike. From May 17 to May 23, the ORTF furnished only the barest of broadcast services. A faction briefly seized control of the news bureau to deliver unvarnished news interspersed with music in lieu of regular programming. "Of all the occupations," writes H. R. Kedward, speaking of the takeover of the ORTF, "it was this action that conveyed to the widest public the message of revolt in May '68. Authoritarian control and tutelage were no longer acceptable."[12] On June 6, ORTF personnel and other print and visual media colleagues launched *Opération Jéricho*, a weeklong series of marches outside the ORTF to break down the "wall" of government censorship.[13] The results of the election favoring the Gaullists and the transition to summer diverted attention from calls for change, André François, the new director of the ORTF's TV-1 channel, directed an internal purge. More than one hundred ORTF journalists were terminated or reassigned, in what some called the "time of *charrettes*," an allusion to the livestock carts that transported the condemned to the guillotine during the Reign of Terror. When questioned about his methods, François bluntly replied, "When I reorganize, I flatten a system. I see where I am and I start building again. That is what I am doing now."[14] Despite efforts to crush the rebellious energy inside the ORTF, however, some remaining members of the massive state media bureaucracy found creative outlets for their contrarian feelings toward the status quo.

Out of the Past: DAEC *Dramatics* and *Short Masterpieces*

In January 1969, as a consequence of a post-May '68 internal reorganization, DAEC took control of ORTF foreign-language broadcast services, which included outreach to more than one hundred countries in almost twenty languages. DAEC's English-language radio section produced original programming under several series titles: *Dramatics, Short Masterpieces, French Drama and Literature, French in the Air,* and *Press Review.* Several of the series had been running in different forms since before the establishment of the ORTF. To give a sense of proportionate emphasis, at the point of the creation of DAEC, English-language radio programming comprised only 3–4.5 percent of the ORTF's total budgeted international effort. In real terms, however, this slight percentage afforded a significant amount of programming. "Each [DAEC English-language] series of thirteen is built around a central theme in the manner of a documentary, interspersed with dramatic themes," explained a report on the *Dramatics* and *Short Masterpieces* series. "We have covered famous men and women, sports, history, art, writers, gastronomy, wines, and dozens of other subjects. These are half-hour programs presented in an instructive and entertaining manner."[15] The unit commissioned scripts in French from ORTF and freelance writers that were translated into English and recorded in Paris by U.S., English, and French actors, including some who had experience with the *Comédie française*. (The series *French Drama and Literature* was presented partly in French and partly in English.)[16]

Programs in the *Dramatics* series, such as *De la Bastille à l'Arc de Triomphe*, presented history lessons through the eyes of two contemporaries who traveled into the past to observe events as they unfolded. The series manipulated present time and historical time through the rhetorical device of the historical present. Describing past events as if they were occurring before the eyes of "He" (the narrator), "She" (an inquisitive foil), and the listening audience, the technique of immediacy created an immersive experience unlike conventional uses of the past tense. The technique allowed modern and historical characters to inhabit a shared present, whose happenings could be simultaneously dramatized and evaluated by the present-day observers and narrator. In a typical example, the contemporary witnesses joined French inspector Dutard in postrevolutionary Paris as he surreptitiously observed the citizenry and recorded the public mood in reports to the information minister: "Even while the citizens are cutting each other's throats, while there's fighting along the borders, and civil war within them . . . here's a crowd of sentimental people [in the Louvre museum] ready to sigh over subjects like *The Good Mother*."[17] Historical and contemporary characters did not interact in this series but through placement together in narrative time, the characters and listener could perceive the past vividly unfolding.

In *De la Bastille à l'Arc de Triomphe*, the Revolutionary era was brought into the present through eyewitnessing of notorious episodes featuring lurid description. "I'm not relating horrors without reason," the male character explained, perhaps disingenuously, as He and She relived eyewitness testimony to the September Massacres of prisoners and captive priests in 1792: "A man with a sword in his hand jumped onto the step of one of the coaches and plunged his sword into one of the priests inside. Blood spurted forth in great gobs."[18] Likewise, the frenzied desecration of the royal tombs at St. Denis, in which revolutionaries disinterred and defiled the remains of France's monarchs, garnered ghoulish attention: "Souvenir gatherers grabbed a tooth, a lock of hair, or a piece of cloth [from the mummified remains]." When Henri IV's corpse was exhumed, "The commissioner of the school of Beaux-Arts, Alexandre Lenoir, . . . was so impressed that he shook the hand of the king, although [Lenoir] was a true republican."[19] The eyewitnesses to revolutionary history absorbed scenes of a "bloodthirsty 'royalist hunt,'" "priests bled to death like cattle," and "butchery" and joined spectators of all ages gazing at "the bleeding headless body [of Madame Roland] placed in the Madeleine charnel house."[20] For a U.S. audience accustomed to representations of violence in Hollywood films, in radio dramas, photographic and broadcast journalism, and on entertainment television, the combination of historical-present narration and macabre description brought the frightening excesses of the revolutionary past a bit closer to the present. The series dispensed with dispassionate historical recitation to bring the listener to the action, even if the scenes could be edgy or even ugly. The listener's exposure to the witnessing of the two time travelers symbolically pulled events of revolutionary history forward for contemporary reflection.

The depiction of ruthless violence and disorder that made one contemporary character "sick of all those horrible things" produced an evocative case against the destructive forces unleashed by the French Revolution. Having deposed and executed the king and queen, the narrator reported, "the revolutionaries found something worse and put it into practice with a relapse into either all that is imbecile or all that is revolting."[21] He continued, "the liberals, the moderates, or those who offended petty vanities or inspired jealousy [were] packed off to the guillotine without consideration of their individual merits . . . a tragic waste!"[22] Reaching the site of *la Place de la Révolution* (now *La Place de la Concorde*), the two contemporary characters reflected on the thousands of public executions by guillotine there. As they did so, they heard the imagined voice of Madame de Staël, the author, essayist, and host of one of the most famous Paris salons, who sparred with Napoleon and survived to tell the tale, remarking, "Would you mind, Sire, if, in a country where women's heads are cut off, they might at least know the reason why?" The narrator continued, "Since the Revolution wanted to make men equal from the lowest, it decimated the highest. It was the leaders, the thinkers, the great characters who were sacrificed, as much in the case of the commoners as the nobility." The series drew out themes of pathos in its presentations of the words and personalities of martyrs of the Revolution (Mme. Roland, Antoine Lavoisier, André Chénier) and others who were executed or took their own lives. It portrayed the sorry days of an abdicated and disgraced Napoleon confined to his palace at Fontainebleau.[23]

The series presented what appeared to be a cautionary tale about revolution that used narrative and aesthetic techniques to render brutal violence palpable and uncomfortably close to listeners. History unfolded simultaneously from the vantage point of late-eighteenth-century participants and from the watchful contemporary pair, "He" and "She," who along with the listener inhabited an era in which political violence and even revolutionary talk were not far removed from the daily headlines. Released in the aftermath of the events of May 1968, *De la Bastille à l'Arc de Triomphe* warned of the dangers of violence and retribution, absolutism, and political zealotry, as well as the dangers of romanticizing revolutionaries or sanitizing the destructive extent of historical events, such as the French Revolution. The radio drama left it to listeners to grapple with the sobering insinuation that the chaotic extremes of the past could be prologue for either France or the United States.

"It Isn't All That Funny, the History of France!"

With characters including a surly French customs officer, William the Conqueror, General Dwight D. Eisenhower, and a wheel of fast-talking Camembert, the thirteen-episode DAEC series *Légendes et merveilles* (Legends and Wonders) used whimsy and the gimmick of a contemporary U.S. couple on their honeymoon to explore French history. Written by Alain Franck, an author and award-winning radio scriptwriter, the irreverent 1969 DAEC series chronicled the adventures of two U.S. newlyweds, Jack and Jill. With their corny names and high-spirited cluelessness, Jack and Jill were cartoonish U.S. characters with whom listeners could humorously identify. The series began with the couple's arrival at the port of Cherbourg. They acquired a car to drive to Paris and became instantly lost. Their hunt for the right road to Paris took them thirteen false starts as each episode took them through a different French province. They encountered colorful locals; experienced flashbacks to French history; learned about legends and myths; ate frequently; and had plenty of time to bicker in the car like a real couple. The series used the excursion to delve into French history and also to brush up against more contemporary events such as World War II and the Occupation.

In episode 1, the listeners met Jack and Jill passing through the gantlet of French customs to begin their journey. Jill was stereotypically innocent, wide-eyed, and a bit loopy, with a passion for cathedrals. Jack was a recent Harvard graduate with a headful of facts and a pedantic tendency. He also was an atrocious navigator who ignored Jill's advice and sent the couple careening into Normandy instead of on the correct road to Paris. Resigned to what they imagined to be a slight detour, the couple encountered regional historical personages through flashback dissolves in the manner of *De la Bastille à l'Arc de Triomphe*. They learned about the tryst of Robert I, the duke of Normandy, that produced William the Conqueror. They indulged in a high-calorie Norman lunch, which induced a surreal encounter between Jill and a talking Camembert that flirtatiously proposed coming home in her suitcase. Through the power of time-travel dissolves, the couple also met Joe Knirim, an eccentric 1920s U.S. physician, who treated his sick patients with Norman dairy products, which he believed were invested with curative powers.[24] Unlike the previously discussed series, present-day and historical figures could sometimes converse in *Legends and Wonders*, which was consistent with its light and fantastical tone.

In episode 2, the couple passed into Brittany, where Jack and Jill found unexpected connection with the interwoven French past and present. Jill had a series of mystical experiences in the ancient forest of Brocéliande with the fairy Viviane, Merlin the magician, and Saint Michel, whom Jill conjured to life with the fairy Viviane's magic wand. Unlike the hardheaded Jack, Jill's willingness to believe in magic made her receptive to elements of French culture that he could not apprehend. It seemed perfectly plausible that by episode 3 Jill conversed with the Loire, a female-voiced character that scolded Jill for referring to France's longest river as a "stream." Jack, by contrast, discovered a France that appealed to his stereotypical masculine interests. He studied a modern French power plant that used tidal energy to produce electricity and commented admiringly on the connection between Breton ingenuity and technological advance. Even if he got testy occasionally about Jill's desire to visit every church and monastery on the trip, Jack shared her enthusiasm for the unexpected discoveries that accompanied their indirect route to Paris.[25]

As the series developed (apparently sponsored by the *Guide Michelin* and the French tourist board), the fruitless search for the highway to Paris gave way to a more reflective tone about time and space, in which the past and the present folded, touched, and diverged again. In episode 7, in the Savoie-Dauphine region, the light tone of the series shifted. Jack informed Jill that they were passing near the Vercors Plateau, an area of fierce resistance to the Occupation and the site of a mass execution of resistance fighters and civilians by the German Schutzstaffel (SS). Jack and Jill reluctantly witnessed a scene from that time. The script described an SS officer discovering wounded resistance fighters and shouting, "*Achtung, Soldaten! Ihr sollt die alle toten*" ("Attention, soldiers! You should kill them all), at which point a nun aiding the wounded men pleaded,

SISTER: You can't do this! It's inhuman!

SS OFFICER: Feuer!

SOUND: *salvo of gunfire, screams and groans, then total silence. A single, measured drumbeat (like a heartbeat), hold . . .*

SS OFFICER (FURIOUS): Soldaten, you will destroy every town in Vercors! Shoot anyone who offers the slightest resistance! Raus!

Sounds of footsteps hurrying out of a cavern. Bring in sound of machine guns firing, screams of dying. The heartbeat effect (established during the deaths of the wounded fighters) holds throughout then grows weaker and fades out altogether.

JACK (HEAVILY): And that's the tragic story of the Vercors Plateau.

JILL: How ghastly! Those poor, poor people!

JACK: You mustn't think about it too much, Jill.

JILL (SIGHS): I know, but it's difficult not to.

JACK (CHANGE OF MOOD): Hey, look! That big city over there in the valley! Is that Paris?

JILL: Paris!

Of course, they were mistaken, since they were in the French Alps, but the distraction helped the two recover (along with listeners) from the traumatic detour they had just taken into contemporary French history. The grim incident contrasted starkly with the comic tone of the series to that point. Jill and Jack did not speak again about what they saw at the Vercors Plateau. Their role, along with that of the listener, was to witness, acknowledge, and move on to the next destination. A merciful distraction from the car window (Paris!) pulled them back into the year 1969, but it was not obvious there was safety in the present from the period they had just left. Having seen the Vercors massacre for herself, Jill countered that it would be a "difficult" task to suppress reflection about "those poor, poor people" and the uncomfortably proximate relationship between the France of 1944 and the France of the present.

Another episode addressed a theme of U.S.–French history introduced in the Normandy episode, when U.S. General Eisenhower had a cameo appearance at D-Day. In a subsequent episode, Jack mentioned to Jill that his grandfather was buried in France. "Your grandfather? Was he French?" she asked. It turned out that Jack's grandfather was a Doughboy who served under General John J. Pershing and died in the Meuse-Argonne region. Jack explained that his grandfather's remains lay, along with those of more than fourteen thousand other combatants, in the U.S. cemetery World War I at Romagne-sous-Montfaucon.[26] Jack and Jill stopped to pay their respects and then moved on to the area of the Battle of Verdun. They viewed trenches, the "boneyard of Douaumont," containing bones of an estimated one hundred thirty thousand soldiers, and the "bayonets trench" where two companies of French soldiers reportedly took shelter during a German bombardment on June 10, 1916:

JACK: It was so violent and sudden that two full companies were buried alive in the trench. They were caught by surprise as they stood there, and when the gunfire died down, only the bayonets they had fixed to the end of their rifles stuck out from the ground.

JILL: What a terrible story! Please, Jack, let's go! I don't want to stay here any longer.

The car drives off. Short pause.

JILL (SOFTLY): It isn't all that funny, the history of France![27]

If certain historical events could be playfully incorporated into Jack and Jill's sojourn through the French provinces, the battlegrounds of D-Day, Vercors, and Verdun proved more complex. Stumbling upon dramatically rendered violence contrasted sharply with Jack and Jill's goofy encounters with talking rivers and eccentric diet doctors. Juxtaposing precocious wheels of talking Camembert with wounded resisters being killed in cold blood set emotional notes in unexpected tension with one another. The juxtaposition complicated a facile portrayal of French history as a source of trivia and amusing distraction for U.S. tourists or an unremitting litany of seriousness. The swerves between emotional registers created discomfort for Jack, Jill, and the audience but also made the series an opportunity for reflection by pulling the weight of the past into the present. The experiments in tone and mood cut against the grain of expectations set by prior historical and cultural radio programming furnished to U.S. listeners by French broadcasting. Along with the amusing and diverting "Legends and Wonders" of French history, the series suggested were painful and unresolved events whose challenges and troubling implications merited reflection for their relevance to the present alongside the happier memories of serendipitous discovery that foreigners might accumulate when visiting France.[28]

"The Heat Doesn't Bother an Arab the Way It Does Others"

DAEC scriptwriters also used experiments in dramatized historical biography to deliver socially conscious messages. Christiane Mallarmé, one of the few female directors in DAEC's English-language unit, coordinated *Plus haut, plus loin, plus vite* (Higher, Further, Faster), a dramatic series devoted to French sport. Written by Bernard Véron, a longtime ORTF drama writer, the series merits attention for its treatment of unconventional high achievers, including two French-Algerian athletes, boxer Marcel Cerdan and competitive runner Alain Mimoun. With various degrees of sympathy, Véron and Mallarmé used dramatized episodes from the lives of mostly male athletes (prizefighters, runners, cyclists, skiers, and sailboat racers) to explore some of the challenges they faced over their lifetimes.

The profile of Marcel Cerdan introduced U.S. listeners to a remarkable boxing talent, whose ethnocultural differences the episode implied, adversely affected his life choices. Born in Sidi Bel Abbès in northwestern Algeria, Marcel Cerdan established a professional boxing career in Casablanca. Cerdan's athleticism eventually won him fame throughout France and international success. Distinguished for his astonishingly high won-lost percentage and tenacity against bigger opponents, Cerdan also gained celebrity for an extramarital affair with singer Édith Piaf. Cerdan won the European Middleweight Championship in 1947 and defeated U.S. boxer Tony Zale in Jersey City in 1948 to become the middleweight champion of the world. Cerdan lost the title the following year to Jake LaMotta. Before he could fight to regain the title, however, Cerdan died in a plane crash.[29]

The DAEC dramatization of Cerdan's life struggled to establish a consistent narrative framework that acknowledged his national credentials as Algerian-born and also a native son of France. The narrator's prologue addressed a U.S. listener presumed to know little or nothing about French colonialism or the contentious topic of Franco-Algerian identity and politics.

> Without a doubt, the famous American "melting pot" gives rise in the United States to an expression similar to "black-feet" in France . . . which does not mean that you will know what black-feet are in France. They are Frenchmen born and raised in Algeria. After the last world war, the brusque decolonization of the French Empire brought them surging back, often dramatically, to France with the feeling that she had not done everything possible for their existence abroad, nor later for their return. *Whatever the truth of the matter, very few black-feet suspected before the War that they would one day be forced to leave "their" countries.* Not Mr. Cerdan, Sr., in any case, a colonist from Roussillon, who came to settle in Sidi Bel Abbès, first home of the famous Foreign Legion. . . . [T]his flamboyant personality had one ambition in life: to make boxers out of his four sons.[30]

Listeners might be forgiven for finding this cryptic synopsis of modern Franco-Algerian political history confusing. Because Cerdan's death occurred in 1949, prior to "the War," a reference to the yet-unnamed Algerian War, the listener might question the need to speculate about the reaction of Marcel Cerdan Sr. to an event that would occur years *after* his son's death. The prefatory remarks appeared designed to alert U.S. listeners to the politics of identity surrounding a figure known for punches, not politics, and one who came of age within a colonial dynamic that devalued men like him in metropolitan France.

Episodes of *Higher, Further, Faster* typically portrayed their subjects affectionately, but this program grew tangled up in the challenge of acknowledging Cerdan's ethno-racial difference and his life's arc and deciding on an evaluative claim about how one shaped the other. The profile described how Cerdan escaped extreme poverty by cultivating his boxing talents under the influence of two domineering men: his father, Marcel Cerdan Sr., and his trainer, Lucien Roupp. The script described the senior Cerdan as a despot who forced all his sons into the ring. It also made an unflattering racist comparison between Georges Carpentier, the famed boxer from Pas-de-Calais, and Marcel Cerdan, a black-foot. The former "conducted his career, himself, clear headedly, like a businessman . . . whereas we can say that Lucien Roupp, following Cerdan, Sr.'s wishes, made Marcel Cerdan from A to Z." Young Marcel was presented in patronizing fashion as simple and passive with little capacity to control his own life.[31]

The episode described a talented athlete, but a rather hapless human being, whose most articulate moment was recounted when Cerdan convinced the parents of his Spanish heartthrob to sever their daughter's engagement so that he could pursue her instead: "For once in his life, Marcel Cerdan was eloquent." The attempt at humor appeared more sarcastic than sympathetic. Although Cerdan surmounted many obstacles to rise to the top of the boxing world, he was repeatedly portrayed in the DAEC drama as a passive subject rather than a self-directing force: "He was like Ferdinand, Walt Disney's peaceful bull, if it weren't for the fact that once in the arena he fought like a wild animal." Portrayed as a beast in the ring and a daydreaming subhuman outside it, Cerdan did not receive a respectful or insightful treatment of the obstacles he faced.[32]

Compounding the patronizing assertions about Cerdan's mental fitness, the boxer was presented as morally lax, which reportedly adversely affected his fighting (a claim that his actual record does not appear to support). "The matter with Cerdan was that he was greedily tasting the dangerous pleasures of Parisian life. His new friends, male and female, gave him nothing but poor examples and advice . . . but on his side, Roupp continued to fight with tenacity."[33] Édith Piaf offered Cerdan protection, which threatened Roupp, who reportedly saw her as an impediment to the project to create a world champion: "It is an established fact," stated the narrator, "that Piaf had a great influence over this weak and dazzled being."[34] The episode culminated with Cerdan's finest hour, when he was able (despite himself, it seems) to rise up and defeat Tony Zale. Cerdan's professional separation from Roupp, however, was presented as a grave error: "Let us simply deplore that an agreement of fifteen years' standing and crowned with success had been broken."[35] As if by prophecy, the newly anointed champ injured his shoulder in the ring, resulting in a loss by decision to Jake LaMotta. Before having a chance to regain his crown, Cerdan died in a plane crash, which lowered the curtain on a life and the ambivalent portrayal of a champion tragically fated by his birth to be something less than he might otherwise have been.

The prologue to the Cerdan profile introduced the boxer and his father as figures caught between national spaces as a result of political and historical events. This observation established a potentially illuminating context for exploring Marcel Cerdan's career as illustrative of the challenges and constrained opportunities for French-Algerians. It is surprising, however, after such a pointed beginning, that the script focused intently on Cerdan's personal failings, which were explained as character flaws that he refused to correct rather than possible indicators of his alienation from mainstream French society. As a result, the program portrayed Cerdan as a tragic but ultimately self-defeating hero, brought down by his weaknesses, which had the unfortunate effect of lending implicit support for negative stereotypes associated with ethnic and racial minorities as undisciplined and mentally unfit.

The profile of champion runner Alain Mimoun offered a more effective and satisfying critical treatment of an outsider battling prejudice in French society. Born Ali Mimoun Ould Kacha, the future star grew up in an Arab-Berber family in Algeria. As historian Philip Dine notes, during the Algerian War, Mimoun "opted definitively for France," though by his own report he remained warmly regarded by Algerians as one of their own, too.[36] Establishing Mimoun's loyalties to France and his Arab-Berber identity, the episode treated his rise as the story of an intrepid striver who strengthened France's republican ideals by insisting that his talents be recognized along with his ethnic difference

The drama portrayed Mimoun's humanity and his athletic prowess repeatedly called into question by a racist French establishment. During World War II, Mimoun evaded the Vichy deportation of North African soldiers from France and joined the Allied forces in Tunisia. He was gravely wounded but rehabilitated himself to become a competitive runner. After the war, he faced recurring incidences of European racism. In the episode, Mimoun was repeatedly addressed as "my boy" or simply "boy." He earned a slot on the French national running team, but only because the Croix-Catelan track clubhouse reportedly needed an extra waiter. A scene described Mimoun serving tea under the snooty gazes of Parisians. Outside work, he took solitary runs in the Bois de Boulogne to train for the French championships. In the competition, Mimoun performed very well but lost to the Czech runner Emil Zátopek. Afterward, the French team trainer refused to treat Mimoun's aching muscles: "Sorry, boy, I don't have the time. I have to give Hansenne his massage now." Racist comments dismissed Mimoun's accomplishments when he did run well: "Nothing extraordinary about him, he was just lucky," said a judge. "It's a hot day, and the heat doesn't bother an Arab the way it does others. Look at the Scandinavian runners, they dropped out of the race like flies."[37] These biting lines leave no ambiguity about with whom a listener is expected to identify. Mimoun is persecuted unjustly on the basis of his ethnicity and race.

The episode showed Mimoun stoically absorbing these slights until a confrontation with the captain of the French team at the Cross of Nations championship in Dublin in 1949. In the final yards of the race, Mimoun sprinted past team captain Raphaël Pujazon and another teammate, Charles Cérou, to take first place. After the race, the captain scolded Mimoun for violating "team spirit" by not deferring to custom and allowing him to cross first. When Mimoun retorted that Pujazon's egotism, not team spirit, motivated the order for teammates to slow down, Pujazon erupted.

PUJAZON: Oh shut up! Why don't you go back to your own country!
MIMOUN: I'm in my own country! I became French when I fought with the French army. I guess that makes me just as much of a Frenchman as someone who was born here by chance. Right?
PUJAZON: What's that supposed to mean?
MIMOUN: I mean just what I said. With a name like Pujazon, your parents or your grandparents were Spanish or something, but they certainly were not French.[38]
CÉROU (DIPLOMATICALLY): Look fellows, Mimoun is Arab and Pujazon is Spanish, so I guess I'm the only real Frenchman here. I was born in Clermont-Ferrand, as everybody knows, Clermont-Ferrand is the belly button of France.
Big laugh.[39]

We might see Cérou's tension-breaking joke as the signal for a retreat from the program's critique of racial inequality in French society, but that is not the case. The harsh tone of Pujazon's attack was typical, not exceptional, and Mimoun's unflinching defense of his rights left no doubt of the program's intention to draw attention to anti-Arab racial discrimination in France. At the end of the program, writer Bernard Véron, speaking as the narrator, disclosed that he interviewed Mimoun for the program and added that Mimoun was still running competitively in 1971. Bringing the living Mimoun out of the historical past and into the narrative present underscored the message that besides being an exceptional achiever, Mimoun represented a class of racial minorities continuing to struggle for their rights and recognition in a social system where discrimination remained a significant structural issue.[40]

Efforts to overcome racial prejudice and xenophobia and promote internationalism are treated in a broad conceptual way in the series profile of Pierre,
baron de Coubertin, the aristocratic champion of physical education in France,
who helped establish the modern Olympics in 1894 and founded the International Olympic Committee. Coubertin promoted the Olympic motto *Citius,
Altius, Fortius* (Faster, Higher, Stronger).[41] The DAEC biographical drama
focused on several instances in which Coubertin rallied French support for
adapting the physical fitness tradition popularized in English public schools.

> COUBERTIN (POLITE BUT IRONIC): Look at it this way. It seems wise to me to
> borrow from [England] what they have gained to compensate ourselves for
> the harm they've done us.
> OLD FOGY: Absolutely right, my dear Coubertin. Our youth today is as limp as
> a rag. And what a bunch of lame ducks in the barracks! Besides, we saw the
> result in the last war! You're right: we must prepare our boys to the mastery
> of arms even in the classroom. They must learn to shoot, to ride . . .
> COUBERTIN (POLITE BUT FIRM): Easy! . . . My desire is not to militarize youth
> but to make it more virile, more vital. . . . It's not at all the same.[42]

Coubertin apparently accepted conventional gendered assumptions about
athletics as for males and as a means of benefiting virility, but the dialogue
also suggested that his motives were different from the traditional view of
physical fitness as solely useful for training soldiers. The profile also criticized
ethnocentrism and class bias by drawing attention to Coubertin's progressive vision of a multinational modern Olympics that included a diversity of
nations and social groups.

> SNOB 1: And if the Chinese and Negroes want to participate in your games?
> COUBERTIN: I'd hope they'll ask! They'll be welcomed with open arms.
> LADY: It'll be a real hodge-podge of anybody and anything!
> COUBERTIN: That's precisely what I'm looking for, my friend.
> SNOB 1: You may even get Jews.
> COUBERTIN: Quite likely.
> SNOB 1: And even laborers.[43]

Recalling the examples of bigotry and elitism that Alain Mimoun confronted
and overcame, this episode showed Coubertin striving to overcome France
and Europe's prejudices and parochial tendencies. The thematic message
in both the Mimoun and Coubertin programs stressed contributions by a
diverse array of French (as opposed to Franco-French) individuals building
a vital republic that upheld its own principles.

Like fellow scriptwriter Alain Franck, who created Jack and Jill for *Legends
and Wonders*, Véron used playful and surreal techniques to grab the listener's

attention, violate radio drama conventions, and even draw philosophical attention to the historical form itself. In a profile of Alain Gerbault, the long-distance sailor, who navigated a perilous Atlantic crossing solo in 1923, the narrator declared, "After a useful stopover in Gibraltar, the big adventure began . . . and for the author of this program, this poses an immediate problem. What kinds of words can I put into the mouth of a man all alone in the middle of the ocean for it to seem 'real'? I am sure that Alain Gerbault must have talked to himself: one cannot remain dumb for 102 days; he must have sung also, sea chanteys, and recited poems that he loved."[44] The narrator's aside in the midst of the drama drew attention to a practical problem of reliable sources in constructing the storyline but also exposed the goal of conventional historical dramatization to conceal its artifice in order to deliver what passes for an objective account. In this case, the narrator reassured listeners that they could trust the voice of Gerbault. The sailor had chronicled the voyage, and presumably such a primary source would be more authoritative and trustworthy than a scriptwriter's attempt to imagine Gerbault's solitary thoughts.

In another episode, Véron again used narrative self-reflexivity to satirize the traditional mode of omniscient historical documentary. In this instance, the description of Émile Allais and the story of how Alpine (downhill) skiing reached France via Austria and Switzerland was literally interrupted by the voice of another skier intent on delivering a competing narrative of the sport's national origins.

> VOICE OF ARNOLD LUNN (ECHO CHAMBER): My dear fellow, will you please allow me to add a word to your résumé?
> NARRATOR: Ah, Sir Arnold! First of all, let me introduce you to our listeners. The voice you are hearing is that of Sir Arnold Lunn, the pope of Alpine skiing.
> LUNN: Oh, come, come, my dear boy, you flatter me. Let's say disciple rather than pope, please. But what I want to add to your résumé is that you forget to mention that the taste for skiing . . . and, in many cases, the skis themselves . . . were first introduced to the Swiss and Austrians by the British. . . .
> NARRATOR: My dear Sir Arnold, far be it from me to overlook the important . . . rather, the leading role, that you and your fellow countrymen played in developing Alpine skiing, but, you see, this program is devoted to Émile Allais, and I'm afraid we'll have to stick to the subject.[45]

The narrator resumed his account but was cut off by the pesky Sir Arnold Lunn, who kept inserting competitive asides about British accomplishments in skiing, until the narrator asked for permission to "get started" with the story of Émile Allais, to which the voice of Lunn pompously replied, "Oh, please don't let me interrupt you, dear friend."[46]

Skewering the illusions of narrative authority and conventional dramatic aesthetics in these ways reflected more than experimental creative techniques or anarchic play (though these may well have been motivations). After decades of drama production for U.S. audiences, a cohort of ORTF scriptwriters was taking risks with content and form. The break from institutional and aesthetic convention could not be uncoupled from the contextual challenges of the events of May '68 as they criticized the ORTF as an ideological tool of information control, propaganda distribution, and cultural legitimation of a status hierarchy. Programs and aesthetic techniques that departed from conventions even in modest ways reflected agency on the part of writers and producers to use broadcasting to engage audiences with alternative messages about the relationship of the past to the present and, most of all, to the future. The ungovernable voices of history that barged into these DAEC programs came from the creative minds of the authors, but once liberated, they signified a challenge to French radio's orthodox conventions and assumptions about the purpose of broadcasting and cultural production. These series adopted humor, provocation, emotional manipulation, and subversive gestures at the level of narration and narrative itself to reshape conventional uses of historical radio dramatization into a field of critique and meditation on history's ultimate uses. These provocations challenged U.S. listeners to reexamine assumptions about the function of radio histories and to carefully consider the stories of France that the ORTF wanted them to hear.

"She's Not Very Pretty. . . . What's Her Name?"

DAEC's dramatic productions also advanced the tradition of U.S.–French radio programs that addressed women. *Les femmes dont on parla au XIXe siècle* (Women We Spoke about in the 19th Century) and *Ces hommes et femmes qui ont fait Paris* (The Men and Women Who Made Paris) featured notable female figures in arts and letters. *Autour de la Belle Époque* (Around the Belle Époque) used a tabloid concept to recount dramatic stories about famous public figures and controversies, such as profiles of great actors like Sarah Bernhardt and Eleonara Duse and investigations of the mysterious disappearance and death of Baroness Yvonne de Cazaubon.

Higher, Further, Faster, the DAEC series devoted to athletic strivers, included a portrait of Suzanne Lenglen, the teen prodigy who excelled in women's tennis after World War I. Lenglen's privileged upbringing afforded her the leisure to pursue a tennis career full-time and gain access to challenging playing partners, both female and male. What appeared a conventional portrait of a glamorous sportswoman, however, turned into a fascinating description of her controversial entry into professional tennis as a teenager, and the polarized public responses to the power and speed of her game, her fashion tastes (turbans), and her repeated defiance of conventional gender roles.[47]

SPECTATOR 1: She's not very pretty. . . . What's her name?

SPECTATOR 2: Suzanne Lenglen. . . . Not pretty, perhaps, but much better than that. What grace—she's like a dancer!

SPECTATOR 1: And her dress—hardly below her knee—it's indecent!

SPECTATOR 2: Bah! She's a child, she's not yet fifteen!

SPECTATOR 1: Goodness, she serves like a man—above the head!

SPECTATOR 2: Why not? And see how she aims her balls. Her father taught her to aim at a handkerchief on the ground.

SPECTATOR 1: A circus animal.

SPECTATOR 2: An infant prodigy—like Mozart.[48]

Here, a booster and a critic furnished examples of the polarized reception that greeted Lenglen's rise in a male-dominated sport with rigid gender norms. Lenglen helped popularize women's tennis in France and brought Jazz Age glamour to the game. Beyond her professional example to other female athletes, Lenglen's career helped introduce comfortable sportswear for women. But the governing theme of this episode concerned how gender politics surrounded her career.

The drama described Lenglen's lone loss in amateur lawn tennis at Forest Hills, New York, in 1921. To the disappointment of paying spectators, Lenglen left the court in the middle of a match. "She withdrew to the boos of the crowd," the narrator explained, and was accused by the president of the American Tennis Association of "pretending to be ill." Lenglen, an informal ambassador of France, returned home humiliated, only to face an interrogation from male members of the recently established French Tennis Federation. "You behaved in a very free and easy manner, and with an unforgivable lack of sportsmanship. Retiring because you lost the first set!" accused one official. Lenglen explained to her inquisitors that she was seriously ill (the script calls for sound effects of "whooping cough" as she prepares for the trip to Forest Hills), and that she had been pressured to play by a U.S. tennis promoter (against the advice of her father-coach). "[The promoter] told me that the American public would be so disappointed if I didn't play that they might attack me."[49] The dialogue evoked the pressures affecting professional athletes and performers, as well as the added physical and psychological pressures sometimes imposed on women when they refused to cooperate with men's demands. Perhaps hyperbolic, the threatened violence of the crowd brought the symbolism of gender politics to the fore. Portraying Lenglen as physically strong, self-confident, and creative but perpetually locked in struggles with male figures trying to dictate the conditions of her life (conservative father, male-dominated professional associations, promoters) made her story timely for a U.S. listening audience growing more attuned to women's progress in professional endeavors, but also growing more cognizant of underlying conventions of gender discrimination and sexism that still constrained independent young women like Suzanne Lenglen almost fifty years after her battles on and off the tennis court.[50]

"We've Lost the Thread"

Using fresh approaches and techniques to engage late-1960s radio listeners, the DAEC drama series appeared poised to build on the successes of French broadcast distributions of the past several decades. An informal 1969 inventory of more than three hundred U.S. stations carrying ORTF radio programs, including DAEC's new drama series, yielded mostly positive responses. Station KTCF in Cedar Falls, Iowa, had carried RTF and ORTF material since 1962. "Throughout the seven years, we have been consistently pleased with the programs you have made available to us," wrote the program director. "[T]he high technical standards . . . combine to make of the programs a worthwhile educational experience and an enjoyable listening experience. The comments we have received from our listeners have been very encouraging." Other correspondence from stations described ORTF programs as "well-received by our listeners" and "excellent."[51]

Though DAEC dramas did not enjoy the widespread distribution accorded the platter series, they were available to listeners in college towns and metropolitan centers via the distribution path pioneered by the NAEB. WNYC remained a stalwart supporter of the bicycle network, as did some broadcasters large and small, such as KFJC-FM, the station of tiny Foothill College in Los Altos Hills, California, which boasted significant listenership because its broadcast signal reached metropolitan San Francisco. Programmers and audiences appreciated what French programs brought to their ears, namely an alternative to mainstream broadcasting. "All other radio here is commercial, and generally appealing to average tastes," wrote Joseph Kirkish of WGGL-FM, which served an audience in remote northern Michigan. "Because of our relative isolation, we feel we should provide an informative yet entertaining glimpse of the 'outside world' to our listeners (who are both members of the campus community and the community at large). . . . All of your programs help us in that manner. . . . Audience response is very good;

those listeners who appreciate our motives in presenting foreign programming are especially grateful, and our rather large group of local residents with a French background also enjoy it."[52]

Despite indicators of demand for more programs from the ORTF, the distribution system developed by the NAEB and BFA in the 1950s was fraying from a lack of sustaining support and transatlantic oversight. The retirement of Pierre Crénesse diminished the FBS New York operation. The subsequent reshuffling of international program-distribution duties tested the durability of the relationships that Crénesse and U.S. colleagues had painstakingly built over many years. Signs of trouble appeared as early as summer 1966, when the French government shifted responsibility for distributing French radio content in the United States from the ORTF's New York office to the cultural services wing of the French consulate in New York.[53] It was a blow to France's first permanent radio bureau in North America. Since Paul Gilson arrived in New York after World War II, French broadcasters and distributors of the platter system and other RDF, RTF, and ORTF content had worked directly with their U.S. radio counterparts. Pierre Crénesse had fought hard to keep such radio exchange work separate from the consular services and insulated from persons unfamiliar with the radio business. Times had changed, however. The resources and direction needed to support professional U.S. distribution of French content were not forthcoming from Paris. Busy consular officials without training or expertise in French or U.S. broadcasting inherited the job of coordinating the distribution of ORTF content with U.S. stations.

Signs of difficulty with the consular arrangement appeared in the winter of 1969, when Ben Smith, former FBS employee, *Bonjour Mesdames* announcer, and now editor of DAEC's English-language production services, wrote to Yvette Mallet, head of the radio-television office at the New York consulate, asking for ORTF program circulation data. "It's a number that has always been maintained around two or three hundred [stations], since we had a New York bureau," Smith wrote, "but, since [the consular takeover] we've lost the thread."[54] DAEC officials were stunned to discover in response to this routine request that no one at the consulate was assigned to keep systematic records of program circulation or to act as a regular liaison with U.S. stations. With Crénesse out of the picture, it also appeared that links with the NAEB had frayed considerably. The consulate made an ill-fated decision to outsource national distribution and tracking responsibilities of ORTF content to the North American Broadcasting Corporation (NABC), a fledgling educational organization near San Francisco. Initially, consular officials and DAEC representatives received glowing reports from the NABC on the distribution of taped programs and engagement of client stations. Testimonial letters from pleased listeners attested to an apparently successful and growing base for DAEC content. Verifying the NABC reports proved difficult, however. San Francisco, New York, and Paris were sufficiently separated that communication lines were not as robust as they needed to be to keep track of where ORTF programs were traveling and which series were receiving audience support. DAEC officials began to doubt the story coming out of the NABC and the competence of its officers.[55] Producers in Paris craved audience feedback on the new drama programs and lamented the loss of informed and motivated ORTF allies in New York willing to contact stations for specific reactions to the new programs. Relations between the consulate and the ORTF grew extremely strained as it became clear that consular officials were not prioritizing the fortunes of French broadcasting in the United States. The consulate did not appear to recognize or chose to ignore that anything was wrong in San Francisco. "Our big problem is broadcasting itself," complained a DAEC official. "We have little or, as it were, no contact with listeners. We don't even know if our programs are broadcast!!!"[56] Despite a recognized problem in coordination, tracking, and responsibility for station relations, disagreement about authority and responsibility in New York and Paris produced an impasse.

In January 1971, the French consulate in New York requested that DAEC supply six of its English-language productions every week. The productions consisted of newsmagazine and public-affairs programs and more episodes of *Priscilla in Paris*, the replacement for Marjorie Dunton's *Bonjour Mesdames*.[57] None of the requested programs included any DAEC drama series. DAEC continued producing new series, however, which it forwarded hopefully to New York for possible distribution via the consulate through the underfunded, but still operating, NAEB bicycle system. The lack of accountability for systematic distribution and shortage of data on where these programs traveled and aired remained an issue. *Priscilla in Paris* reportedly performed well, but the overall picture for French radio in the United States had degraded. The number of stations carrying ORTF programs, including dramatic series, had plunged from the mid-1960s, when 434 stations reported carrying one or more series, to 250 stations by the early 1970s. The platter series continued to reach most of the fifty states, but other programs, including the DAEC dramatics, lacked the duplication and distribution support they needed to command a national audience. Out of the estimated universe of 6,349 commercial U.S. stations and some five hundred educational stations, the DAEC dramas were represented on only 27 percent of U.S. stations.[58] Despite signs of demand among university and nonprofit educational stations exposed to the tape programs of DAEC, there remained no concerted effort to fix and adequately fund the next generation of U.S.–French radio exchanges.[59]

The "Object of a Shared Agenda"

On January 31, 1973, Raymond Poussard, assistant director general of the ORTF, and the creator of DAEC, delivered a report to ORTF and Ministry of Foreign Affairs officials. The "Report on the End of the Mission of Mr. Raymond Poussard, the DAEC 4 Years after Its Creation" delivered a mixed assessment of the organization charged to bring French culture to the world. "The results of these four years of action by the DAEC make it clear that the reform of 1968–69 has been beneficial in all areas," Poussard began.[60] The department produced live or recorded content in nineteen languages and programs reached 119 countries. The department provided 184 hours of daily programs and dedicated seventy-six hours of additional programs to France's overseas *départements* and territories, for a total of 260 hours.

The list of accomplishments seemed less impressive, however, when Poussard compared DAEC's output to that of the leading world powers. Where France allotted twenty transmitters to international service, the BBC dedicated eighty-seven. In cumulative hours of daily international services, France trailed far behind the Soviet Union (1,929), the United States (1,908), China (1,461), Germany (724), and England (719). France obviously could elevate its output from 260 total hours, he noted, but the political will to commit the resources necessary to expand further into the global arena would have to be mustered. Poussard conceded such a commitment was unlikely because of political dissatisfaction with the ORTF externally and internally.[61]

Having delivered a sobering message about France's relative status in the international broadcast arena and explained the economic and political reasons for the bleak prospects for further growth, Poussard praised DAEC's English-language service for its significant progress and programming accomplishments. Despite limited resources, in four years DAEC had achieved a "spectacular" increase in its shortwave broadcasts (200%) and prerecorded programs (150%).[62] Moreover, the number of original musical and spoken-English programs, such as the *Dramatics* series, had leaped 62 percent. What Poussard avoided mentioning, however, was the distribution breakdown in DAEC's dealings with the New York consulate. Poussard briefly alluded to the problems in New York, stating that "The distribution [of programs] to the United States did not seem to reach the scope possible due to not having been the object of a shared agenda on the part of the ORTF."[63] But the obstacles to arriving at a "shared agenda" went unexplored in the report, as did the facts of the matter, which pointed to a combination of bureaucratic mismanagement and inertia, irresponsibility, lack of leadership, and lack of resources, which collectively placed the legacy of U.S.–French radio in jeopardy.

The affair between the ORTF and the French consulate reflected a broader drift in France's international broadcast policies toward the United States. The troubles with the distribution system emerged at approximately the same moment that the French economy began to constrict after nearly three decades of prosperity. The global oil crisis of 1973 and global recession also affected the United States. Resources at the ORTF and those available to nonprofit educational broadcasters in the United States were limited. Although the NAEB gamely cycled along, it could not provide the robust support for French broadcasting that it once had, and it lacked an experienced and motivated partner like Pierre Crénesse. Regrettably, despite the innovative characteristics of the DAEC dramatics series, too few U.S. stations beyond the major NAEB stalwarts appear to have been exposed to their full range.[64]

Unfortunately, DAEC editor Ben Smith's worry that "we've lost the thread" that once linked French broadcasting to U.S. stations proved more accurate than first recognized. The statement could easily be applied to the entire ORTF system, which had not been functioning well since the upheaval of May 1968. The public broadcaster had made institutional changes, such as creating DAEC, but the government had not been able to mollify an angry and impatient French national audience. The public monopoly model had grown incompatible with the wants and needs of the French people. On August 7, 1974, Jacques Chirac, speaking for the new French president Valéry Giscard d'Estaing, announced the breakup of the ORTF into seven separate bodies.[65] The breakup began a restrained advance toward a more economically competitive and independent framework for French broadcasting, which took many years to enact. Media privatization and deregulation only began in earnest under the Socialist government of François Mitterrand.[66] During the 1980s and early 1990s, the emergence of *radios locales* (community radio stations), the rise of commercial advertising, and the addition of popular music stations prompted James Miller to hyperbolically describe 1990s French radio as "a Gallic version of North American FM."[67] Although they hardly resembled commercial U.S. broadcasting's abundant offerings across metropolitan France, the rise of commercial offerings and the slight loosening of governmental control over news and information augured well for further diversification of voices and influences in the French media environment.

Unlike the slow blooming of post-ORTF national broadcasting, however, international services to the United States never recovered the levels they had enjoyed during the 1950s and 1960s. To save money, French officials slashed international media production. International service plummeted from nineteen to three foreign languages. The English-language program services from France continued, but only at a nominal level. Many factors contributed to the cooling of U.S.–French exchange via radio. Above all, the postwar geopolitical crisis that stirred France and the United States to collectively support a massive French radio campaign to "resell itself" and to "rebuild the respect of America" and the Cold War urgency to supplement transatlantic communications between the two allies had passed; France stood on a firm foundation with a thriving tourist industry buoyed by U.S. consumption and with a solid political alliance with the United States.

Transatlantic broadcasting could hardly take credit for France's postwar rebound, but in a period of distress and uncertainty it had contributed sounds of France to boost the nation's recovery and helped strengthen U.S.–French relations. Throughout the postwar period and ending with the experimental dramas of DAEC, French radio services diversified the programs on U.S. airwaves. Exchanges contributed original music, drama, and talk radio programs for more than a generation. Even if the topics of French culture, history, art, drama, and literature tended to be orthodox and narrowly focused on metropolitan France, these programs stimulated U.S. listeners' interest in France. Hundreds of stations across the United States aired thousands of hours of programs thanks to the FBS's platter exchange and tape circulation via the NAEB and BFA bicycle network. Some of the nation's most influential public broadcast stations from WQXR and WNYC in New York to KQED in San Francisco supported French radio and grew stronger through their programming additions from Paris. The FBS platter series brought sounds of France to college and university cities and towns and to untold numbers of students and community listeners. These sustaining programs contributed to the further development of college and nonprofit educational stations, where students, volunteers, and paid staff learned to make their own programs, train for careers in the media industries, and experience the creative possibilities of radio. For five decades, U.S.–French broadcasting traveled across the waves with regularity, carrying ideas back and forth, and shaping listener experiences instantaneously on a mass scale in ways that enriched a transatlantic relationship nurtured by curiosity and a mutual desire to connect.

Afterword

Radios at the Heart of Nations

At the 1931 French Colonial Exposition, the United States and France bet together on the future of transatlantic broadcasting. Many motives informed the wager. Some were principled and others pragmatic, but neither party could explore its fullest options without help from an ally across the waves. From the interwar shaping of techno-aesthetic difference and complementarity, to the call-and-response pattern of U.S.–French broadcasting during the Occupation, to the Cold War calculus that brought programs from France into U.S. living rooms, interdependence characterized U.S.–French broadcasting.

U.S.–French broadcasting developed relationally through the cross-border circulation of persons, sonic artifacts, aesthetic techniques, and institutional practices. Human and technical infrastructure developed across national borders as part of cycles of international production and exchange. These kinds of dynamics blurred national differences under certain conditions and reconstituted them in others. In many cases, the U.S. and French governments played an active part in the story. The geopolitics of international broadcasting enabled national presences beyond fixed borders. The porous membrane separating U.S. and French international broadcasting that Simon J. Copans observed in the early 1950s proved to be less anomalous to broadcast history than it first appeared.

Efforts by the French and U.S. governments to shape the Cold War–era landscape of international broadcasting raise broad questions about the manipulated cultural politics of broadcasting and other international media. Although intention and motives are difficult to fix historically and otherwise, the politically motivated quest to elevate popular approval of France in the

United States through the FBS platter series justified a U.S.–French geopolitics of cultural exclusion rather than inclusion. The FBS platter distribution brought sounds of France across North America and nourished noncommercial broadcasting in the United States. International music, drama, and cultural programs appealed mostly to an educated audience eager to see their international interests supplied by U.S. radio. As an example of how international broadcasting might have illuminated new geopolitical configurations, however, the platter series and bicycle exchanges fell short of their potential. Only at the point of the DAEC dramas of the late 1960s did the decolonizing Francophone world garner more than a cursory inspection by U.S.–French broadcasters. Inevitably, perhaps, state-managed program exchanges performed the cultural work of legitimation in some areas and disavowal in others. International broadcasting helped develop modern U.S. and French cultural imagination along many dimensions, whether fostering insight and providing aesthetic benefits or contributing to mythological caricatures. U.S. and French people learned to listen to one another in certain ways partly because of radio. In the twenty-first century, previously discounted, repressed, or not widely available voices and music of North America and the Francophone world are more widely available in more forms for transatlantic circulation than ever before. Although constraints in resources, technology, and politics remain, voices and expressive traditions can circulate through an infrastructure of diverse and decentralized communication technologies and media, including digital radio forms and digitally supported platforms and social media technologies whose existence started with the internationalization of broadcasting.[1]

Radios at the Heart of Nations

On June 18, 1990, a giant radio appeared at the Place de la Concorde in the center of Paris. The mock replica receiver soared 115 feet into the air. From it came snippets of French and English radio programs from the 1930s. At regular intervals, a voice familiar to millions interrupted the music to intone the words of an iconic French media event: the Appeal of June 18, 1940. On that date, Charles de Gaulle broadcast from London on the BBC to oppose an armistice with the German conquerors. He called on France to continue to fight. "The flame of French resistance must not be extinguished and will not be extinguished," de Gaulle vowed.[2]

To mark the fiftieth anniversary of the appeal and the centennial of de Gaulle's birth, the postmodern artist Catherine Feff draped painted canvases over a superstructure enclosing the Luxor obelisk and created a trompe-

In June 1990, a gigantic radio towered over the Place du la Concorde to commemorate the silver anniversary of Charles de Gaulle's *appel de 18 juin 1940.* (AP Images/Pierre Gleizes)

l'œil of a massive vintage radio. The installation echoed the monumental sculptures of Christo and Jeanne-Claude, who, five years earlier, temporarily swaddled the four-hundred-year-old Pont Neuf in golden-hued fabric. Asked to explain his attraction to ephemeral public art, Christo explained, "All these projects have this strong dimension of missing, of self-effacement, that they will go away, like our childhood, our life."[3]

It is not known whether Feff (a devotee of Christo and Jeanne-Claude) had a similarly elegiac concept in mind when she conceptualized the homage to de Gaulle and the technology he expertly manipulated over his career. The installation symbolically linked an ephemeral live medium to the fading living memories of the war, the Occupation, and of de Gaulle himself. The giant radio represented a nostalgic repository of memories of broadcasting's place during France's worst crisis of the twentieth century. The installation practiced its own kind of effacement, however, by obscuring the fact that the *reception* of de Gaulle's radio address, and its subsequent *canonization* as text and touchstone (the actual broadcast was not recorded), were phenomena of a different order. As historians point out, amid the chaos of June 1940, with the French army defeated and hundreds of thousands of civilians in flight or otherwise dislocated from their routines, the legendary broadcast reached only a small audience of French listeners. The content of the message spread rapidly, however, and listeners heard often thereafter from de Gaulle and his supporters via radio. The Appeal represented a "landmark in retrospect," not a galvanizing force coming over the loudspeaker in 1940.[4]

In 1990, such buzz-killing qualification clashed with the popular commemoration and binding of de Gaulle's memory and a more general celebration of the power of radio in French cultural memory. "De Gaulle's symbolic act of defiance and resistance has entered national French mythology as a turning-point in France's recovery of its self-esteem; and into Gaullist mythology as the first heroic appearance of their national savior," wrote a contemporary observer.[5] Radio had entered national mythology, too. Listening to international radio during the Occupation allowed the French to conjure an imagined national community when unity in real political terms was impossible. The voices from listener letters added particularity to the imagined community. As much as de Gaulle motivated the commemoration, so did the broadcast medium, which pulsed with fantastical hope between 1940 and 1944 for national integration and deliverance from conflict.

The power ascribed to radio to thwart crisis, to bind, and to restore national purpose fuels the cultural narratives of the United States, too. Less than a decade after the 1990 commemoration in France, the National Park Service dedicated the Franklin Delano Roosevelt (FDR) Memorial in Washington, D.C. The permanent installation included a series of bronzes sculpted by George Segal. One depicts a middle-aged male in working clothes, barefoot and seated on a wooden chair with a broken rail. He sits hunched forward, hands clasped, brow furrowed, while listening intently to a radio set on a table. The *Fireside Chat* appears at first to be a scene of isolation and human vulnerability. Its symbolic meaning must be completed by the historically aware observer, who understands that this solitary figure is hardly alone. He is linked simultaneously to millions of invisible, concerned others across the United States listening to the explanatory reassurances of FDR during the Great Depression. As Jason Loviglio demonstrates, FDR's mastery of radio ranked him among the most effective political communicators and nation-builders of his time. Like the installation in Paris, the *Fireside Chat* memorialized a period of crisis, a defining moment in the political career of a great leader, and was a testimonial to a communication device that is given credit for its power to forge mass connection, uplift listeners, and restore confidence in the nation.[6]

By blending the sounds of BBC and French radio programs, the de Gaulle installation acknowledged the importance of international cross listening. Left out, however, were the contributions of U.S.–French radio before, during,

George Segal's *Fireside Chat* at the Franklin Delano Roosevelt Memorial in Washington, D.C., attests to the significance of broadcasting during the Great Depression. (Library of Congress/Carol M. Highsmith)

and after the Occupation. Likewise, the *Fireside Chat* celebrated a U.S. president and a formative moment in the shaping of a U.S. radio nation, but it left out the ways that international broadcasting radiated FDR's speeches outward and shaped perceptions of the United States in the world. Just as George Segal's listener hunched forward to hear the president's words, French listeners like Jean Guéhenno strained to hear the president's words cutting through the static of Occupation-era jamming. The consequences of the economic and political crises of the 1930s and the uses of international broadcasting fatefully linked nations together around the world. The instantaneous long-distance affordances of shortwave brought Roosevelt's inaugural addresses and communiqués on foreign policy, and U.S. attitudes toward fascism, Vichy, and numerous other issues, to millions of listeners outside the United States. In such cases, the international work of one radio nation sustained the hopes and resolve of another.

Over the course of the twentieth century, U.S.–French broadcast communication evolved from tentative experiments into regular patterns of interaction. The beauty and mystery of aural communication without wires at vast distances and on a mass scale captured the imaginations of many users and developers. Radio helped breach the physical confines of nation-states while giving new life to the particulars and differences of national cultures that resisted erasure in the cross-border processes of mediated geopolitics. The history of U.S.–French broadcasting reflected commercial and political motives, but also human-level concerns, such as the desire to speak, to tell, and be heard, as well as to listen, to grow, and to learn from others. Radio's international age yielded a remarkable body of cultural material conveying ideas, values, and aspirations for active forms of connection.

Appendix

U.S.–French Radio Time Line

1865

Twenty nations meet in Paris at the first International Telegraph Convention. They create the International Telegraph Union.

1869

Submarine cable connects France and the United States.

1890

Physicist Édouard Branly invents the coherer to detect radio signals.

1899

Guglielmo Marconi transmits a wireless telegraphic signal across the English Channel.
Marconi Wireless Telegraph Company of America (American Marconi) is incorporated in New Jersey.

1901

Marconi transmits a wireless telegraphic signal across the Atlantic Ocean.

1906

Lee De Forest patents the audion, a three-element vacuum tube capable of detecting and boosting radio signals.
United Wireless Company forms in the United States.
Reginald Aubrey Fessenden conducts successful wireless telephony broadcast of human speech.

1912

Lee De Forest perfects audion amplification technology.

1913

AT&T acquires rights to De Forest's audion amplifier.

1914

World War I begins.

1915

First wireless telegraphy transmission from the United States to France is received at the Eiffel Tower station.

1918

Edwin Howard Armstrong perfects the superheterodyne circuit that can significantly improve radio signal reception.
U.S. Navy purchases coastal and marine stations of American Marconi.
World War I concludes.

1919

Versailles Peace Conference convenes.
Radio Corporation of America (RCA) is incorporated.

1920

U.S. Navy relinquishes control of American Marconi stations; RCA assumes their operation.
AT&T and GE sign cross-licensing patent agreements.
Station KDKA begins regular broadcasting in Pittsburgh.

1921

Eiffel Tower radiotelegraph station is transferred from the military to the PTT. It begins regular broadcasts in late December.
Westinghouse signs a cross-licensing agreement with AT&T, GE, and RCA.

1922

British Broadcasting Company (BBC) is formed. By Royal Charter, it becomes the British Broadcasting Corporation (BBC) in 1927.
PTT Poste l'École supérieure begins broadcasting in Paris.
Private station Radiola is launched. It operates privately as Radio-Paris until its public annexation by the PTT in 1933.
Westinghouse forms station WJZ.
AT&T establishes WEAF.

1923

PTT monopoly over posts and telegraphs is extended to wireless telephony and broadcasting.

1924

Le Petit Parisien newspaper establishes a radio station, Poste-Parisien.
AT&T broadcasts using multiple-station hookups.

1925

The International Broadcasting Union (IBU), a nongovernmental policy organization, is established in Geneva.
The French government legalizes the use of commercial advertising on French airwaves.
Radio LL established. It will later become Radio-Cité.

1926

The so-called Bokanowski décret confirms governmental authority over French broadcasting. Private stations are warned that their right to exist is contingent on governmental approval and that the government reserves the option to annex private stations in the future.
RCA acquires AT&T station WEAF.
National Broadcasting Company (NBC) established.
NBC Red network launches operations.

1927

The U.S. Congress passes the Radio Act of 1927. The Federal Radio Commission (FRC) is established.
AT&T launches trans-Atlantic telephone service via radio signaling to London.
NBC Blue network is formed.
Columbia Broadcasting System (CBS) is formed. It is purchased in 1928 by William S. Paley.

1928

French government decree gives statutory recognition to thirteen existing private stations of their right to continue, but adds that no further private broadcast licenses will be permitted.
AT&T launches telephone service between New York and Paris.

1930

An estimated 500,000 radio receivers are in France.
U.S. Census reports 45 percent of U.S. households own a radio set.
David Sarnoff is named president of RCA.

1931

NBC and PTT partner in transatlantic broadcast of the Colonial Exposition from France to the United States.
Backers of private broadcasting in France, and Radio-Paris specifically, arrange with the French government to establish a commercial station "périphérique" operating on foreign soil and serving French listeners.
John F. Royal is appointed NBC vice president of programming.

1933

PTT introduces an annual radio set licensing fee.
The French government annexes private station Radio-Paris, which joins Paris-PTT as the flagships of French public broadcasting.

L'annuaire de la radiodiffusion reports nineteen radio-related periodicals appearing in France.

1934

February riots between Far Right and Communist factions in Paris.

1935

PTT stations cease running all commercial advertising.
Germany renounces the antirearmament rules of the Treaty of Versailles.

1936

Popular Front (PF) coalition is elected in France and institutes radio reforms.
Telephone service using shortwave directly links Paris and Washington, D.C.
Lenox Lohr is appointed NBC president.

1937

French radio elections of 1937 pit partisan slates against one another. Radio-Liberté, headed by Socialist Léon Blum, loses to Catholic conservative Radio-Famille.
NBC establishes an International Division and launches daily, multilingual overseas shortwave service.

1938

Germany annexes Austria in the *Anschluss*.
CBS runs its first international news "roundup" in response to the *Anschluss*. Program features Edward R. Murrow and William Shirer. Reports link London, Paris, Rome, Berlin, and Vienna.
Munich agreement involving France, Germany, Great Britain, and Italy permits the German annexation of the *Sudetenland* region of Czechoslovakia.
French government tightens ministerial oversight of the content of private broadcasters and orders screening of news reports and scripts.

1939

The French government takes over administration of French broadcasting from the PTT.
Germany and Russia sign a nonaggression pact.
Germany invades Poland.
World War II begins.

1940

Five million radio sets are estimated for forty-one million French inhabitants.
French president Édouard Daladier resigns.
The new French president, Paul Reynaud, orders the establishment of a Ministry of Information.
Germany invades, defeats, and partially occupies France.
Charles de Gaulle makes *l'appel du 18 juin*, calling for resistance to the armistice with Germany.

Franco-German armistice divides France into militarily occupied and unoccupied zones. Radio-Paris broadcasts with a French staff under German command.

1941

Germany launches an offensive against Soviet Russia.

William Donovan is named as head of the U.S. government's Office of the Coordinator of Information (COI).

A German ordinance requires Jews in France to surrender their radios.

Occupation ban on international listening to nonaligned countries is instituted.

United States enters World War II.

1942

Office of War Information (OWI) is established.

U.S. government's Voice of America (VOA) begins broadcast services to France.

Vichy France government creates a new national broadcasting system, *Radiodiffusion nationale*.

U.S. and British forces land in French North Africa.

The German military occupies the entirety of France.

1943

Industrial production of radio sets in France for the public is banned. The ban expands to ready-to-assemble kits, and finally, to the sale of radio sets of any kind.

NBC sells its Blue network. The independent network becomes American Broadcasting Company (ABC) in 1945.

1944

Liberation of Paris.

French provisional government dissolves Vichy's *Radiodiffusion nationale*.

Radiodiffusion française (RDF) is established.

RDF and VOA relay arrangements begin.

1945

French private broadcasting is terminated. RDF is to operate as a monopoly under control of French Ministry of Information, with a supplementary budget and government-appointed director.

United States Information Service (USIS) establishes a radio section in Paris. The Roosevelt Studios are built.

The OWI is abolished.

Control of U.S. government international broadcasting is transferred to the U.S. State Department.

1946

The Office of Information and Cultural Affairs (OIC) is formed in the U.S. State Department.

France adopts the constitution of the Fourth Republic.

1947

U.S. Secretary of State George C. Marshall proposes a U.S.-financed program to aid European rebuilding.

NBC International Division ceases its functions. U.S. State Department takes over international programming services from CBS and NBC.

1948

Congress passes the United States Information and Educational Exchange Act of 1948 (USIE), also known as the Smith-Mundt Act. It authorizes the State Department to utilize international broadcasting and other media to promote U.S. policy abroad.

Congress authorizes the European Recovery Program (the Marshall Plan).

1949

Radiodiffusion-télévision française (RTF) replaces RDF.

RTF officials call for the elevation of France's international broadcast profile to promote French culture, but must confront the reality of limited resources.

1950

The European Broadcasting Union (EBU) is established in Geneva as a nongovernmental organization to inform international broadcast policymaking. It succeeds the IBU.

U.S. government establishes the Radio Free Europe service to Eastern Europe and the Soviet Union.

1953

The United States Information Agency (USIA) is created by the President's Reorganization Plan No. 8 and Executive Order 10477 as a consolidation of all the foreign information activities of the U.S. government.

1954

French forces are defeated by the Viet Minh at the Battle of Dien Bien Phu.

France withdraws its colonial claims in Indochina. The Geneva Accords divide Vietnam in two.

National Liberation Front (FLN) launches sustained attacks against French military and civil authority in Algeria.

1955

Europe No1 is created as a *périphérique* serving metropolitan France.

1958

Amid the Algerian Crisis, Charles de Gaulle returns to power to become president of France. France adopts the constitution of the Fifth Republic.

1962

The Evian Accords end the Algerian conflict. Algeria wins independence from France.

1963

France has an estimated fifteen million radio sets and four million television sets.

1964

The Office de radiodiffusion-télévision française (ORTF) replaces the RTF. Two television channels operate regularly in France.

1966

Charles de Gaulle withdraws France from NATO joint military command (though not the alliance), declaring "It is the will of France to dispose of its own fate."

1967

Congress approves the Public Broadcasting Act. The Corporation for Public Broadcasting (CPB) is established.

1968

Massive protests erupt in Paris and throughout France.

1969

Charles de Gaulle leaves office.

1970

National Public Radio (NPR) is established.

1974

French president Valéry Giscard d'Estaing ends the government monopoly of broadcasting and the ORTF is broken up.

Notes

Introduction

1. "The Basis for *Ici New York* relay by RDF," restricted memo, 4 March 1953, Simon J. Copans to Charles K. Moffly, box 5, Records of the Foreign Service Posts of the Department of State, 1788–ca. 1991 (RG 84), National Archives and Records Administration, College Park, MD.

2. Ibid. RDF representative Pierre Crénesse reported, and *Téléradio*, the annual broadcast entertainment guide, confirms, that FBS programs *Bonjour Mesdames* and *Paris Star Time* aired on Paris-Inter. See, for example, *Téléradio 58* (September 1958), no. 726: 33.

3. Broadcast pioneers joined other vanguard media producers (art/design, text, photograph, cinema) who redefined their aesthetic vocabularies by stretching internationally. See Thomas Bender, *Rethinking American History in a Global Age* (Berkeley: University of California Press, 2002); Thomas Parke Hughes, *Human-Built World: How to Think about Technology and Culture* (Chicago: University of Chicago Press, 2004); Bernhard Rieger, *Technology and the Culture of Modernity in Britain and Germany, 1890–1945* (New York: Cambridge University Press, 2005); Charles Musser, "Nationalism and the Beginnings of Cinema: The Lumière Cinématographe in the U.S., 1896–1897," *Historical Journal of Film, Radio and Television* 19, no. 2 (1999): 149–76.

4. For Atlantic crossings and circulation as a means to trace North America's ties to Europe and beyond, see Nancy F. Cott, "Revisiting the Transatlantic 1920s: Vincent Sheean vs. Malcolm Cowley," *AHR* Forum, *American Historical Review* 118, no. 1 (2013): 46–75; Daniel T. Rodgers, *Atlantic Crossings: Social Politics in a Progressive Age* (Cambridge, MA: Belknap, 1998); Paul Gilroy, *The Black Atlantic: Modernity and Double Consciousness* (Cambridge, MA: Harvard University Press, 1993); Gijs Mom, *Atlantic Automobilism: Emergence and Persistence of the Car, 1895–1940* (New York: Berghahn, 2015).

5. I speak of the field after its conceptualization by Pierre Bourdieu as "a certain distribution structure of some kind of capital." The sociological concept captures the point that international radio production and distribution helped structure social relations in France and the United States as it circulated mediated forms of cultural capital across borders.

Quote in Pierre Bourdieu, *Questions de sociologie* (Paris: Éditions de Minuit, 1980), 138–42, referenced in David Swartz, *Culture and Power: The Sociology of Pierre Bourdieu* (Chicago: University of Chicago Press, 1997), 95. See also Pierre Bourdieu, *Distinction: A Social Critique of the Judgment of Taste* (Cambridge, MA: Harvard University Press, 1984).

6. I came to this concept thanks to Joseph Masco, "Nuclear Technoaesthetics: Sensory Politics from Trinity to the Virtual Bomb in Los Alamos," *American Ethnologist* 31, no. 3 (2004): 349–73. Among the influential calls for critical attention to asymmetrical power relations in the history of technology are Ruth Schwartz Cowan, *More Work for Mother: The Ironies of Household Technology from the Open Hearth to the Microwave* (New York: Basic Books, 1983); Ruth Oldenziel, "Boys and Their Toys: The Fisher Body Craftsman's Guild, 1930–1968, and the Making of a Male Technical Domain," *Technology and Culture* 38, no. 1 (1997): 60–96; Rayvon Fauché, "Say It Loud, I'm Black and I'm Proud," *American Quarterly* 58, no. 3 (2006): 639–61.

7. The technical problem of spectrum scarcity, that is, the finite space on the electromagnetic spectrum for radio communications constrained European powers through international law. William Uricchio uses the notion of constraint to contrast post–World War II ideological differences in U.S. and European broadcasting. See William Uricchio, "Contextualizing the Broadcast Era: Nation, Commerce, and Constraint," *Annals of the American Academy of Political and Social Science* 625 (September 2009): 60–73.

8. See Simon James Potter, *Broadcasting Empire: The BBC and the British World, 1922–1970* (Oxford: Oxford University Press, 2012); James Schwoch, *The American Radio Industry and Its Latin American Activities, 1900–1939* (Urbana: University of Illinois Press, 1990); Holly Cowan Shulman, *The Voice of America: Propaganda and Democracy, 1941–1945* (Madison: University of Wisconsin Press, 1990).

9. On the history of U.S. cultural politics in Europe in an era of transnational corporate expansion, see especially Rob Kroes, *If You've Seen One, You've Seen the Mall: Europeans and American Mass Culture* (Urbana: University of Illinois Press, 1996); Richard F. Kuisel, *Seducing the French: The Dilemma of Americanization* (Berkeley: University of California Press, 1993); Richard F. Kuisel, *The French Way: How France Embraced and Rejected American Values and Power* (Princeton, NJ: Princeton University Press, 2012). On cultural diplomacy and Marshall Plan–era programs in France, see Brian Angus McKenzie, *Remaking France: Americanization, Public Diplomacy, and the Marshall Plan* (New York: Berghahn, 2005), and Reinhold Wagnleitner and Elaine Tyler May, ed., *Here, There, and Everywhere: The Foreign Politics of American Popular Culture* (Hanover, NH: University Press of New England, 2000). On French cultural diversity policies in the late twentieth century, see, for instance, Philip H. Gordon and Sophie Meunier, *The French Challenge: Adapting to Globalization* (Washington, DC: Brookings Institution Press, 2001).

10. Charles Rearick, *The French in Love and War: Popular Culture in the Era of the World Wars* (New Haven, CT: Yale University Press, 1997); Ludovic Tournès, *New Orleans sur Seine* (Paris: Favard, 1999); Richard H. Pells, *Not like Us: How Europeans Have Loved, Hated, and Transformed American Culture since World War II* (New York: Basic Books, 1997); Vanessa R. Schwartz, *It's So French!: Hollywood, Paris, and the Making of Cosmopolitan Film Culture* (Chicago: University of Chicago Press, 2007).

11. On the specific theme of "appropriation of Cold War discourse for alternative projects," see, for example, the introduction to Jadwiga E. Pieper Mooney and Fabio Lanza, ed., *De-Centering Cold War History* (New York: Routledge, 2013).

12. French national and international cinema, radio, and other media often served as instruments of imperial manipulation. See, for example, Francis B. Nyamnjoh, "Broadcasting in Francophone Africa: Crusading for French Culture?" *Gazette* 40, no. 2 (1988): 81–92; Rosemary Chapman and Nicholas Hewitt, ed., *Popular Culture and Mass Communication in Twentieth-Century France* (Lewiston, NY: E. Mellen, 1992); Herrick Chapman and Laura L. Frader, ed., *Race in France: Interdisciplinary Perspectives on the Politics of Difference* (New York: Berghahn, 2004); David Henry Slavin, *Colonial Cinema and Imperial France, 1919–1939: White Blind Spots, Male Fantasies, Settler Myths* (Baltimore: Johns Hopkins University Press, 2001); Tony Chafer and Amanda Sackur, *Promoting the Colonial Idea: Propaganda and Visions of Empire in France* (New York: Palgrave, 2002).

13. On international broadcasting as an institutional story, see Jerome S. Berg, *On the Short Waves, 1923–1945: Broadcast Listening in the Pioneer Days of Radio* (Jefferson, NC: McFarland, 1999). On radio communications and geopolitical power, see Michael Krysko, *American Radio in China: International Encounters with Technology and Communications, 1919–1941* (New York: Palgrave Macmillan, 2011), and Schwoch, *American Radio Industry*. On approaching European regionalism in technological and communications history, see, for example, Alexander Badenoch and Andreas Fickers, *Materializing Europe: Transnational Infrastructures and the Project of Europe* (New York: Palgrave Macmillan, 2010); Suzanne Lommers, *Europe—on Air: Interwar Projects for Radio Broadcasting* (Amsterdam, Neth.: Amsterdam University Press, 2012); Rob Kroes, "Imaginary Americas in Europe's Public Space," in *We Europeans? Media, Representations, Identities*, ed. William Uricchio (Bristol, UK: Intellect, 2008): 23–41.

14. From the amateur wireless era to the broadcast age of all-wave receivers, radio listeners often sought international encounters. In France, Radio Strasbourg catered explicitly to a listenership connected by a regional linguistic and cultural heritage that antedated the boundaries set by the 1919 Paris Peace Conference. On Radio Luxembourg's multinational services, see Denis Maréchal, *Radio Luxembourg, 1933–1993: Un media au cœur de l'Europe* (Nancy, Fr.: Presses universitaires de Nancy, 1994); Jennifer Spohrer, "Ruling the Airwaves: Radio Luxembourg and the Origins of European National Broadcasting, 1929–1950" (PhD dissertation, Columbia University, 2008). In the United States, "border radio" listening practices along the Canadian and Mexican frontiers made cross-cultural and multilingual elements relevant to listening. See, for instance, Mary Vipond, *Listening In: The First Decade of Canadian Broadcasting, 1922–1932* (Montreal: McGill-Queen's University Press, 1992); Gene Fowler, *Border Radio: Quacks, Yodelers, Pitchmen, Psychics, and Other Amazing Broadcasters of the American Airwaves* (Austin: University of Texas Press, 2002); Dolores Inés Casillas, *Sounds of Belonging: U.S. Spanish-Language Radio and Public Advocacy* (New York: New York University Press, 2014). A key work that models how to hold the international and national in analytical view is Michele Hilmes, *Network Nations: A Transnational History of British and American Broadcasting* (New York: Routledge, 2012).

15. For examples of the radio nation as a heuristic, see Joy Hayes, *Radio Nation: Communication, Popular Culture, and Nationalism in Mexico, 1920–1950* (Tucson: University

of Arizona Press, 2000); Hilmes, *Network Nations*; Rebecca Scales, *Radio and the Politics of Sound in Interwar France, 1921–1939* (New York: Cambridge University Press, 2016).

16. On the importance of grappling with transnational and comparative approaches to communication and media history, see, for example, Sonia Livingstone, "On the Challenges of Cross-National Comparative Media Research," *European Journal of Communication* 18, no. 4 (2003): 477–500, and C. A. Bayly, Sven Beckert, Matthew Connolly, Isabel Hofmeyr, Wendy Kozol, and Patricia Seed, "On Transnational History," *AHR* Conversation, *American Historical Review*, 3, no. 5 (December 2006): 1441–64.

17. Historical work on sound, technology, aesthetics, and politics encompasses a vast and fascinating array of methods, perspectives, and questions. See, for example, Peter Bailey, "Breaking the Sound Barrier: A Historian Listens to Noise," *Body and Society* 2, no. 2 (1996): 49–66; Emily Thompson, *The Soundscape of Modernity* (Cambridge, MA: MIT Press, 2002); Christine Ehrick, *Radio and the Gendered Soundscape: Women and Broadcasting in Argentina and Uruguay, 1930–1950* (New York: Cambridge University Press, 2015); James Lastra, *Sound Technology and the Modern Cinema: Perception, Representation, Modernity* (New York: Columbia University Press, 2000); Veit Erlmann, *Hearing Cultures: Essays on Sound, Listening, and Modernity* (New York: Berg, 2004); Jonathan Sterne, *The Audible Past: Cultural Origins of Sound Reproduction* (Durham, NC: Duke University Press, 2003); T. J. Pinch and Karin Bijsterveld, ed., *The Oxford Handbook of Sound Studies* (New York: Oxford University Press, 2012).

18. The phrase appears in Gabrielle Hecht, *Entangled Geographies: Empire and Technopolitics in the Global Cold War* (Cambridge, MA: MIT Press, 2011), 2. On the social construction of technology and technical systems, see Wiebe E. Bijker, Thomas Parke Hughes, and T. J. Pinch, ed., *The Social Construction of Technological Systems: New Directions in the Sociology and History of Technology* (Cambridge, MA: MIT Press, 1987); Nelly Oudshoorn and T. J. Pinch, "Introduction: How Users and Non-Users Matter." In *How Users Matter*, ed. Nelly Oudshoorn and T. J. Pinch, 1–28 (Cambridge, MA: MIT Press, 2003); John M. Staudenmaier, "Rationality, Agency, Contingency: Recent Trends in the History of Technology." *Reviews in American History* 30, no. 1 (2002): 168–81; Patrice Flichy, *Understanding Technological Innovation: A Socio-Technical Approach* (Northampton, MA: Edward Elgar, 2007); Bruno Latour, *Reassembling the Social: An Introduction to Actor-Network-Theory* (New York: Oxford University Press, 2005). This book acknowledges the "Tensions of Europe" collective as it pursues the interlaced histories of technology, nationalism, and border phenomena. On transatlantic electro-acoustical culture and technology, see Steve J. Wurtzler, *Electric Sounds: Technological Change and the Rise of Corporate Mass Media* (New York: Columbia University Press, 2007), and David Suisman, *Selling Sounds: The Commercial Revolution in American Music* (Cambridge, MA: Harvard University Press, 2009).

19. Jean-Noël Jeanneney, *L'écho du siècle: dictionnaire historique de la radio et de la télévision en France* (Paris: Hachette, 1999), 546.

Chapter 1. At the Speed of Sound: Techno-Aesthetic Paradigms in U.S.–French Broadcasting

1. "Tells of Radio Research Abroad," *New York Times*, 30 August 1924, 10; "Statement to the Press on Return from Europe," 30 August 1924, reprinted in E. E. Bucher, "Radio

and David Sarnoff," unpublished manuscript (1943), Sarnoff Library, Sarnoff Research Center, Princeton, NJ, 59.

2. RCA spawned NBC in 1926. Quote ProQuest Historical Annual Reports, Radio Corporation of America, *Annual Report for the Year 1930*, 20; NBC Annual Program Highlight List for the Period 1927–37 (unpublished), folder 96, NBC History Files, Recorded Sound Section, Motion Picture, Broadcasting and Recorded Sound Division, Library of Congress [hereafter, NBC-LOC]; "Coste Lands in New York after Hop from Paris," *Los Angeles Times*, 3 September 1930, 1; Rebecca Scales, *Radio and the Politics of Sound in Interwar France, 1921–1939* (New York: Cambridge University Press, 2016), 32–33.

3. C. W. Horn, "International Broadcasting," in *Radio and Its Future*, ed. Martin Codel, 85–87 (New York: Harper and Brothers, 1930). Alfred H. Morton, RCA's European Manager in Paris, handled the 1931 inaugural transatlantic transmission and subsequent NBC/Poste Coloniale programs from Paris that year. "Morton Gets Important Post," *RCA Family Circle*, January 1937, 3, box 151, Oversized, Lenox Lohr Papers, University of Illinois, Chicago; "International Broadcasts, Red Network," folder 9, box 38, National Broadcasting Records, State Historical Society of Wisconsin, Madison [hereafter, NBC-WHS]; "Colonial Exposition Opens in Paris Today," *New York Times*, 6 May 1931, 8; "Mayors Broadcast from Paris Exposition," *New York Times*, 7 June 1931, 13. On the Poste Coloniale, see Caroline Ulmann-Mauriat, *Naissance d'un média: histoire politique de la radio en France (1921–1931)* (Paris: Harmattan, 1999), 146; Robert Prot, *Dictionnaire de la radio* (Grenoble, Fr.: Presses universitaires de Grenoble–Institut national de l'audiovisuel, 1997), 168–69. On international shortwave broadcasts mounted by other U.S. providers, such as CBS, see "Spain, France, and Japan Will Send Programs Here," *New York Times*, 26 April 1931, XX9; "President of France to Be Heard over Air," *Los Angeles Times*, 30 June 1931, 4; "Patriotism to Ride on All Radio Waves," *New York Times*, 4 July 1931, 3. The French state's pedagogical uplift ambitions embraced numerous media, including cinema. See Robert J. Young, *Marketing Marianne: French Propaganda in America, 1900–1940* (New Brunswick, NJ: Rutgers University Press, 2004), and Kenneth Garner, "Seeing Is Knowing: The Educational Cinema Movement in France, 1910–1945" (PhD dissertation, University of Michigan, 2012).

4. In the 1920s and 1930s, major communications firms, such as Westinghouse and General Electric, developed shortwave broadcast facilities. They participated in various pooling arrangements for intercontinental transmission of programs produced by NBC. RCA Communications provided for most of NBC's shortwave transmission and reception equipment, circuitry and other technologies, engineering, and systems expertise essential to making transatlantic broadcasts and national communications relays throughout the United States and the world possible. For institutional overviews of shortwave in other national and hemispheric contexts, see Harold N. Graves Jr., *War on the Short Wave* (New York: Foreign Policy Association, 1941); Michael Kent Sidel, "A Historical Analysis of American Short Wave Broadcasting 1916–1942" (PhD dissertation, Northwestern University, 1976); Jerome S. Berg, *Broadcasting on the Short Waves, 1945 to Today* (Jefferson, NC: McFarland, 2008). Many histories focus on state-directed shortwave operations for purposes of propaganda and persuasion from the mid-1930s into the Cold War. See Holly Cowan Shulman, *The Voice of America: Propaganda and Democracy, 1941–1945* (Madison: University of Wisconsin Press, 1990); Michael Nelson, *War of the Black Heavens: The*

Battles of Western Broadcasting in the Cold War (Syracuse, NY: Syracuse University Press, 1997); H. J. P. Bergmeier, *Hitler's Airwaves: The Inside Story of Nazi Radio Broadcasting and Propaganda Swing* (New Haven, CT: Yale University Press, 1997); Timothy Stoneman, "A Bold New Vision: The VOA Radio Ring Plan and Global Broadcasting in the Early Cold War," *Technology and Culture* 50, no. 2 (2009): 316–44. On the concept of technological affordance, see Ian Hutchby, *Conversation and Technology: From the Telephone to the Internet* (Cambridge, UK: Polity, 2001).

5. The term *production* is used to describe the array of technical methods and processes used to generate a live or prerecorded radio program at all levels and stages. Production can refer to how sound elements are created and gathered. It also can refer to how they are assembled, mixed, edited, and packaged into forms delivered to a listener. Radio production is contiguous to, but not reducible to, *continuity*, a word referring to the scripted words an announcer speaks in the lead-in/intro, and back announce/outro of a program, such as a concert, performance, or news report. See Max Wylie, *Radio Writing* (New York: Farrar and Rinehart, 1939).

6. Kristen Haring speaks of "technological culture," that is, notions of an identity and preferred use pattern of a technological object or system as a national formation. Kristen Haring, *Ham Radio's Technical Culture* (Cambridge, MA: MIT Press, 2007), 7.

7. Quote ProQuest Historical Annual Reports, Radio Corporation of America, *Annual Report for the Year 1930*, 24. Classified as an experimental medium by international law, shortwave broadcasting could not be used for direct advertising into or out of Europe, which forced U.S. networks to cut commercial messages from national network programs beamed abroad. Some Latin American countries accepted international commercial programs from U.S. networks on an ad hoc basis. See, for example, Michael B. Salwen, "Broadcasting to Latin America: Reconciling Industry-Government Functions in the Pre–Voice of America Era," *Historical Journal of Film, Radio and Television* 17, no. 1 (1997): 67–89; "MacDonald Opens Daily Radio Talks," *New York Times*, 23 January 1930, 2; Geoffrey T. Hellman, "Thirsty Sponge," *New Yorker*, 18 October 1952, 31.

8. International shortwave broadcasts were live phenomena that required regimens of international coordination and technical coordination. On the impact of foreign technologies on French cinema in this period, and the hybrid approach that resulted, see Charles O'Brien, *Cinema's Conversion to Sound: Technology and Film Style in France and the U.S.* (Bloomington: Indiana University Press, 2005).

9. Pascal Griset, "*Je t'aime non plus*: The Development of Atlantic Submarine Cables and the Complexity of the French–American Dialogue, 1870–1960," in *Communications under the Seas: The Evolving Cable Network and Its Implications*, ed. Bernard S. Finn and Daquing Yang (Cambridge, MA: MIT Press, 2009), 268–69. On the rise of systems and information processing, and U.S. capitalism prior to and throughout the electrical revolution of the nineteenth century, see Alfred D. Chandler Jr. and James W. Cortada, ed., *A Nation Transformed by Information: How Information Has Shaped the United States from Colonial Times to the Present* (New York: Oxford University Press, 2000).

10. On sound, society, and culture, see, for example, Raymond Murray Schafer, *The Soundscape: Our Sonic Environment and the Tuning of the World* (Rochester, VT: Destiny, 1994); Peter Bailey, "Breaking the Sound Barrier: A Historian Listens to Noise," *Body and Society* 2, no. 2 (1996): 49–66; Steve J. Wurtzler, *Electric Sounds: Technological Change and*

the Rise of Corporate Mass Media (New York: Columbia University Press, 2007); Emily Thompson, *The Soundscape of Modernity* (Cambridge, MA: MIT Press, 2002); Michael Bull and Les Back, ed., *The Auditory Culture Reader* (Oxford, UK: Berg, 2003); T. J. Pinch and Karin Bijsterveld, ed., *The Oxford Handbook of Sound Studies* (New York: Oxford University Press, 2012). On listener affection for French private radio's adaptation of U.S. commercial broadcasting's rhythms and program genres, see Philip Nord, *France's New Deal from the Thirties to the Postwar Era* (Princeton, NJ: Princeton University Press, 2010).

11. Prot, *Dictionnaire de la radio*, 597, and "Overview of ITU's History," http://www.itu.int/en/history. On the imperial, geopolitical characteristics of the electrical age, see Yakup Bektas, "The Sultan's Messenger: Cultural Constructions of Ottoman Telegraphy, 1847–1880," *Technology and Culture* 41, no. 4 (2000): 669–96; Jill Hills, *Telecommunications and Empire* (Urbana: University of Illinois Press, 2007); Dwayne Roy Winseck and Robert M. Pike, *Communication and Empire: Media, Markets, and Globalization, 1860–1930* (Durham, NC: Duke University Press, 2007); Simon James Potter, *Broadcasting Empire: The BBC and the British World, 1922–1970* (Oxford: Oxford University Press, 2012). On tensions between private U.S. cable firms and the PTT, France's monopoly holder of telegraph communications within France, see Griset, "*Je t'aime non plus.*"

12. Formed in spring 1865, the International Telegraph Union (ITU) developed regulations for electrical communications, including wireless telegraphy, telephony, and eventually broadcasting. Both France and the United States were founding members. Hugh G. J. Aitken, *Syntony and Spark: The Origins of Radio* (New York: Wiley, 1976).

13. "Radio Technology," *Encyclopaedia Britannica: Britannica Academic* (Chicago: Encyclopædia Britannica, 2015), http://academic.eb.com.proxy.lib.umich.edu/EBchecked/topic/1262240/radio-technology; "Guglielmo Marconi," *Encyclopaedia Britannica: Britannica Academic* (Chicago: Encyclopædia Britannica, 2015), http://academic.eb.com.proxy.lib.umich.edu/EBchecked/topic/364287/Guglielmo-Marconi. Essential accounts of the technology progression of radio communication in the U.S. context from the nineteenth century through the early 1930s are Aitken, *Syntony and Spark*, and Susan J. Douglas, *Inventing American Broadcasting, 1899–1922* (Baltimore: Johns Hopkins University Press, 1987).

14. Depending on the context, the abbreviation "TSF" can indicate either wireless telegraphy (télégraphie sans fil) or wireless telephony (téléphonie sans fil). The Radio Society of Great Britain also participated in these multinational exercises. Le Bleis Marie, "Le radio-amateurisme et la découverte des ondes courtes" (Bordeaux, Fr.: Université Michel de Montaigne–Bordeaux III, 1995), 19; "Radio Amateurs Span the Atlantic," *Literary Digest* 73, 1 April 1922, 27–28; "More than 300 Amateurs Transmit to Europe," *Literary Digest* 76, 27 January 1923, 29; K. B. Warner, "International Amateur Radio Union Formed!," *QST* 10, no. 6 (1925), 9. Scales, *Radio and the Politics of Sound in Interwar France, 1921–1935*, 111–57.

15. This discussion follows Hugh G. J. Aitken, *The Continuous Wave: Technology and American Radio, 1900–1932* (Princeton, NJ: Princeton University Press, 1985.

16. Adam Tooze, *The Deluge: The Great War, America, and the Remaking of the Global Order, 1916–1931* (New York: Viking, 2014); H. R. Kedward, *France and the French: A Modern History* (Woodstock, NY: Overlook Press, 2006); Eugen Weber, *The Hollow Years: France in the 1930s* (New York: W. W. Norton, 1994).

17. Casualties as reported to the U.S. War Department in February 1924 and amended in 1957. Casualties included the total of combatants killed and died, wounded, and listed as prisoners or missing. See table 4 "World War I." *Encyclopaedia Britannica: Britannica Academic* (Chicago: Encyclopædia Britannica, 2015), http://academic.eb.com.proxy.lib .umich.edu/EBchecked/topic/648646/World-War-I. Even by 1939, France's total exports to the United States had not recovered to their prewar levels. "Exports (Including Reexports) and General Imports of Merchandise, by Continents, Commercial Regions, and Countries: 1921 to 1939 [Selected Years and Periods]," *Statistical Abstract of the U.S. 1940*, ed. ProQuest, 1940 (ProQuest Statistical Abstract 03/17), http://statabs.proquest.com/sa/docview.html?table -no=570&acc-no=C7095–1.22&year=1940&z=E52B918EA5679A836318FB9A4A1EC74 CDD8BE51E. French debt to the United States in 1940 amounted to more than $4.2 billion. "Indebtedness of Foreign Governments to United States [Principal and Accrued Interest, With Payments Received, As of March 31, 1940]," ed. ProQuest, 1940 (ProQuest Statistical Abstract 03/17), http://statabs.proquest.com/sa/docview.html?table-no=209&acc -no=C7095–1.9&year=1940&z=2EDC8ABF9AD52B03387CB63D645531B62DC53D4A.

18. For an overview of interwar U.S.–French diplomatic relations in this period, see David Hastings Dunn, "Isolationism Revisited: Seven Persistent Myths in the Contemporary American Foreign Policy Debate," *Review of International Studies* 31, no. 2 (2005): 237–61, and Tooze, *Deluge*. On U.S. attitudes, see Alan Brinkley, *American History, a Survey* (New York: McGraw-Hill, 1995).

19. See Aitken, *Continuous Wave*. See also "RCA Corporation," *Encyclopaedia Britannica* online, https://www.britannica.com/topic/RCA-Corporation; P. J. Kingston, "A Survey of the French Radio Industry 1940–1944 as Seen by the BBC," *Historical Journal of Film, Radio and Television* 3, no. 2 (1983), 151; Asa Briggs, *History of Broadcasting in the United Kingdom*, vol. 2, *The Golden Age of Wireless* (London: Oxford University Press, 1965), 353.

20. See Peter J. Hugill, *Global Communications since 1844: Geopolitics and Technology* (Baltimore: Johns Hopkins University Press, 1999), 118–19. On global strategy, imperialism, and transatlantic communications, see also Paul Starr, *The Creation of the Media: Political Origins of Modern Communications* (New York: Basic Books, 2004); David Paul Nickles, *Under the Wire: How the Telegraph Changed Diplomacy* (Cambridge, MA: Harvard University Press, 2003); Daniel R. Headrick, *The Invisible Weapon: Telecommunications and International Politics, 1851–1945* (New York: Oxford University Press, 1991). On U.S.–French communications, see Raymond Kuhn, *The Media in France* (New York: Routledge, 1995); Michel Amoudry, *Le général Ferrié et la naissance des transmissions et de la radiodiffusion* (Grenoble, Fr.: Presses universitaires de Grenoble, 1993). On English radio and U.S.–UK connectivity, see Asa Briggs, *The History of Broadcasting in the United Kingdom*, vol. 1, *The Birth of Broadcasting* (London: Oxford University Press, 1961); Edward Pawley, *BBC Engineering 1922–1972* (London: Broadwater Press, 1972); Michele Hilmes, *Network Nations: A Transnational History of British and American Broadcasting* (New York: Routledge, 2012). On the suboceanic cable, communications, and U.S.–French relations, see Pascal Griset, *Les télécommunications transatlantiques de la France (XIXe–XXe siècles)* (Paris: Rive Droite, 1996); Silas Bent, "International Broadcasting," *Public Opinion Quarterly* 1 (July 1937): 117–21; ProQuest Historical Annual Reports, RCA, *Annual Report for the Year Ended December 31, 1922*, 10; ProQuest Historical Annual Reports, RCA, *Annual Report for the Year Ended December 31, 1923*, 5. PTT ministry concerns about British spying on

French radio communications appear a perennial concern. See Fred Bate, London Office Report, 30 August 1935, 9, folder 47, box 91, NBC-WHS.

21. For a brief overview of national information control programs, see Robert J. Young, *French Foreign Policy, 1918–1945: A Guide to Research and Research Materials*, rev. ed., Guides to European Diplomatic History Research and Research Materials (Wilmington, DE: Scholarly Resources, 1991), 11–16. See also Donald Baker, "The Surveillance of Subversion in Interwar France: The Carnet B in the Seine, 1922–1940," *French Historical Studies* 10, no. 3 (1978): 486–516. On the political economy of interwar French broadcasting, see André-Jean Tudesq, "La politique de la radio en France 1926–1932," in *Mélanges offerts à Jean Prinet* (Saint-Julien-du-Sault: F. P. Lobies, 1980), 141–52; Cécile Méadel, *Histoire de la radio des années trente: du sans-filiste à l'auditeur* (Paris: Anthropos Economica, 1994).

22. An increase in transatlantic broadcasting by NBC could bring more business to RCA through the use of its transmitting and receiving stations and sales of electronics equipment around the world. On U.S. broadcasting and regulation, see Erik Barnouw, *The Golden Web: A History of Broadcasting in the United States, 1933–1953* (New York: Oxford University Press, 1968), and Christopher H. Sterling and John M. Kittross, *Stay Tuned: A Concise History of American Broadcasting* (Belmont, CA: Wadsworth, 1978).

23. On liberal ideology and U.S. communications regulation, see Thomas Streeter, *Selling the Air: A Critique of the Policy of Commercial Broadcasting in the United States* (Chicago: University of Chicago Press, 1996). See also "Radio," *Encyclopaedia Britannica: Britannica Academic* (Chicago: Encyclopædia Britannica, 2015), http://academic.eb.com.proxy.lib .umich.edu/EBchecked/topic/488788/radio; Susan Smulyan, *Selling Radio: The Commercialization of American Broadcasting 1920–1934* (Washington, DC: Smithsonian Institution Press, 1994); Michele Hilmes, *Radio Voices: American Broadcasting, 1922–1952* (Minneapolis: University of Minnesota Press, 1997); Susan Douglas, *Listening In: Radio and the American Imagination* (New York: Times Books, 1999). On struggles to shape radio for populist, public, and alternative ends, see, for example, Nathan Godfried, *WCFL, Chicago's Voice of Labor, 1926–78* (Urbana: University of Illinois Press, 1997); Elizabeth A. Fones-Wolf, *Waves of Opposition: Labor and the Struggle for Democratic Radio* (Urbana: University of Illinois Press, 2006); Hugh Richard Slotten, *Radio's Hidden Voice: The Origins of Public Broadcasting in the United States* (Urbana: University of Illinois Press, 2009); Victor Pickard, *America's Battle for Media Democracy: The Triumph of Corporate Libertarianism and the Future of Media Reform* (New York: Cambridge University Press, 2015).

24. The first transatlantic broadcast of speech from the Eiffel Tower occurred in 1915. On France's role in the international development of radio, see Clinton B. DeSoto, *Two Hundred Meters and Down* (West Hartford, CT: American Radio Relay League, 1936); Douglas, *Inventing American Broadcasting*; Amoudry, *Le général Ferrié*; Aitken, *Syntony and Spark*; James Wood, *History of International Broadcasting* (London: P. Peregrinus, 1992), 17–22; Jean-Claude Montagné and Bernard Ducretet, *Eugène Ducretet: Pionnier français de la radio* (Bagneux, Fr.: Autoédition J.-C. Montagné, 1998); Finn and Yang, *Communication under the Seas*.

25. Tudesq, "La politique," 141–52; Gabrielle Hecht, *The Radiance of France: Nuclear Power and National Identity after World War II* (Cambridge, MA: MIT Press, 1998), 15.

26. Quoted in Caroline Ulmann-Mauriat, "L'émergence de la radiodiffusion dans la vie publique française (1921–1931)" (PhD dissertation, University of Lyon, 1984), 85. See also

Ulmann-Mauriat, "Après l'enterrement du statut, la coexistence des deux réseaux—public et privé—est organisée," *Cahiers d'histoire de la radiodiffusion*, no. 64 (2000): 5.

27. Prot, *Dictionnaire de la radio*, 448–49.

28. Ulmann-Mauriat, *Naissance d'un média*, 45. On the annexation, see Ruth Thomas, *Broadcasting and Democracy in France* (Philadelphia: Temple University Press, 1977), and Fabrice d'Almeida and Christian Delporte, *Histoire des médias en France: de la grande guerre à nos jours* (Paris: Flammarion, 2003), 75. The décret of 24 November 1924 declared that the government would "tolerate" the unauthorized private stations, but left some doubt about the government's long-term commitment to honoring its pledge. See Prot, *Dictionnaire de la radio*, 7. Another décret on 28 December 1926 reaffirmed the state's monopoly over radio and declared that any authorization of private broadcasting represented a temporary privilege, subject to review. The precarious status quo inhibited growth of independent stations for fear of government interference or annexation. Statistic for 1930 stations from Ulmann-Mauriat, "Après l'enterrement du statut," 5.

29. Ulmann-Mauriat, *Naissance d'un média*, 245, 248; Pascal Griset, "La société Radio-France dans l'entre-deux-guerres," *Histoire, économie et société* 2, no. 1 (1983): 83–109; Prot, *Dictionnaire de la radio*, 240, 487.

30. The preceding discussion synthesizes the work of scholars who have mapped the complex institutional history of interwar broadcasting, including René Duval, *Histoire de la radio en France* (Paris: A. Moreau, 1979); André-Jean Tudesq, "La politique de la radio en France"; Pierre Albert, *Histoire de la radiotélévision en France* (Paris: PUF, 1981); Méadel, *Histoire de la radio*. These uncertain dynamics help explain why broadcasting developed more slowly as a popular medium in France than in the United States, England, and Germany. See also Maréchal, *Radio Luxembourg*; Spohrer, "Ruling the Airwaves"; International Programs, Misc. (1924–1929), folder 9, box 38, NBC-WHS. Networks also were engaged with the BBC. In 1924, the BBC shortwave station at Daventry broadcast British dance music to RCA's WJZ. As the 1920s wore on, it also grew clearer that RCA's transoceanic radio messaging business might be able to compete effectively with suboceanic cable companies like Western Union. "Cables Combat Rule of Radio," *Los Angeles Times*, 27 September 1928, 4. Citing the work of David Noble, *America by Design, Science, Technology, and the Rise of Corporate Capitalism* (New York: Oxford University Press, 1980), Robert McChesney links the corporate-friendly partnership between U.S. engineering and the regulation of U.S. airwaves in the late 1920s and early 1930s. Robert W. McChesney, *Telecommunications, Mass Media, and Democracy* (New York: Oxford University Press, 1993), 22–24.

31. "Report to Owen D. Young, Chairman of Board of Directors, RCA, 30 January 1920, in Bucher, "Radio and David Sarnoff," pt. 1, 299, quoted in David Sarnoff, *Looking Ahead: The Papers of David Sarnoff* (New York, 1968), 15.

32. If necessary, signals could also travel under the ocean via transatlantic telephone cables to a receiving facility that could feed the (low-quality) signal to a broadcast transmitter. On the relative efficiency of shortwave signaling to radiotelegraphy, see "Transoceanic Radio Shows Big Gain," *New York Times*, 2 January 1930, 35. On the reflection of the shortwave signal, see "Salzburg Music Will 'Bounce' through Ionosphere to America," *Daily News Report, NBC*, box 55, folder 96, NBC-LOC. On routing a transatlantic transmission, see Correspondence, Fred Bate to Phillips Carlin, 9 August 1939, National Broadcasting Records, folder 8, box 95, NBC-WHS.

33. A deputy (*député*) is the rough equivalent of a member of the U.S. Congress. Quote in Ulmann-Mauriat, "L'émergence de la radiodiffusion," 119. The United States boasted forty-one such stations. "Les stations de radiodiffusion des États-Unis," *Le Petit Radio*, 20 August 1927, 4. Unless otherwise stated, all translations are the author's.

34. "L'emploi du micro aux États-Unis," *Le Petit Radio*, 1 June 1929, 2. The discourse was charged on multiple levels, not least of which was gender and the equation of technological abundance with (masculine) potency and power. On gendered politics in modern U.S. and European technological history, see, for example, Cowan, *More Work for Mother*; Oldenziel, "Boys and Their Toys"; Judy Wajcman, "Reflections on Gender and Technology Studies: In What State Is the Art?," *Social Studies of Science* 30, no. 3 (2000): 447–64. On radio, see also Douglas, *Inventing American Broadcasting*; Haring, *Ham Radio's Technical Culture*; Lacey, *Feminine Frequencies*.

35. Mid-nineteenth-century observers, including Charles Baudelaire and Edmond and Jules de Goncourt, used *américanisation* to refer to loss of consciousness of a distinction between the physical and the moral world. "As these critics saw it," explains Rob Kroes, "industrial progress ushered in an era where quantity would replace quality and where a mass culture feeding on standardization would erode established taste hierarchies" (Rob Kroes, *Them and Us: Questions of Citizenship in a Globalizing World* [Urbana: University of Illinois Press, 2000], 154). See also Jean-Philippe Mathy, *Extrême-Occident: French Intellectuals and America* (Chicago: University of Chicago Press, 1993), and Roxanne Panchasi, *Future Tense: The Culture of Anticipation in France between the Wars* (Ithaca, NY: Cornell University Press, 2009).

36. "Aux États-Unis," *Le Petit Radio*, 5 December 1934, 3. See also Derek W. Vaillant, "Sounds from the Life of the Future: Making Sense of U.S. Radio Broadcasting in France, 1921–1939," in *Radio's New Wave: Global Sound in the Digital Era*, ed. Michele Hilmes and Jason Loviglio, 180–93 (New York: Routledge, 2013).

37. For a historical synthesis of this theme, see Philippe Roger, *The American Enemy: A Story of French Anti-Americanism*, trans. Sharon Bowman (Chicago: University of Chicago Press, 2005).

38. The hallmarks of the French public radio system could be registered at the level of cultural knowledge, sophistication, and discriminating taste in the use of the medium. The concept of cultural competence and aesthetic discrimination in power relations is treated in Pierre Bourdieu, *Distinction: A Social Critique of the Judgment of Taste* (Cambridge, MA: Harvard University Press, 1984).

39. Hans Bodenstedt, "La radio aux États-Unis," *Le Petit Radio*, 4 January 1930, 3. On the intersection of European and U.S. practices of acoustics and concert hall design, see Thompson, *Soundscape of Modernity*.

40. Bodenstedt, "La radio aux États-Unis," 3. For an introduction to critiques of the so-called culture industries, see Andrew Arato and Eike Gebhardt, ed., *The Essential Frankfurt School Reader* (New York: Continuum, 1998). On technological innovation and its implications for musical life, creativity, and perception, see Mark Katz, *Capturing Sound: How Technology Has Changed Music* (Berkeley: University of California Press, 2005); Timothy Dean Taylor, *Strange Sounds: Music, Technology and Culture* (New York: Routledge, 2001); David Byrne, *How Music Works* (San Francisco: McSweeneys, 2012). On the gendered dimensions of technologically enhanced performance and radio, see

Allison McCracken, *Real Men Don't Sing: Crooning in American Culture* (Durham, NC: Duke University Press, 2015).

41. Bodenstedt, "La radio aux États-Unis," 3.

42. "Un gratte-ciel radiophonique," *Le Petit Radio,* 22 June 1929, n.p.; "Item," *Le Petit Radio,* 12 July 190, 2.

43. Michel Ferry, "À New York—Une visite à Radio-City," *Le Petit Radio,* 7 April 1934, 1.

44. Ibid. Emphasis added.

45. The program included appearances by the Republican Guard (performing the "Star-Spangled Banner") and a quartet of tubas playing Handel's *Largo.* "France Greets Radio City," folder 3, box 21, NBC-WHS; "Radio Programs Scheduled for Broadcast This Week," *New York Times,* 12 November 1933, X10.

46. David E. Nye, *American Technological Sublime* (Cambridge, MA: MIT Press, 1994). Quote in Alberto Caprile Jr., "From the Argentine Angle," in *You Americans: Fifteen Foreign Press Correspondents Report Their Impressions of the United States and Its People,* ed. B. P. Adams (New York: Funk and Wagnalls, 1939), 92.

47. George Kao, "Your Country and My People," in Ibid., 229.

48. ProQuest Historical Annual Reports, Radio Corporation of America, *Annual Report for the Year 1933,* 6.

49. On broadcasting and propaganda in Germany and Europe, see Karl Van Gelderland, "The War in the Ether," *The Nation,* 12 March 1938, 300–301; Ortwin Buchbender, *Radio humanité: Les émetteurs allemands clandestins 1940* (Paris: France-Empire, 1986); H. J. P. Bergmeier, *Hitler's Airwaves: The Inside Story of Nazi Radio Broadcasting and Propaganda Swing* (New Haven, CT: Yale University Press).

50. Paul Campargue, "La course à la puissance," *Parole Libre,* 28 May 1933, 1.

51. Raoul Roussy de Sales, "What Is This Aloofness?" in *You Americans,* 32.

52. For a contemporary reflection on global techno-boosterism, see Susan Douglas, "The Turn Within: The Irony of Technology in a Globalized World," *American Quarterly* 58, no. 3 (2006): 619–38.

53. *Le Petit Parisien,* 9 December 1934, 1. On the gendered themes of space-binding in U.S. radio advertising in this period, see Smulyan, *Selling Radio.*

54. Georges Duhamel, *America the Menace, Scenes from the Life of the Future,* trans. Charles Miner Thompson (Boston: Houghton Mifflin, 1931), 15, 202. On the work's legacy in articulating a critique of U.S. culture, see Richard F. Kuisel, *Seducing the French: The Dilemma of Americanization* (Berkeley: University of California Press, 1993), and Panchasi, *Future Tense.*

55. On commercial culture and French politics, see, for example, Herman Lebovics, *True France: The Wars over Cultural Identity, 1900–1945* (Ithaca, NY: Cornell University Press, 1992); Kedward, *France and the French;* Nord, *France's New Deal.* For close readings of French radio programs of the 1930s, see Joelle Neulander, *Programming National Identity: The Culture of Radio in 1930s France* (Baton Rouge: Louisiana University Press, 2009).

56. Paul Virilio offers the provocative concept of "dromology," which critiques the accelerated tempo of modern life as a form of tyranny. By his reckoning, "the more speed increases the faster freedom decreases." Paul Virilio, *Speed and Politics: An Essay on*

Dromology, trans. Mark Polizzotti (New York: Columbia University Press, 1986), 142. See also John Tomlinson, *The Culture of Speed: The Coming of Immediacy* (Los Angeles: Sage, 2007). According to W. T. Lhamon, "The implicit aesthetic of a deliberately speedy style" shaped a post–World War II U.S. ethos, notably in the area of a "consumer electronics revolution." W. T. Lhamon, *Deliberate Speed: The Origins of a Cultural Style in the American 1950s* (Washington, DC: Smithsonian Institution Press, 1990), 7. Kristin Ross writes, "The unusual swiftness of French postwar modernization seemed to partake of the qualities of what [Fernand] Braudel has designated as the temporality of the event: it was headlong, dramatic, and breathless." Kristin Ross, *Fast Cars, Clean Bodies: Decolonization and the Reordering of French Culture* (Cambridge, MA: MIT Press, 1995), 4. As scholars argue, however, modernity and modernization theory run up against complications when it comes to social and cultural analysis of Western Europe. See Geoff Eley, *A Crooked Line: From Cultural History to the History of Society* (Ann Arbor: University of Michigan Press, 2005), 75–81.

57. Fernand Braudel, *The Mediterranean and the Mediterranean World in the Age of Philip II*, trans. Siân Reynolds (London: Collins, 1972); Moishe Postone, *Time, Labor, and Social Domination: A Reinterpretation of Marx's Critical Theory* (New York: Cambridge University Press, 1993); Mechal Sobel, *The World They Made Together: Black and White Values in Eighteenth-Century Virginia* (Princeton, NJ: Princeton University Press, 1987). A key moment in the history of speed and life in the West occurred during the Industrial Revolution with the development of what E. P. Thompson dubbed "industrial time" and the emergence of rationalized scientific management in service of mass industrial production, consumption, and efficiency. See E. P. Thompson, *The Making of the English Working Class* (New York: Pantheon, 1964).

58. David Montgomery, *The Fall of the House of Labor* (New York: Cambridge University Press, 1987), and David Harvey, *The Condition of Postmodernity: An Inquiry into the Origins of Cultural Change* (Cambridge, UK: Basil Blackwell, 1990). An essential account of the history of technology and shifting perceptions of time, space, and sound is Alain Corbin, *Village Bells: Sound and Meaning in the Nineteenth-Century French Countryside*, trans. Martin Thom (New York: Columbia University Press, 1998).

59. Among transportation and communications scholars, for instance, shifts in perception accompanied changes in how physical bodies and information moved together and separately, and how embodied and disembodied identities rooted in space and time were conceptualized. See Wolfgang Schivelbusch, *The Railway Journey: The Industrialization of Time and Space in the 19th Century* (Berkeley: University of California Press, 1986); James W. Carey, *Communication as Culture: Essays on Media and Society* (Boston: Unwin Hyman, 1989); Richard R. John, *Spreading the News: The American Postal System from Franklin to Morse* (Cambridge, MA: Harvard University Press, 1995); John Durham Peters, *Speaking into the Air: A History of the Idea of Communication* (Chicago: University of Chicago Press, 1999); Siegfried Zielinski, *Deep Time of the Media: Toward an Archaeology of Hearing and Seeing by Technical Means* (Cambridge, MA: MIT Press, 2006).

60. Christopher Todd, "Georges Duhamel: Enemy-cum-Friend of the Radio," *Modern Language Review* 92, no. 1 (1997): 48–59. Some of the discomfort in France with U.S.-style speed has passing resemblance to the pejorative label of "chaos" that proponents of a public monopoly model for the BBC used to denigrate U.S. commercial radio. See Michele

Hilmes, "British Quality, American Chaos: Historical Dualisms and What They Leave Out," *Radio Journal* 1, no. 1 (2003): 13–27. British followers of U.S. radio were sometimes moved to comment on the faster pace, too. An implicit critique of the haste of mainstream journalism shaped a culture of difference at the BBC by the late 1920s. "The whole aim and object of our news service is to avoid the errors into which journalists, as such, seem inevitably to fall (sensationalism, inaccuracy, partiality and overstatement), and to present news of all that is happening the world in a clear, impartial and succinct language" (Jeffrey Strutt, Head of BBC News Division, quoted in Paddy Scannell and David Cardiff, *A Social History of British Broadcasting* [Oxford: Basil Blackwell, 1991], 113).

61. Historical work on broadcasting in France's provinces reveals an eclectic cross-pollination of programs and sponsors. See André-Jean Tudesq, "La radiodiffusion en Languedoc avant la deuxième guerre mondiale," in *Économie et société en Languedoc-Roussillon* (Montpellier, Fr.: Presses universitaires de la Méditerranée, 1978); Élisabeth Cazenave, "Histoire de la radio à Bordeaux et dans le Sud-Ouest" (PhD dissertation, University of Bordeaux III, 1977).

62. On the diversity of pre–World War II U.S. broadcast genres, see, for example, Smulyan, *Selling Radio*; Douglas, *Listening In*; and Michele Hilmes and Jason Loviglio, ed., *Radio Reader: Essays in the Cultural History of Radio* (New York: Routledge, 2001).

63. *Le Petit Radio*, 14 May 1932, 1. On French politicians on air, see André-Jean Tudesq, "L'utilisation gouvernementale de la radio," in *Édouard Daladier, chef de gouvernement*, ed. René Rémond and Janine Bourdin (Paris: Presses de la Fondation nationale des sciences politiques, 1977). A systematic content analysis partially debunks the view that private and public French broadcasters programmed dramatically different music. See Christophe Bennet, *La musique à la radio dans les années trente: La création d'un genre radiophonique* (Paris: Harmattan, 2010).

64. This is not to adopt a McLuhanesque posture on international broadcasting. Rather, it is an attempt to tease out the layered historical specificities of experiencing transatlantic broadcasting via shortwave at multiple levels of production and reception. See Marshall McLuhan, *Understanding Media: The Extensions of Man* (New York: McGraw-Hill, 1964). On the phenomenology of listening, see Paddy Scannell, *Broadcast Talk* (London: Sage, 1991).

65. "Moins de snobisme . . . et plus de bon sens," *Le Petit Radio*, 5 March 1932, 3. "Les beautés de la radio-publicité," *Le Petit Radio*, 22 June 1929, 5.

66. Thompson, *The Soundscape of Modernity*. On modernity as nationally experienced, see Bernhard Rieger, *Technology and the Culture of Modernity in Britain and Germany, 1890–1945* (New York: Cambridge University Press, 2005); Karl Christian Fuhrer, "A Medium of Modernity? Broadcasting in Weimar Germany, 1923–1932," *Journal of Modern History* 69, no. 4 (1997): 722–53. On the prospect of multiple modernities, see Herrick Chapman, "Modernity and National Identity in Postwar France," *French Historical Studies* 22, no. 2, (spring 1999): 291–314.

67. Eugen Weber, *Peasants into Frenchmen: The Modernization of Rural France, 1870–1914* (Stanford, CA: Stanford University Press, 1976); Marcel Bleustein-Blanchet, *La rage de convaincre* (Paris: Robert Laffont, 1970); Nord, *France's New Deal*, 245. A useful sketch of the commercial radio situation in France is Briggs, *History of Broadcasting in the United Kingdom* 2: 362–69.

68. Translates literally as "Radio City." Bleustein-Blanchet traveled frequently to the United States and by his own report grilled David Sarnoff for the secrets of NBC's most lucrative program genres. Marcel Bleustein-Blanchet, *Les ondes de la liberté sur mon antenne 1934–1984* (Paris: Jean-Claude Lattès, 1984), 86. See also Bleustein-Blanchet, *La rage de convaincre* and Lise Elina, *Le micro et moi* (Paris: Pierre Horay, 1978). Private stations Radio-Paris and Poste-Parisien also selectively appropriated elements of U.S. programming and style.

69. U.S. listeners enjoyed the "vox pop" approach where the person on the street had a chance to opine before the microphone. See Warren Susman, *The Transformation of American Society in the Twentieth Century* (New York: Pantheon, 1984); Hilmes, *Radio Voices*; Jason Loviglio, *Radio's Intimate Public: Network Broadcasting and Mass-Mediated Democracy* (Minneapolis: University of Minnesota Press, 2005). On independent broadcasting in France and the impact of Radio-Cité on French broadcasting, see Almeida and Delporte, *Histoire des médias en France*; Neulander, *Programming National Identity*; Nord, *France's New Deal*.

70. Prot, *Dictionnaire de la radio,* 386–87.

71. Mandel also brought the Poste Coloniale more closely under his control by dissolving the National Federation of Colonial Broadcasting, which had previously managed the station. On Mandel's career, see John M. Sherwood, *Georges Mandel and the Third Republic* (Stanford, CA: Stanford University Press, 1970); Jean-Noël Jeanneney, *Georges Mandel, l'homme qu'on attendait* (Paris: Seuil, 1991); Prot, *Dictionnaire de la radio*; Nord, *France's New Deal*. The annual licensing fee began in 1933.

72. Listener quoted in Sherwood, *Georges Mandel,* 152–53.

73. The center's transmitters would reportedly easily reach the "Far East/IndoChina; the Near East and East Africa; West and Equatorial Africa; South America (Guyana and Antilles) and North America." "Rapport sur le centre émetteur colonial," 18 September 1937, 1–12, article 2, dossier 2, Cote 870714, Archives Nationales, Fontainebleau, France [hereafter, CAC]. The outmoded Poste Coloniale operated two transmitters at a rated power level of 10–12 kilowatts apiece. By contrast, Germany and England operated eight and six transmitters respectively at considerably higher power levels.

74. Quoted in Sherwood, *Georges Mandel,* 200. See also Kedward, *France and the French,* 176–83.

75. Document, Annexe du rapport de M. Pellenc sur la Poste Coloniale, "Extrait des travaux de la Commission d'enquête du Sénat," 1; Procès-verbal, Conseil supérieur des émissions, 15 January 1937, article 2, dossier 1, 5, CAC.

76. "Extrait des travaux," 5. Emphases added.

77. Jacques Attali and Yves Stourdze, "The Birth of the Telephone and Economic Crisis: The Slow Death of Monologue in French Society," in *The Social Impact of the Telephone,* ed. Ithiel de Sola Pool (Cambridge, MA: MIT Press, 1977), 97.

78. Méadel, *Histoire de la radio*; Neulander, *Programming National Identity*; Nord, *France's New Deal*. Neulander singles out a "conservative-bourgeois" ideology that persisted on French airwaves during the 1930s. French public broadcasting would expand in later years to nourish artistic, experimental projects in music and electroacoustics. See, for example, Jane F. Fulcher, "From 'the Voice of the Maréchal' to Musique Concrète: Pierre Schaeffer and the Case of Cultural History," in *The Oxford Handbook of the New Cultural History of Music,* ed. Jane F. Fulcher, 381–402 (New York: Oxford University Press, 2011).

79. Document, "Annexe du rapport de M. Pellenc sur la Poste Coloniale." Quoted passage in "Extrait des travaux de la commission d'enquête du Sénat," 1, CAC. Emphasis added.

80. Document, "Annexe du rapport de M. Pellenc sur la Poste Coloniale;" "Radio's Shortwaves," *New York Times*, 27 February 1938, 158; Prot, *Dictionnaire de la radio*, 168–69. For an exploration of how security issues affected radio in metropolitan France and beyond, see Derek Vaillant, "*La Police de l'Air*: Amateur Radio and the Politics of Aural Surveillance in France, 1921–1940," *French Politics, Culture and Society*, no. 1 (Spring 2010): 1–24; and Scales, *Radio and the Politics of Sound in Interwar France*.

81. Fernand Auberjonois, "French Broadcasting Stations to Build 'American Programs' Here," [1938?], folder 61, box 60, NBC-WHS. Emphasis added.

82. Bulletin. "Your Audience the French: Tips for the Field Broadcaster," [1943?], "E: France 9," folder 10, box 288, Records of the Office of War Information (RG 208), National Archives and Records Administration, College Park, MD.

83. Weber, *Peasants into Frenchmen*, 222.

Chapter 2. We Won't Always Have Paris: U.S. Networks in France and Europe

1. Prior to placing managers in Europe, the networks coordinated news reports with freelance print journalists abroad. Established in 1934, the Mutual Broadcasting System (MBS), a small consortium of stations, also pursued international broadcast opportunities. See "Mutual Broadcasting System," *Encyclopaedia Britannica: Britannica Academic* (Chicago: Encyclopædia Britannica, 2015), http://academic.eb.com.proxy.lib.umich.edu/EBchecked/topic/1586228/Mutual-Broadcasting-System. The MBS was "a very minor part of the broadcasting picture," according to John MacVane, *On the Air in World War II* (New York: William Morrow, 1979), 11. The major networks also engaged the broadcast systems of Latin America and elsewhere. See, for example, Fred Fejes, *Imperialism, Media, and the Good Neighbor: New Deal Foreign Policy and United States Shortwave Broadcasting to Latin America* (Norwood, NJ: Ablex, 1986); Michael Krysko, *American Radio in China: International Encounters with Technology and Communications, 1919–1941* (New York: Palgrave Macmillan, 2011). On radio's international applications before 1938, see, for example, Michael J. Socolow, *Six Minutes in Berlin: Broadcast Spectacle and Rowing Gold at the Nazi Olympics* (Urbana: University of Illinois Press, 2016).

2. On the European crisis and shortwave news reporting, see William L. Shirer, *Berlin Diary* (New York: Alfred A. Knopf, 1941); David Holbrook Culbert, *News for Everyman: Radio and Foreign Affairs in Thirties America* (Westport, CT: Greenwood, 1976); Stanley Cloud and Lynne Olson, *The Murrow Boys: Pioneers on the Front Lines of Broadcast Journalism* (Boston: Houghton Mifflin, 1996); Edward Bliss, *Now the News: The Story of Broadcast Journalism* (New York: Columbia University Press, 1991).

3. On regulation and print journalism in France, see, for example, Jean-Noël Jeanneney, *Une histoire des médias: des origines à nos jours* (Paris: Seuil, 1998), and Christian Delporte, *Histoire du journalisme et du journalistes en France: du XVIIe siècle à nos jours* (Paris: Presse Universitaire de France, 1995).

4. César Saerchinger, *Hello America! Radio Adventures in Europe* (Boston: Houghton Mifflin, 1938); Max Jordan, *Beyond All Fronts: A Bystander's Notes on This Thirty Year's*

War (Milwaukee, WI: Bruce, 1944). Bate also handled programs from Belgium and Holland (Memorandum, Alfred H. Morton to R. C. Patterson, 9 October 1934, folder 46, box 91, National Broadcasting Company Records, Wisconsin Historical Society Archives, Madison, WI) [hereafter, NBC-WHS].

5. Obituary, "Frederick Bate, 84, N.B.C. European Aide," *New York Times*, 30 January 1970, 28; academic transcript, University of Chicago, 1907–8; telephone interview by the author with Judith Bate Acheson, stepdaughter of Fred Bate, 17 May 2009 [hereafter, JBA]. On Vera Bate and her social circle, see Axel Madsen, *Chanel: A Woman of Her Own* (New York: H. Holt, 1990), 142.

6. JBA; "Owen D. Young," Encyclopædia Britannica Online, http://search.eb.com .proxy.lib.umich.edu/eb/article-9078062; http://www.ge.com/company/history/bios/ owen_young.html; obituary, "Frederick Bate"; interdepartmental memorandum, 17 September 1932, John W. Elwood to M. J. Woods, folder 55, box 6, NBC-WHS. Quote from Alistair Cooke, *Six Men* (New York: Knopf, 1977), 61. See Saerchinger, *Hello America*, 253.

7. Obituary, "Frederick Bate"; JBA; various email correspondence with Judith Bate Acheson; "Owen D. Young," http://www.ge.com/company/history/bios/owen_young.html; interdepartmental memorandum, 17 September 1932, M. J. Woods to John W. Elwood, folder 55, box 6, NBC-WHS; https://history.state.gov/milestones/1921–1936/dawes; press release, "Fred Bate Heads NBC International Division," 15 April 1942, folder 140, Library of Congress, Recorded Sound Section, Motion Picture, Broadcasting and Recorded Sound Division, Washington, DC [hereafter, NBC-LOC].

8. See Jordan, *Beyond All Fronts*. The BBC dispatched a permanent representative to the United States in 1935. On NBC's ties with the BBC during this period, see Michele Hilmes, *Network Nations: A Transnational History of British and American Broadcasting* (New York: Routledge, 2012).

9. For a typical lampoon of NBC and commercial hucksterism, see "Les beautés de la radio-publicité" ("The beauties of radio advertising"), *Le Petit Radio*, 22 June 1929, 5.

10. Radio Corporation of America, *Annual Report for the Year 1931*, 3; *Annual Report for the Year 1933*, 6; *Annual Report for the Year 1934*, 1.

11. Fred Bate, "London Office Report, April 1934," 6, folder 61, box 90, NBC-WHS.

12. Saerchinger, *Hello America*, 253–54. On the climate of domestic competition, see Michael J. Socolow, "'Always in Friendly Competition': NBC and CBS in the First Decade of National Broadcasting," in *NBC: America's Network*, ed. Michele Hilmes and Michael Henry (Berkeley: University of California Press, 2007): 25–43; A. J. Liebling, *The Road Back to Paris* (New York: Doubleday, Doran, 1944), 46.

13. Hilmes, *Network Nations*, 106–15.

14. Ira Nelson Morris, *Heritage from My Father, an Autobiography* (New York: Privately printed, 1947), 243.

15. "International Radio Forum, American and French Committee membership," circa 1933, folder 56, box 18, NBC-WHS; http://www.nobelprize.org/nobel_prizes/peace/laureates/ 1931/butler-bio.html.

16. "Our London Correspondence," *Manchester Guardian*, 7 May 1932, 12; "Ira N. Morris, Once Envoy to Sweden, Dies," *Chicago Daily Tribune*, 16 January 1942, 16.

17. "International Radio Forum Speakers, 1931–32," n/d, folder 56, box, 18, NBC-WHS; Morris, *Heritage from My Father*, 247.

18. "Less Sarcasm Is Jusserand's Plea to America," *Chicago Daily Tribune*, 11 April 1932, 9; "Jusserand Urges 'Charity' to France," *New York Times*, 11 April 1932, 8.

19. Correspondence, Fred Bate to John W. Elwood, 9 September 1933, folder 28, box 90, NBC-WHS; quote from press release, "Committee on International Broadcasting," n/d, folder 28, box 90, NBC-WHS; "Friendship among Nations," *London Times*, 9 September 1933, np.

20. The RC's stated aim was "the development of a closer friendship between America and France, and the furtherance of international good will through the channels of radio exchange" (correspondence, Franka Gordon to Colonel Richard E. Patterson, 17 November 1934, folder 28, box 31, NBC-WHS).

21. Correspondence, Frank E. Mason to John F. Royal, 1 November 1933, folder 14, box 27, NBC-WHS.

22. Correspondence, Alice Langelier to Fred Bate, 27 September 1933, folder 14, box 27, NBC-WHS.

23. Correspondence, Fred Bate to Alice Langelier, 14 October 1933, folder 14, box 27, NBC-WHS.

24. Ibid.

25. Ibid.

26. On the cultural history of U.S. radio audiences, see, for example, Jason Loviglio, *Radio's Intimate Public: Network Broadcasting and Mass-Mediated Democracy* (Minneapolis: University of Minnesota Press, 2005); Elena Razlogova, *The Listener's Voice: Early Radio and the American Public* (Philadelphia: University of Pennsylvania Press, 2011); Kathy M. Newman, *Radio Active: Advertising and Consumer Activism, 1935–1947* (Berkeley: University of California Press, 2004). On political discourse and U.S. radio listening, see Douglas B. Craig, *Fireside Politics: Radio and Political Culture in the United States, 1920–1940* (Baltimore: Johns Hopkins University Press, 2000); Bruce Lenthall, *Radio's America: The Great Depression and the Rise of Modern Mass Culture* (Chicago: University of Chicago Press, 2007). On "distracted listening," see David Goodman, *Radio's Civic Ambition: American Broadcasting and Democracy in the 1930s* (New York: Oxford University Press, 2011). For a cross-national perspective on listening and civic engagement, see Kate Lacey, *Listening Publics: The Politics and Experience of Listening in the Media Age* (Cambridge, UK: Polity).

27. Correspondence, Fred Bate to Alice Langelier, 14 October 1933, folder 14, box 27, NBC-WHS.

28. On the contrast between natural soundscapes and their manipulation in the age of electroacoustical studio production, see Raymond Murray Schafer, *The Soundscape: Our Sonic Environment and the Tuning of the World* (Rochester, VT: Destiny, 1994), and Emily Thompson, *The Soundscape of Modernity* (Cambridge, MA: MIT Press, 2002). On the creative applications of engineering and studio production techniques in the 1930s and afterward for aesthetic effects, see Neil Verma, *Theater of the Mind: Imagination, Aesthetics, and American Radio Drama* (Chicago: University of Chicago Press, 2012). On the regulation of core cultural principles in France as a nationalist exercise, see Herman Lebovics, *True France: The Wars over Cultural Identity, 1900–1945* (Ithaca, NY: Cornell University Press, 1992).

29. Correspondence, Fred Bate to Alice Langelier, 14 October 1933, folder 14, box 27, NBC-WHS.

30. Ibid.

31. Ibid.

32. Correspondence, Fred Bate to John F. Royal, 17 October 1933, folder 14, box 27, NBC-WHS.

33. Memorandum, Alfred H. Morton to John F. Royal, 16 October 1933, folder 41, box 27, NBC-WHS.

34. Correspondence, Fred Bate to John F. Royal, 21 November 1933, folder 41, box 27, NBC-WHS.

35. "International Broadcasts," folder 9, box 38, NBC-WHS; folders 9, 49, 55, box 18, NBC-WHS.

36. Correspondence, C. W. Horn to Alfred H. Morton, 5 January 1934, folder 14, box 27, NBC-WHS; quotes in correspondence, Alfred H. Morton to Fred Bate, 6 January 1934, folder 14, box 27, NBC-WHS; correspondence, Alfred H. Morton to John F. Royal, 16 November 1934, folders 41 and 14, box 27, NBC-WHS; minutes, 21 January 1935, Committee of Broadcast Improvement, 3, dossier 2, article 2, Culture et Communication/Société nationale de la radiodiffusion française/RDF Bureau A du N, Fonds de l'ORTF, Archives nationales, Fontainebleau [hereafter, CAC]. On the general upsurge of domestic radio in the latter half of the decade, see Jean-Noël Jeanneney, *Une histoire des médias*, and Philip Nord, *France's New Deal from the Thirties to the Postwar Era* (Princeton, NJ: Princeton University Press, 2010).

37. "Barthou Sends U.S. Message of Amity," *New York Times*, 13 May 1934, E7; "Wireless Error Gives New York Crowd a Laugh," *Chicago Daily Tribune*, 6 May 1934, 1.

38. "Le Centenaire de La Fayette [*sic*]," *Le Temps*, 20 May 1934, 4.

39. "Lafayette Relics Put on Exhibition," *New York Times*, 6 May 1934, N4.

40. "Comedy Skit Supplants Barthou on the Radio," *New York Times*, 6 May 1934, N4. On the competitive mood between print journalism and broadcasting, see, for example, Robert McChesney, "Press-Radio Relations and the Emergence of Network, Commercial Broadcasting in the United States, 1930–1935," *Historical Journal of Film, Radio and Television* 11, no. 1 (1991): 41–57; Michael Stamm, *Sound Business: Newspapers, Radio, and the Politics of New Media* (Philadelphia: University of Pennsylvania Press, 2011).

41. Fred Bate, "London Office Report, April 1934," folder 61, box 90, 6, NBC-WHS.

42. On the nature of these ties, see Hilmes, *Network Nations*.

43. More far-flung targets of NBC programs were Iceland, Ethiopia, Manila, parts of the Middle East, and Japan: "International Programs, 1935," folder 16, box 47, NBC-WHS.

44. Correspondence, Alfred H. Morton to John F. Royal, 6 June 1935, folder 1, box 40, NBC-WHS; confidential memorandum, Fred Bate to David Sarnoff, 19 September 1935, folder 48, box 91, NBC-WHS.

45. Fred Bate, London Office Report, 30 August 1935, 9, folder 1, box 40, NBC-WHS; quote from correspondence, Alfred H. Morton to John F. Royal, 6 June 1935, folder 1, box 40, NBC-WHS.

46. Letter, Fred Bate to John F. Royal, 18 August 1936, London, Fred Bate, folder 38, box 92, NBC-WHS.

47. "Broadcasting and Peace," International Institute of Intellectual Co-operation, Paris, 1933, quoted in Saerchinger, *Hello America*, 370.

48. Jacques Attali and Yves Stourdze, "The Birth of the Telephone and Economic Crisis: The Slow Death of Monologue in French Society," in *The Social Impact of the Telephone*, ed. Ithiel de Sola Pool (Cambridge, MA: MIT Press, 1977), 100, 102.

49. Cécile Méadel, *Histoire de la radio des années trente: du sans-filiste à l'auditeur* (Paris: Anthropos Economica, 1994); H. R. Kedward, *France and the French, a Modern History* (Woodstock, NY: Overlook Press, 2006), 165–76.

50. Paul Starr, *The Creation of the Media: Political Origins of Modern Communications* (New York: Basic Books, 2004), 4–5. On technological innovation and shifts in information circulation and news practices, see, for example, Michael Schudson, *Discovering the News: A Social History of American Newspapers* (New York: Basic Books, 1978); Richard R. John, *Spreading the News: The American Postal System from Franklin to Morse* (Cambridge, MA: Harvard University Press, 1995).

51. On French press history and news policies, see Claude Bellanger, Jacques Goudechot, et al., ed., *Histoire générale de la presse française*, 3 vols. (Paris: Presses universitaires de France), 1969; Jeanneney, *Histoire des médias*; Élisabeth Cazenave and Ulmann-Mauriat, *Presse, radio et télévision en France de 1631 à nos jours* (Paris: Hachette, 1995).

52. Correspondence, John F. Royal to Alfred H. Morton, 8 February 1935, folder 55, box 36, NBC-WHS. Emphasis added.

53. Morton and Bate had developed a friendship working together in Paris for RCA. They often traded inside jokes in their frequent communiqués, such as mashing together PTT and AT&T. Alfred H. Morton to Fred Bate, 8 February 1935, folder 55, box 36, NBC-WHS; correspondence, Alfred H. Morton to John F. Royal, 15 February 1935, folder 55, box 36, NBC-WHS.

54. Correspondence, Fred Bate to Alfred H. Morton, 26 February 1935, folder 55, box 36, NBC-WHS.

55. Saerchinger, *Hello America*, 301.

56. John W. Elwood quoted in Jordan, *Beyond All Fronts*, 45.

57. Saerchinger, *Hello America*, 253–54.

58. Ibid., 250. "It's always like that" or "That's how it is" serve as approximate translations of the quote. On the effect of commerce on U.S. radio's sense of timing and pace, see Shawn VanCour, "The Sounds of 'Radio': Aesthetic Formations of 1920s American Broadcasting" (PhD dissertation, University of Wisconsin-Madison, 2008) cited in Verma, *Theater of the Mind*, 28.

59. Saerchinger, *Hello America*, 251.

60. Details on the riots are in Charles Rearick, *The French in Love and War: Popular Culture in the Era of the World Wars* (New Haven, CT: Yale University Press, 1997), 183, and Kedward, *France and the French*, 167–83.

61. Saerchinger, *Hello America*, 32.

62. Jordan, *Beyond All Fronts*, 285.

63. CBS reporter William Shirer deemed the broadcast censors in Berlin to be "fairly reasonable" prior to the invasion of France. Their obstructions were less onerous "than [Eric] Sevareid and [Charles] Grandin had to put up with in Paris." See Shirer, *Berlin Diary*, 511.

64. Telegram, 3 March 1937, John F. Royal to Fred Bate, folder 33, box 93, NBC-WHS.

65. MacVane, *On the Air*, 11.

66. A. M. Sperber, *Murrow, His Life and Times* (New York: Freundlich, 1986); RWA_5337_B3 [date 10/19/40, News Special, 6:15–6:25 PM, shortwave from London], "What Does It Mean to Live in an Air Shelter?" Recorded Sound Research Center, Library of Congress, Recorded Sound Section, Motion Picture, Broadcasting and Recorded Sound Division, Washington, D.C.

67. Murrow and Bate recordings can be heard in the NBC collection at the Recorded Sound Research Center of the Library of Congress in Washington, D.C.; Elizabeth McLeod, "Old Time Radio Moments of the Century," http://jeff560.tripod.com/mcleod.html, segment 21; JBA.

68. Correspondence, John F. Royal to Niles Trammell, 28 October 1940, folder 61, box 74, NBC-WHS.

69. "Britain Held Eager for Nazi Invasion," *New York Times*, 1 February 1941, 2; "The Fred Bate Luncheon," transcription recording of broadcast from Waldorf Astoria Hotel, LWO 16798_R65_B3, Recorded Sound Research Center, Library of Congress, Recorded Sound Section, Motion Picture, Broadcasting and Recorded Sound Division, Washington, D.C.

70. "BBC Bombed," *Time*, 20 January 1941, np; correspondence, David Sarnoff to Fred Bate, 11 December 1940; correspondence, A. A. Schechter to Niles Trammell, 19 December 1940; correspondence, A. A. Schechter to Sidney Strotz, 19 December 1940, folder 61, box 74, NBC-WHS. See also Sperber, *Murrow*, 186.

71. John F. Royal to Orrin Dunlap, 21 January 1941, folder 92, box 81, NBC-WHS.

72. Lanfranco Rasponi, "Reporting under Fire," *New York Times*, 16 February 1941, X10; obituary, "Frederick Bate."

Chapter 3. *Voices of the Occupation: U.S. Broadcasting to France during World War II*

1. Correspondence received and translated by NBC International Division, 5 September 1941 and 3 October 1941, reprinted in *France Speaks to America, Letters from a Frenchwoman to the International Division of the National Broadcasting Company* (New York: National Broadcasting Company, 1941). "In spite of drastic rules and repressive measures, several thousand letters have been sent by the French to America." See Fernand Auberjonois, "Letters from France," *New York Times Magazine*, 3 May 1942, 12. The actual number of French listeners to *The French Hour* during the Occupation is unknown.

2. A post-Liberation BBC survey of 269 French listeners conducted between 1 November 1944 and 15 January 1945 estimated that the French audience for the retransmitted programs of the VOA by the BBC was one-third of that for the BBC French Service. "Report on Voice of America Programs Based on a BBC Survey," 2 April 1945, 1, Evaluations Division, Overseas Branch, E: France 9, box 288, Records of the Office of War Information (RG 208), National Archives and Records Administration, College Park, MD [hereafter OWI]. A survey of radio listening conducted in 1973–74 that included selections across 180 residential sectors of France and across nine professional and occupational categories found that 90 percent of male adults reported having access to a radio during the Occupation. When asked to rank their preferences for international broadcasters from

that time, subjects ranked the BBC first and VOA second. See J. L. Crémieux-Brilhac and G. Bensimhon, "Les propagandes radiophoniques et l'opinion publique en France de 1940 à 1944," *Revue d'histoire de la deuxième guerre mondiale* 101 (1976): 3–18; Christian Brochand and Comité d'histoire de la radiodiffusion, *Histoire générale de la radio et de la télévision en France*, vol. 1, *1921–1944* (Paris: Documentation française, 1994), 571–73. Programs furnished by Radio Sottens in Switzerland were also popular news sources.

3. Listener letters obviously represented a small and unrepresentative sample of the actual audience. It is also likely that those broadcast were selected for propaganda value. Selections from letters in the BBC archives have been published. See Aurélie Luneau, *Je vous l'écris de France: lettres à la BBC, 1940–1944* (Paris: L'Iconoclaste, 2014).

4. Kate Lacey, *Listening Publics: The Politics and Experience of Listening in the Media Age* (Cambridge, UK: Polity), 4, 19. Lacey builds from the work of Jürgen Habermas, *The Structural Transformation of the Public Sphere: An Inquiry into the Category of Bourgeois Society*, trans. Thomas Burger (Cambridge, MA: MIT Press, 1992), and critics such as Craig Calhoun, ed., *Habermas: Critical Essays* (Cambridge, MA: MIT Press, 1994); Nancy Fraser, "Rethinking the Public Sphere: A Contribution to the Critique of Actually Existing Democracy," in *Habermas and the Public Sphere*, ed. Craig Calhoun (Cambridge, MA: MIT Press, 1992). See also Benedict Anderson, *Imagined Communities* (New York: Verso, 1991). Unlike Habermas's model, restrictions by gender and economic status did not apply in the example of listening to radio.

5. A key overview of the OWI is Allan M. Winkler, *The Politics of Propaganda: The Office of War Information, 1942–1945* (New Haven, CT: Yale University Press, 1978). On the OWI and visual culture on the home front, see George H. Roeder, *The Censored War: American Visual Experience during World War Two* (New Haven, CT: Yale University Press, 1993). On the VOA, see Alan L. Heil, *Voice of America: A History* (New York: Columbia University Press, 2003); David F. Krugler, *The Voice of America and the Domestic Propaganda Battles, 1945–1953* (Columbia: University of Missouri Press, 2000); Robert Pirsein, "The Voice of America: A History of the International Broadcasting Activities of the U.S. Government, 1940–1962" (PhD dissertation, Northwestern University, 1970); Holly Cowan Shulman, *The Voice of America: Propaganda and Democracy, 1941–1945* (Madison: University of Wisconsin Press, 1990). See also Nicholas John Cull, *The Cold War and the United States Information Agency: American Propaganda and Public Diplomacy, 1945–1989* (Cambridge: Cambridge University Press, 2009). On French nationals in New York who contributed to VOA programs, see Emmanuelle Loyer, *Paris à New York: Intellectuels et artistes français en exil (1940–1947)* (Paris: Bernard Grasset, 2005).

6. "Manuscript, prepared by Major Lenox R. Lohr in collaboration with Charles W. Horn and Percy Winner," 4 January 1938, folder 41, box 94, National Broadcasting Company Records, Central Files, 1921–1969, State Historical Society of Wisconsin [hereafter, NBC-WHS]. NBC aired two daily newscasts in French, three in English, and one each in Italian, German, Spanish, and Portuguese (Interdepartmental Correspondence, L. R. Lohr to C. W. Fitch, 6 August 1937, folder 140, NBC History Files, Recorded Sound Section, Motion Picture, Broadcasting and Recorded Sound Division, Library of Congress [hereafter, NBC-LOC].

7. As early as summer 1936, NBC vice president Frank M. Russell demanded of John F. Royal, "If war should break out in Germany—and it might any night—what is going to

be our position in radio? Has the Radio Commission or the State Department given any thought to this? If anything has been done we ought to know about it so we can prepare, and not wait until the last minute." Correspondence, Frank M. Russell to John F. Royal, 7 August 1936, folder 1275, box 147, Lenox Riley Lohr Papers, Richard J. Daley Library Special Collections and University Archives, University of Illinois at Chicago [hereafter, Lohr].

8. NBC International Division, "General Report of the Division's Recent Activities in Short Wave Broadcasting," National Broadcasting Company, 1937; staff memorandum, 24 November 1937, folder 141, NBC-LOC.

9. John W. Elwood quoted in Earl Sparling, "America Calling All Peoples: The Vital Role Short Wave Radio Plays in America's Fight for Freedom," ed. International Division (New York: National Broadcasting Company, 1942), 13, emphasis added. Fernand Auberjonois, *The French Are Listening In . . . and They Say So* (New York: NBC International Division, 1942), 150–51; obituary, "Fernand Auberjonois: Much Admired Foreign Correspondent. Who Lived a Chronicle of 20th Century," *Pittsburgh Post-Gazette*, 28 July 2004; unpublished report, *Programs of Special International Interest*, "Programs of Interest Presented in French," 6, folder 70, box 95, NBC-WHS; *NBC Short Wave News* Programs for Week of October 3–29, 1938; "Weekly Program Schedule for International Broadcasting Station W3XAL, effective February 28, 1938," folder 64, box 93, NBC-WHS; Fernand Auberjonois, *Entre deux mondes: Chroniques 1910–1953*, 2nd ed. (Geneva, Switz.: Metropolis, 1994), 149.

10. Auberjonois, *Entre deux mondes*, 151.

11. On the significance of listener correspondence to broadcasters before survey research became commonplace, see Elena Razlogova, *The Listener's Voice: Early Radio and the American Public* (Philadelphia: University of Pennsylvania Press, 2011); Kathy M. Newman, *Radio Active: Advertising and Consumer Activism, 1935–1947* (Berkeley: University of California Press, 2004).

12. Senegal, the Belgian Congo, Madagascar, Sudan, Cambodia, and Indo-China were among the areas responding to *The French Hour*, most likely because shortwave listening provided a rare source of French news. In the early stages of the program, Auberjonois complained, "the Canadians were tickled to be hearing French [but] France remained silent. Only the shortwave fanatics were responding." Auberjonois, *Entre deux mondes*, 152. Auberjonois's data tabulation in summer 1937 showed less than 50 percent of correspondence to his program coming from Paris. See NBC International Division, "General Report," 10–11.

13. Auberjonois, *Entre deux mondes*, 153; W3XAL Mail, July–December 1937, F 20/42, pt. 2, folder 64, box 93, NBC-WHS; correspondence, Guy Hickok to C. U. Clark, 7 April 1939, NBC, folder 41, box 68, Response Letters, NBC-WHS.

14. Rebecca Scales, *Radio and the Politics of Sound in Interwar France, 1921–1939* (New York: Cambridge University Press, 2016); "Émission en français sur ondes courtes de New York"; *Dimanche Illustré*, 23 February 1941, n.p.

15. "France Sees Menace in Hitler's Speech," *New York Times*, 13 September 1938, X5; Bulletin, "Your Audience the French: Tips for the Field Broadcaster," [1942–43?], 5, E: France 9, box 288, OWI.

16. Memorandum, Frank E. Mason to Guy Hickok, 18 October 1938, folder 62, box 93, NBC-WHS; Auberjonois, *Entre deux mondes*, 155; "Your Audience the French," [1942–43?], 5, E: France 9, box 288, OWI.

17. "Slavery by Radio, Princeton Listening Center," *Washington Post*, 9 September 1940, 7. See H. J. P. Bergmeier, *Hitler's Airwaves: The Inside Story of Nazi Radio Broadcasting and Propaganda Swing* (New Haven, CT: Yale University Press, 1997), and Derek W. Vaillant, "La Police de l'Air: Amateur Radio and the Politics of Aural Surveillance in France, 1921–1940." *French Politics, Culture and Society* 28 (Spring 2010): 1–24.

18. Jean-Noël Jeanneney, *Une histoire des médias: des origines à nos jours* (Paris: Seuil, 1998), 174, 180; Julian Jackson, *France: The Dark Years, 1940–1944* (New York: Oxford University Press, 2001), 117; Asa Briggs, *The History of Broadcasting in the United Kingdom*, vol. 3, *The War of Words* (London: Oxford University Press, 1970), 222–23.

19. Jean-Louis Crémieux-Brilhac, *Les voix de la liberté: Ici Londres, 1940–1944* (Paris: Documentation française, 1975), xiii. Both black stations continued their operations into the early 1940s. A. F. Panfilov, *Broadcasting Pirates, or Abuse of the Microphone: An Outline of External Political Radio Propaganda by the USA, Britain, and the FRG* (Moscow: Progress, 1981).

20. *France Speaks to America*. Statistics in Jackson, *France*, 246. On 11 November 1942, Germany occupied the entirety of France in response to the Allied invasion of North Africa.

21. Terms such as "the Resistance" and the "French resistance" should be read with the caveat that resistance to the Occupation comprised many factions with shifting alliances to the Free French and should not be mistaken as references to a monolithic entity. Statistics reported in Jackson, *France*, 1, 601. On broadcasting and other media during the Occupation, see, for example, Jean-Pierre Azéma, François Bédarida, and Institut d'histoire du temps présent (France), *Le régime de Vichy et les français* (Paris: Fayard, 1992); Agnès Callu, Patrick Eveno, and Hervé Joly, *Culture et médias sous l'occupation: Des entreprises dans la France de Vichy*, CTHS Histoire, 39 (Paris: CTHS, 2009); Jean-Louis Crémieux-Brilhac, *La France libre: De l'appel du 18 juin à la libération* (Paris: Gallimard, 1996); Hanna Diamond and Simon Kitson, *Vichy, Resistance, Liberation: New Perspectives on Wartime France* (New York: Berg, 2005); Donna Evleth, *France under the German Occupation, 1940–1944: An Annotated Bibliography*, Bibliographies and Indexes in World History, no. 20 (New York: Greenwood, 1991); Robert O. Paxton, *Vichy France: Old Guard and New Order, 1940–1944* (New York: Knopf, 1972).

22. Jackson, *France*, 118–21; "World War II," Encyclopædia Britannica Online, http://search.eb.com.proxy.lib.umich.edu/eb/article-53540.

23. Brochand and Comité d'histoire de la radiodiffusion, *Histoire générale de la radio*, 1: 571.

24. Laure Schnapper-Flender, "La vie musicale sous l'occupation," *Vingtième Siècle* 63 (July–September 1999): 132–43; Karine Le Bail, "Radio-Paris ou Radio-Vichy? Le milieu artistique français face au nouveau marché d'ondes," in *Culture et médias sous l'occupation des entreprises dans la France de Vichy*, ed. Patrick Eveno and Hervé Joly (Paris: Éditions du CTHS, 2009): 329–43; Jackson, *France*, 256.

25. Pierre Laval and Jacques Tremoulet managed private stations and collaborated with the Vichy government to profit during the Occupation. See Brochand and Comité d'histoire, *Histoire générale*, 1: 574–86.

26. Ruth Thomas, *Broadcasting and Democracy in France* (Philadelphia: Temple University Press, 1977), 3; H. R. Kedward, *France and the French: A Modern History* (Woodstock,

NY: Overlook, 2006), 252–54. On the use of film, see Brett Bowles, "Newsreels, Ideology, and Public Opinion under Vichy: The Case of *La France en Marche*," *French Historical Studies* 27, no. 2 (2004): 419–63.

27. The program replaced *Ici la France* (This Is France). Jean-Jacques Ledos, "Les français parlent aux français! 1940–1944: la radio de l'espérance," *Gavroche* 60 (1991): 1–6. See also various intelligence reports, E: France 9, box 288, OWI. In a bit of cheek, a chemist from Marseille opined that "Although the British are not very popular in France, BBC programs are widely listened to and liked." Report, "Unoccupied France-Marseille, May 1942," E: France 9, box 288, OWI.

28. Robert Prot, *Dictionnaire de la radio* (Grenoble, Fr.: Presses universitaires de Grenoble–Institut national de l'audiovisuel, 1997), 252–53, 537; Crémieux-Brilhac, *La France libre*, 218.

29. Excerpts from British Broadcasting Corporation (BBC) European Intelligence Section, "BBC Bi-Monthly Surveys of European Audiences, France, 4 March 1942," in *European Intelligence Papers: Series 1b* (London: European Intelligence Section, BBC, 1942), n.p. All quoted passages from these reports were translated by the BBC. Quote from Crémieux-Brilhac, *La France libre*, 229. Author interview with Paulette Sabarthe, 25 June 2006, Bordeaux, Fr.

30. BBC broadcast, 3 July 1940, reprinted in Crémieux-Brilhac, *Les voix de la liberté*, 11.

31. BBC broadcasts, 24 July 1940, 30 September 1941, 21 October 1940, reprinted in Crémieux-Brilhac, *Les voix de la liberté*, 29, 308–10, 312–13.

32. Transcript, "The French Speak to the French," 2 January 1942, reprinted in Crémieux-Brilhac, *Les voix de la liberté*, 85, 159–60.

33. Transcript, "The French Speak to the French," 3 October 1940, 1 July 1942, and 8 August 1942, reprinted in Crémieux-Brilhac, *Les voix de la liberté*, 101–2, 159–60, 185–86. Other broadcasts on repression of Jews aired throughout 1942.

34. All BBC and Allied intelligence reports translated the remarks of French correspondents and informants into English. European Intelligence Section, 9. On the role of BBC intelligence and radio, see Briggs, *History of Broadcasting in the United Kingdom*, vols. 1–3 (London: Oxford University Press, 1961, 1965, 1970); Martyn Cornick, "The BBC and the Propaganda War against Occupied France: The Work of Émile Delavenay and the European Intelligence Department," *French History* 8, no. 3 (1994): 316–54.

35. "BBC Bi-Monthly Surveys of European Audiences—France," 4 March 1942, European Intelligence Papers, Series 1b, E: 92, BBC Bi-Monthly Surveys, box 254, OWI.

36. Beginning in 1938, and throughout the war, the BBC used "high-power medium-wave transmitters" clustered in the north and south of England. Each group of transmitters used "one medium wavelength" according to Briggs, *Broadcasting in the United Kingdom*, 3: 62.

37. "Your Audience the French," 3. Estimate for sets in winter 1942 in "BBC Bi-Monthly Surveys of European Audiences—France," 4 March 1942. Radio listening commonly occurred in households or other group settings. Crémieux-Brilhac and Bensimhon, "Les propagandes radiophoniques," 6.

38. Report, "Unoccupied France (Cannes), May 1942, E: France 9, box 288, OWI; report to John Houseman et al. from Claire Melson, 22 September 1942, E: France 9, box

288, OWI. Value in estimated labor hours derived from hourly average wage data for a hypothetical thirty-hour week. See International Labour Organization, *Yearbook of Labor Statistics 1935–1955*, www.iisg.nl/hpw/data.php#europe; Janet Flanner, "So You're Going to Paris!" *New Yorker*, 21 June 1941, 36–48; P. J. Kingston, "A Survey of the French Radio Industry 1940–1944 as Seen by the BBC," *Historical Journal of Film, Radio and Television* 3, no. 2 (1983): 149–60.

39. British Broadcasting Corporation (BBC) European Intelligence Section, "BBC Bi-Monthly Surveys of European Audiences France, 1 July 1942," 5 and 4 March 1942, 3; report—Unoccupied France (near Antibes), Unoccupied France (unspecified), n.p., April 1942, E: France 9, box 288, OWI.

40. Briggs, *Broadcasting in the United Kingdom*, vol. 3, *War of Words*; Jackson, *France*, 252–56.

41. European Intelligence Section, "BBC Bi-Monthly Surveys of European Audiences France, 4 March 1942," 7. Daniel Fisher notes how, years later, Frantz Fanon would regard the noisy bursts caused by government jamming of Algerian nationalist radio as a metonym of the fight against French colonialism. Daniel Fisher, "Radio," in *Keywords in Sound*, ed. David Novak and Matt Sakakeeny (Durham, NC: Duke University Press 2015), 157.

42. European Intelligence Section, "BBC Bi-Monthly Surveys of European Audiences France, 4 March 1942," 4.

43. BBC Interviews on 23 April 1944, E: France 9, 288, OWI; European Intelligence Section, "BBC Bi-Monthly Surveys of European Audiences France, 1 July 1942," 3.

44. Scattered incidents of punishments for "black listening" are reported by BBC intelligence, such as "'9 Chateauneuvians' sent to prison 'for having heard the English radio.'" European Intelligence Section, "BBC Bi-Monthly Surveys of European Audiences France, 1 July 1942," 3–4.

45. Quotations from letters and field reports expurgated in "BBC Bi-Monthly Surveys of European Audiences France, 4 March 1942," 2. Claude Lévy, "L'organisation de la propagande allemande en France," *Revue d'histoire de la Deuxième Guerre mondiale* 64 (October 1966): 25–26. On the situation in Alsace, see "BBC Bi-Monthly Surveys of European Audiences France, 4 March 1942," 2, E: France 9, box 288, OWI; "Four Sentenced in France for Tuning British Radio," *Chicago Daily Tribune*, 29 November 1941, 2.

46. Briggs, *Broadcasting in the United Kingdom*, 3: 179. The geography of Western Europe made international listening a hallmark of broadcasting from its earliest inceptions. Radio Strasbourg catered explicitly to a cross-border audience linked by linguistic and cultural heritage. On Radio Luxembourg in this regard, see Denis Maréchal, *Radio Luxembourg, 1933–1993: Un media au cœur de l'Europe* (Nancy, Fr.: Presses universitaires de Nancy, 1994), and Jennifer Spohrer, "Ruling the Airwaves: Radio Luxembourg and the Origins of European National Broadcasting, 1929–1950" (PhD dissertation, Columbia University, 2008).

47. "What joy amidst this horrible disaster to hear at last a voice with a bit of pride," Guéhenno wrote in response to hearing de Gaulle's appeal. Jean Guéhenno, *Journal des années noires (1940–1944)* (Paris: Gallimard, 1947), 13.

48. Ibid., 96.

49. Ibid., 64.

50. Ibid., 70.

51. Quoted in Earl Sparling, "Uncle Sam, Radio Propagandist," *American Mercury* (February 1940), 226–27. "Many of us in shortwave broadcasting feared that our French listeners would stop writing." See *France Speaks to America*, 3.

52. Enclosure, Lunsford P. Yandell to John F. Royal, "Translations of Excerpts from French Hour Letters Pertaining to Raymond Gram Swing," folder 61, box 86, NBC-WHS. The letter about the assassination was written retrospectively and mailed to NBC after the listener reached the United States, 5 March 1944 (Auberjonois digest of letters, folder 42, box 110, NBC-WHS).

53. Auberjonois digest of letters, folder 42, box 110, NBC-WHS.

54. By contrast, WRUL, a private station acting as a secret front for British political interests, praised England and criticized Germany, Vichy, and U.S. isolationism with gusto. See Nicholas John Cull, *Selling War: The British Propaganda Campaign against American "Neutrality" in World War II* (New York: Oxford University Press, 1995), and Auberjonois, *Entre deux mondes*, 160.

55. Memorandum, O. B. Hanson to L. R. Lohr, 6 September 1939, folder 1275, box 147, Lohr.

56. Auberjonois, *Entre deux mondes*, 170.

57. "Historic Words: More than 150 Stations to Carry Roosevelt Inauguration to a World-Wide Audience," *New York Times*, 26 February 1933, X10; "Short Waves Carry the President's Speech to a Dozen Foreign Countries," *New York Times*, 21 January 1937, 16; "Mr. Roosevelt's Talk Sets All-Time 'High'—Greatest Network Carried the Speech," *New York Times*, 1 June 1941, X10.

58. "President Moves," *New York Times*, 16 May 1941, 1. The *Times* noted Roosevelt's desire to speak to the French people directly as evidenced by the broadcast coming on the heels of the text address's release.

59. NBC used two shortwave stations for this purpose: WNBI and WRCA. Press release, "Twenty-Four Hour Broadcasting Continues," 16 May 1941, folder 70, box 95, NBC-WHS; Auberjonois digest of letters, folder 42, box 110, NBC-WHS; text of presidential address reprinted in "Roosevelt's Statement, No Collaboration beyond Terms of Armistice Justified, He Says," *Daily Boston Globe*, 16 May 1941, 16.

60. Quote in Sparling, "America Calling All Peoples," 20; Vichy quote in press release "Twenty-Four Hour Broadcasting Continues."

61. Press release, "French Listeners Use NBC to Relay Mail to England," NBC Trade News Service, folder 72, box 95, NBC-WHS; correspondence, Clay Morgan to John F. Royal, 11 March 1941, folder 72, box 95, NBC-WHS.

62. Correspondence, John F. Royal to Lunsford P. Yandell, 13 March 1941, folder 72, box 95, NBC-WHS.

63. The response to the schoolboy is my own translation (Il avait pourtant acheté une très belle gomme). Quotes in *France Speaks to America*; Luneau, *Je vous l'écris de France*.

64. *France Speaks to America*.

65. Ibid.; correspondence, John W. Elwood to John M. Begg, 16 December 1941, and Begg response, 30 December 1941, box 4026, 811.76, Central Decimal Files, Records of the Department of State (RG 59) [hereafter, CDF]. Auberjonois discusses the letters from the French widow in his memoir. She died prior to the Liberation. See Auberjonois, *Entre deux mondes*, 166–67.

66. Guéhenno, *Journal*, 207.

67. Ibid. *Bamboula nègre* appears to be a reference to Louis Moreau Gottschalk's 1859 composition *Bamboula, danse des nègres* (Bamboula, Dance of the Blacks), which used a syncopated style akin to that of U.S. ragtime. Irving Lowens and S. Frederick Starr, "Gottschalk, Louis Moreau," *Grove Music Online: Oxford Music Online*, Oxford University Press, http://www.oxfordmusiconline.com.proxy.lib.umich.edu/subscriber/article/grove/music/11530.

68. In May 1942, the Armed Forces Radio Service, later Armed Forces Radio, formed as a governmental broadcast network for U.S. military personnel. It broadcast information and entertainment programs without commercials, often using V-Discs, transcription recordings of popular radio programs made in the United States. See Lewis A. Erenberg, *Swingin' the Dream: Big Band Jazz and the Rebirth of American Culture* (Chicago: University of Chicago Press, 1998); David W. Stowe, *Swing Changes: Big-Band Jazz in New Deal America* (Cambridge, MA: Harvard University Press, 1994); Michele Hilmes, *Radio Voices: American Broadcasting, 1922–1952* (Minneapolis: University of Minnesota Press, 1997), 259–64, and Lauren Rebecca Sklaroff, "Variety for the Servicemen: The Jubilee Show and the Paradox of Racializing Radio during World War II," *American Quarterly* 56, no. 4 (December 2004): 945–73.

69. Quote in Shulman, *Voice of America*, 13. See also Lenox R. Lohr, "Broadcasting in Time of War," unpublished manuscript, ca. 10 April 1939, folder 1275, box 147, Lohr.

70. On the U.S. government as a propagandist, see Robert Jackall and Janice M. Hirota, "America's First Propaganda Ministry: The Committee on Public Information during the Great War," in *Propaganda, Main Trends of the Modern World*, ed. Robert Jackall, 137–73 (New York: New York University Press, 1995), and Krugler, *Voice of America*, 12–51.

71. NBC International Division, "General Report," 35; http://www.archives.gov/research/guide-fed-records/groups/208.html; John A. Pollard, "Words Are Cheaper than Blood," *Public Opinion Quarterly* 9, no. 3 (1945): 283–304. In spring 1941, a former Associated Press correspondent, Stanley P. Richardson, was named "coordinator of international broadcasting" on behalf of private shortwave stations and networks. See "Overseas Radio Is Mobilized," *New York Times* 20 April 1941, X12.

72. "Voice of America (VOA)," *Encyclopaedia Britannica: Britannica Academic* (Chicago: Encyclopædia Britannica, 2015), http://academic.eb.com/EBchecked/topic/631859/Voice-of-America. The inaugural program went to Germany. See also Leonard Carlton, "Voice of America: The Overseas Radio Bureau," *Public Opinion Quarterly* 7, no. 1 (1943): 46–64, and T. R. Kennedy Jr., "Classroom of a Hemisphere," *New York Times*, 4 May 1941, X12. See also "What Was OSS?" https://www.cia.gov/library/publications/intelligence-history/oss/art03.htm.

73. The OWI consolidated the work of the OEM's Division of Information, Office of Facts and Figures, and the COI's Foreign Information Service. By spring 1942, thirteen former private U.S. broadcasters had reportedly been assigned to VOA executive positions. Joseph Barnes, "Fighting with Information Overseas," *Public Opinion Quarterly* 7, no. 1 (Spring 1943), 39–40; memorandum, Percy Winner to C. W. Fitch, 24 October 1937, folder 141, NBC-LOC; VOA Program Guide, 1940–44, Shortwaves/220–499, 811.76, box 4027, CDF.

74. Krugler, *Voice of America*, 27. In the period between 1 October 1937 and 31 October 1942, the total cost to NBC-RCA of operating their shortwave services was $825,380.60.

Between 1 November 1942 and the end of the war, NBC recovered $484,990.67 from the U.S. government for furnishing VOA shortwave services. Because the network also was making capital improvements on shortwave capacity during this period, the total NBC-RCA expended was $543,286.39. NBC, Summary of International Short-Wave Operations, 1 October 1937 to 30 April 1945, NBC, folder 141, LOC. At the peak of the war, approximately one dozen privately owned shortwave transmitters supported the VOA. General Electric, NBC, Westinghouse, CBS, Crosley, and World Wide Broadcasting Corporation were among the providers.

75. The VOA broadcast live and transcripted, that is, prerecorded, programs. Evidence suggests that the use of transcription recordings increased once the Allied campaign shifted to North Africa and Europe. See Carlton, "Voice of America," 1.

76. "Report on Voice of America Programs Based on a BBC Survey"; Reports "Unoccupied France (Nîmes)," April 1942; and "Unoccupied France (unspecified)," April 1942, E: France 9, box 288, OWI.

77. "Interview with M. François Navarre," ca. spring 1943, E: France 9, box 288, OWI; "Radio Listeners in France," confidential report, 20 April 1944, E: France 9, box 288, OWI.

78. "Interview with M. Albert Guigui, ca. spring 1943," E: France 9, box 288, OWI.

79. David Krugler writes, "The VOA's broadcasts themselves were propaganda—efforts to convince listeners that the presentation offered was the truth, and that listeners' beliefs and actions should correspond to this truth." Krugler, *Voice of America*, 3. For more on twentieth-century propaganda, see Garth Jowett and Victoria O'Donnell, *Propaganda and Persuasion*, 3rd ed. (Thousand Oaks, CA: Sage, 1999).

80. Auberjonois, *Entre deux mondes*.

81. Report, 7 November 1942, Allied Force Headquarters, Psychological Warfare Branch; *Report on the Divisions in the Psychological Warfare Branch of AFHQ*, dated 6 January 1944, folder 2, box 132, OWI.

82. *Report on the Divisions*, dated 6 January 1944, folder 2, box 132, OWI.

83. Pollard, "Words Are Cheaper," 287; Auberjonois, *Entre deux mondes*; "French Short-Wave Listeners," confidential memorandum, U.S. Department of State, 19 March 1942, box 40227, CDF.

84. Prot, *Dictionnaire de la Radio,* 497. Quote in Bi-Monthly Report, 22 October 1943, Psychological Warfare Branch, Radio Section, box 132, OWI.

85. Memorandum, C. H. Coggins to Overseas Branch, OWI, 27 February 1943, FR-MISC, box 107, OWI.

86. "The French radio had never established a reputation for veracity; it had followed the French poster campaign in making the most of what was to be the silliest of all Phony War–time slogans: 'We shall win because we are stronger.'" Briggs, *Broadcasting in the United Kingdom,* 3: 227; British Broadcasting Corporation (BBC) European Intelligence Section, "BBC Bi-Monthly Surveys of European Audiences France, 26th August 1942," in *European Intelligence Papers: Series 1b* (London: European Intelligence Section, BBC, 1942), 22; E: France 9, box 288, OWI.

87. "BBC Bi-Monthly Surveys of European Audiences France, 1 July 1942," 28, E: France 9, box 288, OWI; "Your Audience the French," 1, 18; "BBC Bi-Monthly Surveys of European Audiences France, 1 July 1942," 27, E: France 9, box 288, OWI; quote in memorandum. C. H. Coggins to Overseas Branch, OWI, 27 February 1943, FR-MISC, box 107, OWI. Emphasis added.

88. Jackson, *France*, 466–68, 75–80.

89. Ibid., 5. On discourses of gendered weakness in the U.S. armed services in France, see Mary Louise Roberts, *What Soldiers Do: Sex and the American GI in World War II France* (Chicago: University of Chicago Press, 2013).

90. Quotes in "Your Audience the French," 2, 13, 15, 16.

91. Ibid., 16. Henry E. Mattox, "One Example of Natural Allies," *American Diplomacy* (August 2000), http://www.unc.edu/depts/diplomat/AD_Issues/amdipl_16/edit_16.html.

92. Quote, *Your Audience the French*, 6; quote, memorandum, C. H. Coggins to Overseas Branch, OWI, 27 February 1943, France-Miscellaneous, box 107, OWI; Irwin M. Wall, *The United States and the Making of Postwar France, 1945–1954* (Cambridge: Cambridge University Press, 1991), 24–25. On the rocky relations between U.S. leaders and both Vichy and the Free French, see, for example, Julian G. Hurstfield, *America and the French Nation, 1939–1945* (Chapel Hill: University of North Carolina Press, 1986).

93. Memorandum, "French Attitudes toward Allied Broadcasts," 14 April 1944, E: France 9, box 208, OWI.

94. Ibid.

95. Translates literally as "The Committee for the Liberation of Radio." Miriam Crénesse, telephone interview with the author, 13 January 2012; Prot, *Dictionnaire de la radio*, 290–91; Philip Nord, *France's New Deal from the Thirties to the Postwar Era* (Princeton, NJ: Princeton University Press, 2010); Hélène Eck, "Radio, Culture and Democracy in the Immediate Postwar Period, 1944–50," in *France and the Mass Media*, ed. Brian Rigby and Nicholas Hewitt (London: Palgrave Macmillan, 1991), 130–31.

96. Pierre Crénesse, *La libération des ondes* (Paris: Berger-Levrault, 1944), 9–10.

97. Crénesse, *Libération des ondes*, 31.

98. Ibid., 7.

99. Ibid., 7, 11. Quote from John MacVane, *On the Air in World War II* (New York: William Morrow, 1979), 295; "Field Report from Captain F. Auberjonois in London for period 24 August to 26 August," Outpost Service Bureau, folder 2, box 132, OWI.

100. Charles de Gaulle, *The Complete War Memoirs of Charles de Gaulle*, 3 vols. (New York: Simon and Schuster, 1964), 652–53.

Chapter 4. Served on a Platter: How French Radio Cracked the U.S. Airwaves

1. "*Variety* plaque awards for 1948–49," *Variety*, 27 July 1949, 33. The RDF comprised four divisions: Artistic Programs, News and Information, Technical Services, and Administrative and Financial ("Organisation des Services," 4, Annexe IV, Organisation des Services Centraux, 10, pièces annexes, *Radio France* finding aid, cote 950218, Archives nationales, Site de Fontainebleau, Fr.). Separate subdivisions handled news broadcasting, Arabic-language broadcasting, broadcasts to France's overseas territories and departments, and central editing and translating.

2. The FBS was sometimes referred to as the "North American Service of the French Broadcasting System," but mostly as the "French Broadcasting System."

3. In 1964, Radiodiffusion-télévision française (RTF), French national radio/TV broadcasting, reorganized as the Office de la radiodiffusion-télévision française (ORTF). The

platter distribution continued under the supervision of the ORTF. In 1966, the French consulate in New York took charge of distributing English-language programs in the United States. This arrangement continued until 1974.

4. Wallace Carroll, "Long-Range Policy Guidance for France," 28 October 1944, 4, Office of War Information, Overseas Branch, Washington, D.C., box 107, Records of the Office of War Information (RG 208), National Archives and Records Administration, College Park, MD [hereafter OWI].

5. Union Internationale de Radiodiffusion, *Bulletin Mensuel*, October 1946, no. 237, 313; quote from "Les services techniques de la radiodiffusion française, leur activité en 1947," 1, 2, 4, Conseil Supérieur des Émissions: 1923–1964 (CSE), cote 900214, Fonds de l'ORTF, Archives Nationales, Site de Fontainebleau, Fr. [hereafter, ORTF-CAC].

6. On postwar economic policy strategy in France, see Philip Nord, *France's New Deal from the Thirties to the Postwar Era* (Princeton, NJ: Princeton University Press, 2010); William I. Hitchcock, *France Restored: Cold War Diplomacy and the Quest for Leadership in Europe, 1944–1954* (Chapel Hill: University of North Carolina Press, 1998).

7. Memorandum, S. J. Campbell to L. S. Brady, 4 January 1954, box 5, Records of the Foreign Service Posts of the Department of State, 1788–ca. 1991 (RG 84), National Archives and Records Administration, College Park, MD [hereafter, FSP]; memorandum, Simon J. Copans to Charles Moffly, 4 March 1953, "The Basis for 'Ici New York' Relay by RDF," restricted memorandum, box 5, FSP; quote from author telephone interview with E. N. Brandt, Bordeaux, Fr., 23 March 2013 [hereafter, Brandt interview].

8. The author filed a Freedom of Information Act (FOIA) request to see whether any prominent U.S. nationals in the employ of the FBS worked directly for the U.S. government, and the response was inconclusive. Ben Smith, a highly visible FBS announcer, who remained with the ORTF for his entire career, had no reported affiliations with the U.S. government. FOIA Request, no. 47717, 26 August 2015; curriculum vitae in E. N. Brandt, interview by James J. Bohning, 1992; Brandt interview; obituary, Robert Carrier, 28 June 2006, *Guardian* (UK); obituary, Robert Carrier, 1 July 2006, *Independent* (UK).

9. Quote in memorandum, Simon J. Copans to Charles Moffly, 4 March 1953, "The Basis for 'Ici New York' Relay by RDF," box 3, FSP; restricted memorandum, 1 April 1953, Charles Moffly, IIA: Payment of Shortwave Rental Charges for VOA Relay of French Radio Information Program, FSP. The two countries split transmission costs. In 1946, the VOA transmitter in Algiers shut down. The relay arrangement is mentioned briefly in Kenneth Carter, "French Broadcasting Today," *Journal of the Association for Education by Radio 7*, no. 3 (1947): 29–30.

10. On postwar anti-American discourse in France and elsewhere in Europe, see, for example, Jessica C. E. Gienow-Hecht, "Always Blame the Americans: Anti-Americanism in Europe in the Twentieth Century," *AHR* Forum, *American Historical Review* 111, no. 4 (2006): 1067–91; Jean-Philippe Mathy, *Extrême-Occident: French Intellectuals and America* (Chicago: University of Chicago Press, 1993); Richard F. Kuisel, *Seducing the French: The Dilemma of Americanization* (Berkeley: University of California Press, 1993).

11. "U.S. Plan for Tangier Radio Stirs Opposition by French," *Christian Science Monitor*, 3 July 1947, 14.

12. On OWI, Armed Forces Radio, and VOA uses of African American popular culture and sounds and symbols of ethno-racial diversity in the United States as an ideological

weapon against fascism and communism, see David W. Stowe, *Swing Changes: Big-Band Jazz in New Deal America* (Cambridge, MA: Harvard University Press, 1994); Lewis A. Erenberg, *Swingin' the Dream: Big Band Jazz and the Rebirth of American Culture* (Chicago: University of Chicago Press, 1998); Penny M. Von Eschen, *Satchmo Blows Up the World: Jazz Ambassadors Play the Cold War* (Cambridge, MA: Harvard University Press, 2004). U.S. officials noted how the program "discusses in a friendly manner American problems and interviews numerous American personalities." Memorandum no. 4271 to the secretary of state, "Transmitting Specific Evidence and Illustrations of the Usefulness of the Activities of the Information and Cultural Program," 3, Paris, 18 January 1946, French Embassy, cat. 842, 2; box 388, FSP.

13. Quotes from Executive Order 9608, Providing for the Termination of the Office of War Information, and for the Disposition of Its Functions and of Certain Functions of the Office of Inter-American Affairs, 31 August 1945, and "Statement by the President upon Signing Order Concerning Government Information Programs," http://trumanlibrary.org/publicpapers/viewpapers.php?pid=127. For a critique of the imperial attributes of postwar U.S. information policies and communications development, see Edward S. Herman and Robert McChesney, "The Rise of the Global Media," in *Planet TV, a Global Television Reader*, ed. Lisa Parks and Shanti Kumar, 21–39 (New York: New York University Press, 2003).

14. "The Basis for *Ici New York* relay by RDF," 3, FSP; International Broadcasting Programs, 30 October 1947, Foreign Service Serial 777, Voice of the United States of America Programs, box 443, FSP.

15. Quote in Nord, *France's New Deal*, 24.

16. De Gaulle fired Guignebert for his criticism of government-controlled broadcasting. See Nord, *France's New Deal*, 115, 338–45; Hélène Eck, "Radio, Culture and Democracy in the Immediate Postwar Period, 1944–50," in *France and the Mass Media*, ed. Brian Rigby and Nicholas Hewitt (London: Palgrave Macmillan, 1991); Robert Prot, *Dictionnaire de la radio* (Grenoble, Fr.: Presses universitaires de Grenoble–Institut national de l'audiovisuel, 1997), 635; Hélène Eck, *La guerre des ondes: histoire des radios de langue française pendant la Deuxième Guerre mondiale* (Paris: A. Colin, 1985); Raymond Kuhn, *The Media in France* (New York: Routledge, 1995), 90–91.

17. Quoted phrase summarizes remarks of Pierre Lazareff, Emil Blan, and Marcel Bleustein-Blanchet in the memorandum "Paris Trip," Fred Bate to William F. Brooks, 14 April 1948, folder 26, box 285, National Broadcasting Company Records, State Historical Society of Wisconsin, Madison, WI [hereafter, NBC-WHS]; Eck quote is from "Radio, Culture and Democracy," 135.

18. Eck, "Radio, Culture and Democracy," 139–40. On the protracted (and mostly unsuccessful) battles to instill a public-mindedness into the RDF, see Christian Brochand and Comité d'histoire de la radiodiffusion, *Histoire générale de la radio et de la télévision en France*, vol. 2, *1944–1974* (Paris: Documentation Française, 1994), 57–69. Some argue that newspapers fared only nominally better in weathering governmental regulation. Jean K. Chalaby, *The De Gaulle Presidency and the Media: Statism and Public Communications* (New York: Palgrave, 2002), 1–19.

19. Prot, *Dictionnaire*, 271–73; No. 4271, unrestricted communication, U.S. Embassy Paris to U.S. Secretary of State, 18 January 1946, box 388, FSP. The document describes Gilson as a "fair and friendly observer of American life."

20. "Via the Shortwaves," *New York Times*, 17 February 1946, 53; "Via Shortwave," *New York Times*, 28 April 1946, X7. Multilingual border areas were an exception to general U.S. listening habits. See, for example, América Rodríguez, "Creating an Audience and Remapping a Nation: A Brief History of U.S. Spanish Language Broadcasting, 1930–1980," *Quarterly Review of Film and Video* 16, nos. 3–4 (1999): 357–74; Dolores Inés Casillas, *Sounds of Belonging: U.S. Spanish-Language Radio and Public Advocacy* (New York: New York University Press, 2014); Gene Fowler, *Border Radio: Quacks, Yodelers, Pitchmen, Psychics, and Other Amazing Broadcasters of the American Airwaves* (Austin: University of Texas Press, 2002).

21. Pierre Crénesse, "Report, 6 October 1949," 5, Culture et communication, Société nationale de la radiodiffusion française, RDF Bureau A du N, cote 870714, Fonds de l'ORTF, Archives nationales, Site de Fontainebleau, Fr. [Hereafter, RDF-NY].

22. "World Magazine to Preach Peace," *New York Times*, 9 June 1938, 21; "Vichy Strips 64 of Citizenship," *New York Times,* 11 June 1942, 7.

23. "France Preps Air Barrage to World with Seg Exchange," *Billboard*, 27 April 1946, 7.

24. Christopher H. Sterling, *Electronic Media: A Guide to Trends in Broadcasting and Newer Technologies, 1920–1983* (New York: Praeger, 1984); David Morton, *Off the Record: The Technology and Culture of Sound Recording in America* (New Brunswick, NJ: Rutgers University Press, 2000); Alex Russo, "Defensive Transcriptions: Radio Networks, Sound-on-Disc Recording, and the Meaning of Live Broadcasting." *Velvet Light Trap* 54 (Fall 2004): 4–17; Stowe, *Swing Changes*, 151–53; "France Wants Yank Air Shows," *Billboard*, 10 April 1948, 4. Some wartime broadcasters used wire-recording technology in the field; John MacVane, *On the Air in World War II* (New York: William Morrow, 1979), 293.

25. "Foreign Lingo's Link-Up," *Billboard*, 25 June 1949, 6. On the major networks' opposition to widespread transcription use, see Morton, *Off the Record*, 48–54.

26. "Plan Radio Interchange," *New York Times*, 25 June 1946, 15; Robert Leiter, *The Musicians and Petrillo* (New York: Bookman, 1953); George Seltzer, *Music Matters: The Performer and the American Federation of Musicians* (Metuchen, NJ: Scarecrow, 1989); Michael James Roberts, *Tell Tchaikovsky the News: Rock 'n' Roll, the Labor Question, and the Musicians' Union, 1942–1968* (Durham, NC: Duke University Press, 2014).

27. "Radio Row: One Thing and Another," *New York Times,* 2 February 1947, X11; "France Preps Air Barrage."

28. The national channel reached the entirety of France and the Parisian channel reached approximately two-thirds of the country (Eck, "Radio, Culture and Democracy," 135–37); confidential OIE memorandum, 3 November 1947, box 58, FSP; secretary of state to the president of the Information Council, "State of expected expenses, payable in dollars, for the first trimester 1947 for the organization and production of special programs retransmitted to the U.S. and Canada," 13 January 1947, article 19, Culture et Communication/Société Nationale de la Radiodiffusion Française/RDF Bureau A du N, cote 870714, Fonds de l'ORTF, Archives nationales site de Fontainebleau, Fr [hereafter FBS-NY].

29. "Com'l Setup Looming as Threat to State-Controlled French Radio," *Variety,* 12 November 1947, 41.

30. Quote in Pierre Crénesse, "Ici Paris . . . radiodiffusion française," *RPM* (1948): 10–11, FBS-NY; Brandt interview; "Gruskin Takes ECA Post for New Drive?" *Billboard,* 19 March 1949, 6.

31. "In 1947, anti-communism was developing in France with fervor equal to if not greater than in Washington" (Irwin M. Wall, *The United States and the Making of Postwar France, 1945–1954* [Cambridge: Cambridge University Press, 1991], 67). During the Fourth Republic, the French parliament included the National Assembly (a lower house) and the Council of the Republic (Senate). See H. R. Kedward, *France and the French: A Modern History* (Woodstock, NY: Overlook, 2006), 317–22, 59; Wall, *The United States and the Making of Postwar France*, 2.

32. "Alleged Scandals in French Ministries," *Manchester Guardian*, 4 January 1949, 8; "French Chambers Close '48 Session," *New York Times*, 3 January 1949, 14.

33. "Paris Radio Execs Fired; Funds Misuse Is Claimed," *Variety*, 19 January 1949, 11.

34. Quote in "Crénesse New Head of French Radio," *Variety*, 17 March 1948, 32; physical description in Lise Elina, *Le micro et moi* (Paris: Pierre Horay, 1978), 101. NBC officials also felt that Crénesse understood the techno-aesthetics of U.S. radio in a way that Lange, a VOA announcer, did not (memorandum "Paris Trip").

35. Andy Lanset, "Ted Cott: WNYC Wunderkind," NYPR Archives and Preservation; list of committee members in Crénesse, "Ici Paris . . . radiodiffusion française," 10.

36. Signed confidential memorandum, 20 January 1948, box 58, FSP. "Troisième Force" (Third Force) referred to the coalition leading the Fourth Republic (1947–1958).

37. "The Basis for *Ici New York* Relay by RDF"; "Les services techniques de la radiodiffusion française, leur activité en 1947," Procès-verbaux du réunion du conseil supérieur de la radiodiffusion française, Conseil supérieur des émissions: 1923–1964 (CSE) 1, 2, 4, ORTF-CAC; Carter, "French Broadcasting Today," 29–32.

38. American Embassy, Paris, to Sec. State, confidential airgram, 13 August 1947; Pierre Crénesse, "Report, 6 October 1948," 5, RDF-NY; correspondence, Stanley F. X. Worris to French Broadcasting System, 27 May 1948, RDF-NY.

39. Quoted in translation in Carter, "French Broadcasting Today," 32.

40. Quote from Acting Secretary of State, Robert Lovett, in 1947 and aid package amounts appear in David F. Krugler, *The Voice of America and the Domestic Propaganda Battles, 1945–1953* (Columbia: University of Missouri Press, 2000), 21, 19. "France accounted for twenty percent of the total financing involved in the Marshall Plan" (Wall, *The United States and the Making of Postwar France*, 75).

41. Data collected by the U.S. attorney general for the U.S. Congress under the "Foreign Agents Registration Act" (FARA) show the FBS as a beneficiary of federal support in the 1950s. See U.S. Department of Justice, "Report of the Attorney General to the Congress of the United States on the Administration of the Foreign Agents Registration Act of 1938, as Amended for the Period January 1, 1950, to December 31, 1954" (Washington, DC: U.S. Department of Justice, 1955). "The Foreign Agents Registration Act (FARA) was enacted in 1938. FARA is a disclosure statute that requires persons acting as agents of foreign principals in a political or quasi-political capacity to make periodic public disclosure of their relationship with the foreign principal, as well as activities, receipts, and disbursements in support of those activities." https://www.fara.gov/.

42. Pierre Crénesse, "La radiodiffusion française en Amérique du Nord," *Radio Informations-Documentation*, no. 11 (December 1949), 5; Foreign Service Operations Memorandum, Projects Bulletin, American Embassy, Paris, to American Consulate General, Marseille, 28 December 1950, "Marseille," box 2, FSP; confidential preliminary report on

ECA-IBD coordination, 21 June 1950, box 4, FSP; Brandt interview. For an analysis of Marshall Plan spending in other economic areas, see Gérard Bossuat, *La France, l'aide américaine et la construction européenne, 1944–1954*, Histoire économique et financière de la France études générales (Paris: Comité pour l'histoire économique et financière de la France, 1992).

43. "France to Increase Radio Service Here," *New York Times*, 27 January 1948, 2; Pierre Crénesse, "Report, 6 October 1949," 2–5, RDF-NY. In the first years, the FBS piloted other series, including *This Week in France* (in which a U.S. journalist residing in France offered commentary and analysis on international events, trends, and French public opinion); miscellaneous "Spots for Women's Shows," produced short pieces to be incorporated into "women's broadcasts" [*émissions féminines*]; and *Farm Letter*, produced for the Rural Radio Network.

44. "Carriage Report, 1949," box 19, RDF-NY; Pierre Crénesse to Jacques Manachem, 8 April 1949, 2, RDF correspondence, RDF-NY; manuscript, Pierre Crénesse, "Radio Executives' Club Luncheon," n.d., ca. summer–fall 1949, RDF-NY; RDF advertisement, *New York Times*, 4 January 1950, 53, RDF-NY.

45. RPM Awards, *RPM, the Radio Programming Magazine*, July 1949, n.p., RDF-NY. See also Alex Surchamp, "Le maillot jaune à la R.D.F.," *La semaine radiophonique*, 14 August 1949, n.p., Fonds Pierre Crénesse, Inathèque, Bibliothèque nationale française, Paris, Fr. [hereafter, PC].

46. Letters appended to 1952 *Annual Report of the French Broadcasting System in North America*, RDF-NY.

47. *RTF Rapport Annuel, 1952*, "Stations NBC diffusant *Stars from Paris*"; correspondence, Bob Wogan to Pierre Crénesse, 6 February 1953, RDF-NY.

48. Pierre Crénesse, "RDF: Link between U.S. and France," *Variety*, 6 January 1954, 102, PC; memorandum, Edmund Souhami to Bob Wogan, 12 October 1953, NBC Wogan—Stars from Paris—1952–54, folder 2, box 356, NBC-WHS.

49. A. M., "Nos meilleures émissions sont entendues aux U.S.A., mais pas en France," *Paris-Presse*, 15 January 1952, n.p., PC. Only Paris-Inter carried any of the FBS programs, which left most of the country unable to listen.

50. Pierre Crénesse, undated and unpublished speech delivered at Radio Executive's Club Luncheon, ca. summer 1949, box 19, RDF-NY; correspondence, Pierre Crénesse to Wladimir Porché, 10 October 1950, box 19, RDF-NY.

51. *Bonjour Mesdames* and *Paris Star Time* aired on Paris-Inter. See, for example, *Téléradio 58* (September 1958), no. 726, du 21.09.58, 33.

52. "Diffusing America," *Newsweek*, 18 April 1949, 61; correspondence, Pierre Crénesse to Wladimir Porché, 7 March 1949. Crénesse explained the IGN exchange component to RDF executives as a way to guarantee that the FBS "could not be attacked by les business men." See Correspondence, Pierre Crénesse to Jacques Manachem, 30 April 1949, RDF-NY.

53. Emphasis added. Speech delivered at National Association of Broadcasters Convention, 16 April 1950, n.p., PC; *RDF News*, IGN, box 14, PC.

54. "Les déguisements de M. Crénesse," *Radio-Liberté*, 14–20 May 1950; Edward Francis Rice-Maximin, *Accommodation and Resistance: The French Left, Indochina, and the Cold War, 1944–1954* (New York: Greenwood, 1986), 78–79. For more on broadcast news and censorship as it affected U.S.–French radio, see chapter 6.

55. Correspondence, Pierre Crénesse to Roger Vaurs, 4 November 1953, RDF-NY. The contents of the reports that Crénesse produced for French listeners are beyond the scope of this study.

56. Correspondence, Pierre Crénesse to Wladimir Porché, 28 April 1952, RDF-NY. Wolfgang Saxon, "Roger Seydoux, French diplomat, dies at 77," 18 July 1985, *New York Times*, A20. In 1949, the RDF became the RTF (Radiodiffusion-télévision française) though many radio broadcasters (as Crénesse did here) continued to refer to the "RDF" by convention or force of habit.

57. Christopher H. Sterling and Michael C. Keith, *Sounds of Change: A History of FM Broadcasting in America* (Chapel Hill: University of North Carolina Press, 2008); Susan Douglas, *Listening In: Radio and the American Imagination* (New York: Times Books, 1999); Michael C. Keith, *Voices in the Purple Haze: Underground Radio and the Sixties* (Westport, CT: Praeger, 1997), 67–99; Matthew Lasar, *Pacifica Radio: The Rise of an Alternative Network* (Philadelphia: Temple University Press, 1999). Ultra-conservatives jumped into the new era of radio, too; see Heather Hendershot, *What's Fair on the Air? Cold War Right-Wing Broadcasting and the Public Interest* (Chicago: University of Chicago Press, 2016). In its postwar report, "Public Service Responsibilities of Broadcast Licensees," also known as the "Blue Book," the Federal Communications Commission (FCC) expressed the view that licensed broadcasters should consider local and nonprofit program initiatives a public-interest concern. See Michele Hilmes, *Network Nations: A Transnational History of British and American Broadcasting* (New York: Routledge, 2012).

58. W. Wayne Alford, *NAEB History*, vol. 2, *1954–1965* (Washington, DC: National Association of Educational Broadcasters, 1966), 16. On the role of the NAEB in public broadcast history, see James Day, *The Vanishing Vision: The Inside Story of Public Television* (Berkeley: University of California Press, 1995); Ralph Engelman, *Public Radio and Television in America: A Political History* (Thousand Oaks, CA: Sage, 1996).

59. On the role of U.S. foundations in supporting cultural initiatives linking the United States and Europe, see Richard H. Pells, *Not like Us: How Europeans Have Loved, Hated, and Transformed American Culture since World War II* (New York: Basic Books, 1997). Biographical information is from Harry J. Skornia Papers, 1937–91, Series 13–6–20, University of Illinois Special Collections, Urbana-Champaign, IL; Alford, *NAEB History*; Jerry M. Landay, "Illinois: The Cradle of Public Broadcasting," *Communications in Illinois History* 14, no. 1 (2007): 3–12.

60. On battles over the political economy of U.S. broadcasting, see Robert W. McChesney, *Telecommunications, Mass Media, and Democracy* (New York: Oxford University Press, 1993). On the politics of public service and localism in tension with the public interest, see Derek Vaillant, "Sounds of Whiteness: Local Radio, Racial Formation, and Public Culture in Chicago, 1921–1935," *American Quarterly* 54, no. 1 (2002): 25–66, and Bill Kirkpatrick, "Localism in American Media Policy, 1920–1934: Reconsidering a 'Bedrock Concept,'" *Radio Journal* 4, nos. 1–3 (October 2006): 87–110.

61. Quote from the preamble to the constitution of the Association of College and University Broadcasting Stations (the forerunner to the NAEB) appears in Harold E. Hill, *The National Association of Educational Broadcasters: A History* (Urbana, IL: National Association of Educational Broadcasters, 1954), 4 [emphasis added].

62. Val Adams, "Education Network," 21 September 1952, *New York Times*, X13; Susan Smulyan, *Selling Radio: The Commercialization of American Broadcasting 1920–1934*

(Washington, DC: Smithsonian Institution Press, 1994); McChesney, *Telecommunications, Mass Media, and Democracy*; Paul Starr, *The Creation of the Media: Political Origins of Modern Communications* (New York: Basic Books, 2004), 357. On regional commercial networks, see Alexander Russo, *Points on the Dial: Golden Age Radio beyond the Networks* (Durham, NC: Duke University Press, 2010).

63. Morton, *Off the Record*, 68; "Ford Grant to Aid Radio Education," *New York Times*, 5 May 1951, 19; Engelman, *Public Radio and Television in America*, 85.

64. Joelle Neulander, *Programming National Identity: The Culture of Radio in 1930s France* (Baton Rouge: Louisiana University Press, 2009), and Nord, *France's New Deal*.

65. A sock offering was industry jargon for an attention-getting project. "News and Notes Gathered from the Studio," *New York Times*, 12 April 1953, X11; "News of TV and Radio," *New York Times*, 7 June 1953, X9; "News of TV and Radio," *New York Times*, 23 August 1953, X9; quote in "C'est Si Bon," *Variety*, 11 March 1953, 26; KPFA Program Folio, 20 September–3 October 1953, vol. 4, no. 19; 13–27 December 1953, vol. 4, no. 19; 21 March–3 April 1954, vol. 4, no. 26.

66. Quote on BFA in Hilmes, *Network Nations*, 239. Hilmes mentions the NAEB's support of the BBC in the United States. The BFA received initial Rockefeller Foundation support as the "Broadcasting Corporation of America." Anne S. Pomex, "America's New Hearing Aid," *ALA Bulletin* 53, no. 9 (1959): 782–83; Pamela K. Doyle, "National Association of Educational Broadcasters," 493–96, Christopher H. Sterling and Cary O'Dell, ed., *The Concise Encyclopedia of American Radio* (New York: Routledge, 2010).

67. "Émissions musicales," Programmes américaines (Ben Smith), CSP 1982, 1356, Direction des Affaires Extérieures et de la Coopération, Section Anglaise Programme Américaine, CSP 1982, 1356, Fonds de l'ORTF, Archives Nationales, Site de Fontainebleau, Fr. [hereafter, DAEC-ORTF].

68. "Conseil des programmes," Informations, no. 8, semaine du 16 au 22 février 1958, SGCC/Synthèses des revues de presse et des rapports d'écoutes effectués par le Contrôle artistique des émissions (CAE): 1956–58, folder 2, box 12, ORTF-CAC; "Programmes américaines (Ben Smith); listes des productions réalisées jusqu'en 1967" and "Premières émissions N.A.E.B.," n.d., Programmes américaines (Ben Smith), CSE 1982, 1356, ORTF-DAEC; NAEB manifest, National Association of Educational Broadcasters (NAEB), National Public Broadcasting Archives, Special Collections, University of Maryland, College Park, MD; Herman W. Land Associates, *The Hidden Medium: Educational Radio, a Status Report on Educational Radio in the United States* (New York: National Association of Educational Broadcasters, 1967). For a general background on public broadcasting, see Hugh Richard Slotten, *Radio's Hidden Voice: The Origins of Public Broadcasting in the United States* (Urbana: University of Illinois Press, 2009).

69. Clare Podetti, *La torture en Algérie à la télévision française, une table ronde animée par Isabelle Veyrat-Masson*, http://www.histoire.ac-versailles.fr/old/magazine/evenements/blois2002/torture.htm. On Europe No1, see https://fr.wikipedia.org/wiki/Europe_1; Kedward, *France and the French*, 456; John L. Hess, "A General Strike to Back Students Starts," *New York Times*, 13 May 1968, 1.

70. In September 1999, the French Assembly established an official retrospective term for the anticolonial struggle in French Algeria, *la guerre d'Algérie* (the Algerian War). Colloquialisms, such as "the war with no name" and "the crisis" were commonly employed in the era. See Kristin Ross, *May '68 and Its Afterlives* (Chicago: University of Chicago Press,

2002), 49; Joshua Cole, "Remembering the Battle of Paris: 17 October 1961 in French and Algerian Memory," *French Politics, Culture and Society* 21, no. 3 (2003): 21–50.

71. "Petites séries," *France and North Africa* (1956), Programmes américaines (Ben Smith), Listes des productions réalisés jusqu'en 1967, CSE 1982, 1356, ORTF-DAEC.

72. "The French Story" (list of episodes), *France and North Africa* (1956), Programmes américaines (Ben Smith), Listes des productions réalisés jusqu'en 1967, CSE 1982, 1356, ORTF-DAEC.

73. In one of thirteen episodes dedicated to French folk music (*The Land of France Sings*, produced in 1956), there were regional treatments of folk music, work songs, love songs, dancing songs, and even Christmas songs. There was a single exploration of songs of Muslim Africa and black French Africa (*Chants de l'Afrique musulmane et de l'Afrique noire françaises*), *France and North Africa* (1956), Programmes américaines (Ben Smith), Listes des productions réalisés jusqu'en 1967, CSE 1982, 1356, ORTF-DAEC.

74. Engelman, *Public Radio and Television in America*, 89.

Chapter 5. The Air of Paris: Women's Talk Radio, Gender, and the Art of Self-Fashioning

1. *Bonjour Mesdames*, produced summer 1948, episode 5, segment 1, The French Broadcasting Service in North America (FBS), J. David Goldin Collection, Marr Sound Archives, University of Missouri–Kansas City [hereafter, Marr Archives]. All quoted passages attributed to the program are from my written transcriptions of recordings of the series. I auditioned a randomly selected assortment of forty episodes of the series across its peak years of activity (1948–60) comprising a total of 120 segments. The FBS series aired at the discretion of the individual station. There is no national "air date" for any given program. For each segment and episode quoted, I provide the fullest citation information for the recording on the basis of the cataloguing information furnished by the different collecting institutions I approached to obtain copies of FBS programs.

2. Ibid. "Bonnie Cashin," *Los Angeles Times*, 3 September 1948, B1; Enid Nemy, "Bonnie Cashin, Who Helped Introduce Sportswear to Americans, Is Dead," *New York Times*, 5 February 2000, C16.

3. Caroline Evans, *The Mechanical Smile: Modernism and the First Fashion Shows in France and America, 1900–1929* (New Haven, CT: Yale University Press); Alexandra Palmer and Royal Ontario Museum, *Couture and Commerce: The Transatlantic Fashion Trade in the 1950s* (Vancouver, BC: UBC Press, 2001); Steve Zdatny, *Fashion, Work, and Politics in Modern France* (New York: Palgrave Macmillan, 2006).

4. Harvey A. Levenstein notes that U.S. travelers made France their top destination for overseas tourism for the bulk of the twentieth century partly because of heavy promotional campaigns underwritten by the French (Harvey A. Levenstein, *Seductive Journey: American Tourists in France from Jefferson to the Jazz Age* [Chicago: University of Chicago Press, 1998]). See also Harvey A. Levenstein, *We'll Always Have Paris: American Tourists in France since 1930* (Chicago: University of Chicago Press, 2004), ix–xi; Alice Yaeger Kaplan, *Dreaming in French: The Paris Years of Jacqueline Bouvier Kennedy, Susan Sontag, and Angela Davis* (Chicago: University of Chicago Press, 2012).

5. Such thematic concerns typified the campaigns of the French Mission of the Marshall Plan's Economic Cooperation Administration (ECA). See Brian Angus McKenzie,

Remaking France: Americanization, Public Diplomacy, and the Marshall Plan (New York: Berghahn, 2005), 197–99.

6. Quote is from Joanne Meyerowitz, "Beyond the Feminine Mystique: A Reassessment of Postwar Mass Culture," *Journal of American History* 79, no. 4 (1993): 1480.

7. I draw on the concept of aesthetic reflexivity after Ulrich Beck, Anthony Giddens, and Scott Lash, *Reflexive Modernization: Politics, Tradition and Aesthetics in the Modern Social Order.* (Stanford, CA: Stanford University Press, 1994), and Tia DeNora, *Music in Everyday Life* (Cambridge: Cambridge University Press, 2000).

8. On the conceptual tension and variations between the nineteenth-century, U.S.-made "new woman" and the cosmopolitan "modern girl," see Alys Eve Weinbaum and Modern Girl around the World Research Group, *The Modern Girl around the World: Consumption, Modernity, and Globalization* (Durham, NC: Duke University Press, 2008); Christine Stansell, *American Moderns: Bohemian New York and the Creation of a New Century* (New York: Metropolitan, 2000); and Kathy Lee Peiss, *Hope in a Jar: The Making of America's Beauty Culture* (New York: Metropolitan, 1998). A key synthesis of the politics of consumption and nationalism is Lizabeth Cohen, *A Consumer's Republic: The Politics of Mass Consumption in Postwar America* (New York: Knopf, 2003). Thanks to Edward Timke for directing me to the Modern Girl project.

9. Quote in Ann Laura Stoler, "Intimidations of Empire: Predicaments of the Tactile and Unseen," in *Haunted by Empire Geographies of Intimacy in North American History,* ed. Ann Laura Stoler (Durham, NC: Duke University Press, 2006), 4. On the intersections of gender, race, and sexuality in national discourse and French history, see Rogers Brubaker, *Citizenship and Nationhood in France and Germany* (Cambridge, MA: Harvard University Press, 1992); Gérard Noiriel, *The French Melting Pot: Immigration, Citizenship, and National Identity,* trans. Geoffrey de Laforcade (Minneapolis: University of Minnesota Press, 1986); Todd Shepard, *The Invention of Decolonization: The Algerian War and the Remaking of France* (Ithaca, NY: Cornell University Press, 2006); Patrick Weil and Catherine Porter, *How to Be French: Nationality in the Making since 1789* (Durham, NC: Duke University Press, 2008).

10. For an overview of ethnocentric racism in French history, see Herrick Chapman and Laura L. Frader, ed., *Race in France: Interdisciplinary Perspectives on the Politics of Difference* (New York: Berghahn, 2004), and Frederick Cooper and Ann Laura Stoler, ed., *Tensions of Empire: Colonial Cultures in a Bourgeois World* (Berkeley: University of California Press, 1997). On the history and exclusionary aspects of the French fashion industry, see Evans, *Mechanical Smile.* On primitivism and racial formation in France, see Bennetta Jules-Rosette, *Josephine Baker in Art and Life: The Icon and the Image* (Urbana: University of Illinois Press, 2006). On the place of French tourism in these vexed issues, see especially Ellen Furlough, "*Une Leçon des Choses*: Tourism, Empire, and the Nation in Interwar France," *French Historical Studies* 25, no. 3 (2002): 441–73.

11. The classic work on the subject of radio and listening is Rudolf Arnheim et al., *Radio* (London: Faber and Faber, 1936). I have immersed myself in the aural text. I listen (as one might read) for a "preferred narrative" that structures, but does not necessarily determine, the possible interpretations of the text by the audience. Through such "close listening," I have tried to enter into the historical worlds of the listener as well as the speaker. On the history of close reading, see Terry Eagleton, *Literary Theory: An Introduction* (Minneapolis: University of Minnesota Press, 1983); Stuart Hall, "Encoding/Decoding," in

Culture, Media, Language, ed. Stuart Hall, Dorothy Hobson, Andrew Lowe, and Paul Willis (London: Hutchinson, 1980).

12. On gender, women, and the U.S. home front, see Elaine Tyler May, *Homeward Bound: American Families in the Cold War Era* (New York: Basic Books, 1988); Joanne Meyerowitz, *Not June Cleaver: Women and Gender in Postwar America, 1945–1960* (Chicago: University of Chicago Press); Maureen Honey, *Creating Rosie the Riveter: Class, Gender, and Propaganda during World War II* (Amherst: University of Massachusetts Press, 1984). On gender politics and the Occupation as interlinked phenomena, see Hanna Diamond, *Women and the Second World War in France, 1939–1948* (New York: Longman, 1999); Julian Jackson, *France: The Dark Years, 1940–1944* (New York: Oxford University Press, 2001); Mary Louise Roberts, *What Soldiers Do: Sex and the American GI in World War II France* (Philadelphia: Temple University Press, 1994). Hanna Diamond also considers the varied forms of French women's agency whether working for the Resistance or as collaborators: Hanna Diamond and Simon Kitson, ed., *Vichy, Resistance, Liberation: New Perspectives on Wartime France* (New York: Berg, 2005).

13. Estimates of the number of "femmes tondues" appears in Jackson, *France,* 581. On women's politics and place during the Occupation, see Hanna Diamond, *Women and the Second World War in France, 1939–48: Choices and Constraints* (New York: Longman, 1999); Hanna Diamond, "A New Dawn? French Women and the Liberation," *Women's Studies International Forum* 23, no. 6 (2000): 729–73.

14. On gender and the politics of modern French national identity, see, for example, Elisa Camiscioli, *Reproducing the French Race: Immigration, Intimacy, and Embodiment in the Early Twentieth Century* (Durham, NC: Duke University Press, 2009), and Edward E. Timke, "Cherchez la Femme: Franco-American Relations through Popular Magazines' Representations of French and American Women, 1945–1965" (PhD dissertation, University of Michigan, 2015).

15. On women's programs in the history of U.S. broadcasting, see Katherine Jellison, *Entitled to Power: Farm Women and Technology, 1913–1963* (Chapel Hill: University of North Carolina Press, 1993); Susan Smulyan, *Selling Radio: The Commercialization of American Broadcasting 1920–1934* (Washington, DC: Smithsonian Institution Press, 1994); Lesley Johnson, "Radio and Everyday Life the Early Years of Broadcasting in Australia, 1922–1945," *Media, Culture and Society,* no. 3 (1981): 167–78; Kate Lacey, *Feminine Frequencies: Gender, German Radio, and the Public Sphere, 1923–1945* (Ann Arbor: University of Michigan Press, 1996); Peter Behrens, "Psychology Takes to the Airwaves: American Radio Psychology between the Wars, 1926–1939," *American Sociologist* 40, no. 3 (2009): 214–27. On "domestication strategy," see Richard Butsch, "Crystal Sets and Scarf-Pin Radios: Gender, Technology and the Construction of American Radio Listening in the 1920s," *Media, Culture and Society* 20, no. 4 (1998), 558. On denigration of women's programs, see Smulyan, *Selling Radio*; Michele Hilmes, *Radio Voices: American Broadcasting, 1922–1952* (Minneapolis: University of Minnesota Press, 1997), 130–50, 271–83. On women and the BBC, see Michele Hilmes, *Network Nations: A Transnational History of British and American Broadcasting* (New York: Routledge, 2012). On interwar programs for French women, see Joelle Neulander, *Programming National Identity: The Culture of Radio in 1930s France* (Baton Rouge: Louisiana University Press, 2009). On the rise of a therapeutic discourse in women's radio programs for listeners on Radio Luxembourg in

the late 1960s, see Judith G. Coffin, "From Interiority to Intimacy: Psychoanalysis and Radio in Twentieth-Century France," *Cultural Critique* 91 (Fall 2005): 114–49.

16. Susan Smulyan, "Radio Advertising to Women in Twenties America: 'A Latchkey to Every Home,'" *Historical Journal of Film, Radio, and Television* 13, no. 3 (1993): 299–314; Roland Marchand, *Advertising the American Dream: Making Way for Modernity, 1920–1940* (Berkeley: University of California Press, 1985); Hilmes, *Radio Voices*, 130–50.

17. Lacey, *Feminine Frequencies*; Neulander, *Programming National Identity*, 99–112; 128–59. On women's programs outside the United States, see, for example, Justine Lloyd, "Intimate Empire: Radio Programming for Women in Postwar Australia and Canada," *Storytelling* 6, no. 2 (2007): 131–39; and Christine Ehrick, *Radio and the Gendered Soundscape: Women and Broadcasting in Argentina and Uruguay, 1930–1950* (New York: Cambridge University Press, 2015). In 1946, the BBC launched *Woman's Hour*, a national program produced and hosted by Englishwomen for other Englishwomen. See David Hendy, *Life on Air: A History of Radio Four* (Oxford, UK: Oxford University Press, 2007).

18. *Programmes de Paris Mondial*, January 1939.

19. Sources indicate that Dunton left Canada in 1928 or 1929. Margaret Ecker, "Oshawa Girl Important in Parisian Society," [Toronto] *Globe and Mail*, 11 May 1945, 10; Eva Lis Wuorio, "Poem Is Turning Point Designing to Broadcasts," [Toronto] *Globe and Mail*, 24 December 1945, 8.

20. Edith Thornton McLeod, "Beauty after Forty, Voices from Foreign Shores," *Pittsburgh Press*, May 8 1951, 26; Ecker, "Oshawa Girl Important"; "Parisian-Made Femme Spots Prepped for U.S.," *Variety*, 2 March 1949, 26.

21. Elizabeth Turnell, "An NAEBer Visits the French Broadcasting System," *NAEB Newsletter* 123, no. 3 (1964): 28–33.

22. Untitled article, *Chicago Daily News*, 27 June 1956, A4; Pamela Wilde Garroway, "I Married Dave Garroway," *Washington Post*, 8 March 1959, AW3.

23. E. N. Brandt interview, 22 March 2013, Bordeaux, France [hereafter, Brandt interview].

24. Quoted in Lotta Dempsey, "Person to Person," 4 April 1949, 16; Brandt interview.

25. FBS Annual Report, Carriage data, 1949, box 19, Culture et communication/Société nationale de la radiodiffusion française/RDF Bureau A du N, cote 870714, Archives nationales, Site de Fontainebleau, Fr.

26. Modern audience measurement techniques arrived in France after the war, but the RDF did not poll in the United States. See Cécile Méadel, "The Arrival of Opinion Polls in French Radio and Television 1945–1960," in *France and the Mass Media*, ed. B. Rigby and N. Hewitt (Basingstoke, UK: Macmillan, 1991), 147–76.

27. *Bonjour Mesdames*, [9 June 1949?], segment 3, episode 7, Marr Archives.

28. Quotes from *Bonjour Mesdames*, [10 June 1949?], segments 1, 2, episode 8, Marr Archives; Margaret Ecker, "Oshawa Girl Important in Parisian Society"; Eva Lis Wuorio, "Poem Is Turning Point Designing to Broadcasts."

29. *Bonjour Mesdames*, [10 June 1949?], segments 1, 2, episode 8, Marr Archives;

30. Ibid.

31. *Bonjour Mesdames*, [10 June 1949?], segment 3, episode 8, DG 41976, Marr Archives.

32. *Bonjour Mesdames*, n.d., side A, program 529, Gotham Recording Company (GRC) 5996, Institut national de l'audiovisuel de France (Inathèque), Bibliothèque nationale de France, Paris, Fr. [hereafter, INA]

33. Ibid.

34. *Bonjour Mesdames*, handwritten on label, 12 August 1949, segment 2, episode 5, Marr Archives; *Bonjour Mesdames*, handwritten on label, 12 August 1949?, program no. 19, Marr Archives; *Bonjour Mesdames*, n.d., 1–49/11438, Historical Music Recordings Collection, University of Texas at Austin Libraries [hereafter, HMRC].

35. *Bonjour Mesdames*, n.d., 1–49/11438, HMRC.

36. *Bonjour Mesdames*, 15–49/11677, HMRC.

37. *Bonjour Mesdames*, handwritten date of 8 June 1948, segment 1, episode 6, Marr Archives.

38. Steve Craig, "'The Farmer's Friend': Radio Comes to Rural America, 1920–1927," *Journal of Radio Studies* 8, no. 2 (2001): 330–46; Jellison, *Entitled to Power*; Smulyan, *Selling Radio*.

39. https://eca.state.gov/fulbright/frequently-asked-questions; Levenstein, *Seductive Journey*; Levenstein, *We'll Always Have Paris*; Christopher Endy, *Cold War Holidays: American Tourism in France* (Chapel Hill: University of North Carolina Press, 2004); Kaplan, *Dreaming in French*. Quote in Whitney Walton, *Internationalism, National Identities, and Study Abroad: France and the United States, 1890–1970* (Stanford, CA: Stanford University Press, 2010), 86. As these experts also note, the French had commensurate concerns about promiscuous and aggressive U.S. women and men.

40. On gender politics and U.S. and French women's magazines, see Carolyn L. Kitch, *The Girl on the Magazine Cover: The Origins of Visual Stereotypes in American Mass Media* (Chapel Hill: University of North Carolina Press, 2001); Timke, "Cherchez la Femme." On Dunton's divorce, see Lotta Dempsey, "Person to Person—Canadian Once Arrested for Singing Lord's Prayer," 4 April 1949, 16.

41. *Bonjour Mesdames*, 69/12893, segment 3, episode 2, HMRC.

42. *Bonjour Mesdames*, 8 June 1949, segments 2 and 3, episode 6, Marr Archives.

43. Kathy Davis, "Beauty (the Feminine Beauty System)," in *Encyclopedia of Feminist Theories* (New York: Routledge, 2000), 38–39.

44. Beth Montemurro, Jennifer Bartasavich, and Leanne Wintermute, "Let's (Not) Talk about Sex: The Gender of Sexual Discourse," *Sexuality and Culture* 19, no. 1 (2015): 139.

45. *Bonjour Mesdames*, handwritten date of 7 June 1949, segment 3, episode 5, Marr Archives.

46. *Bonjour Mesdames*, handwritten date of 10 June 1949, segment 2, episode 7, HMRC.

47. "Jacques Heim," http://www.fashionencyclopedia.com/Ha-Ja/Heim-Jacques .html; "Jacques Heim, Couturier, Is Dead," *New York Times*, 9 January 1967, 36; *Bonjour Mesdames*, handwritten date of 13 June 1949, BL11290 (matrix), program no. 9, Marr Archives.

48. This segment is not typical, but it resembled to some extent the subsequent genre of "makeover" television programs of the 1990s and since, which critics have shown mobilized gender and sexual norms, often using rigid binaries of right and wrong to police boundaries. See Brenda R. Weber, *Makeover TV: Selfhood, Citizenship, and Celebrity* (Durham, NC: Duke University Press, 2009); and Katherine Sender, *The Makeover: Reality Television and Reflexive Audiences* (New York: New York University Press, 2012).

49. *Bonjour Mesdames*, handwritten date of 8 June 1949, segment 1, episode 6, DG 43726, Marr Archives.

50. Indexed liner notes, *Bonjour Mesdames*, 31 August 1949?, program 2, DG 43726, Marr Archives.

51. I acknowledge the difficulties of identity categories in relation to historical sexual practices. I use "same-sex" to include homosexual and lesbian populations after the historical typologies of John D'Emilio and Estelle B. Freedman, *Intimate Matters: A History of Sexuality in America* (New York: Harper and Row, 1988); Lillian Faderman, *Odd Girls and Twilight Lovers: A History of Lesbian Life in Twentieth-Century America* (New York: Columbia University Press, 1991); George Chauncey, *Gay New York: Gender, Urban Culture, and the Making of the Gay Male World, 1890–1940* (New York: Basic Books, 1994).

52. On early modern bohemianism as a national and transnational formation, see, for example, Christine Stansell, *American Moderns: Bohemian New York and the Creation of a New Century* (New York: Metropolitan, 2000). On Paris same-sex history and culture, see Scott Eric Gunther, *The Elastic Closet: A History of Homosexuality in France, 1942–Present* (New York: Palgrave, 2009); Julian Jackson, "Sex, Politics and Morality in France, 1954–1982," *History Workshop Journal* 61, no. 1 (2006): 77–102; Florence Tamagne, "Paris: 'Resting on Its Laurels?'" in *Queer Cities, Queer Cultures: Europe since 1945*, ed. Jennifer V. Evans and Matt Cook, 240–60 (London: Bloomsbury, 2014).

53. On favored haunts of U.S. travelers seeking "sexual adventures," including same-sex encounters, see Brooke Lindy Blower, *Becoming Americans in Paris: Transatlantic Politics and Culture between the World Wars* (New York: Oxford University Press, 2011), 137–43.

54. Robert Aldrich, "Homosexuality and the City: An Historical Overview," *Urban Studies* 41, no. 9 (2004): 1719–37; Sophie Body-Gendrot, "If France Didn't Exist, Americans Would Have to Invent It," *French Politics, Culture and Society* 21, no. 2 (2003): 8–23; Michael Sibalis, "Review Essay: Homosexuality in France," *French Politics, Culture and Society* 19, no. 3 (2001): 108–19.

55. On Montparnasse and the Left Bank's significance to cultural modernism in the interwar era, see, for example, Janet Flanner, *Paris Was Yesterday, 1925–1939* (New York: Viking, 1972); Tyler Edward Stovall, *Transnational France: The Modern History of a Universal Nation* (Boulder, CO: Westview, 2015), 298–301; and Charles Rearick, *The French in Love and War: Popular Culture in the Era of the World Wars* (New Haven, CT: Yale University Press, 1997). African American intellectuals, writers, musicians, and others had a special relationship with Paris. See Tyler Stovall, *Paris Noir: African Americans in the City of Light* (Boston: Houghton Mifflin, 1996), and James Baldwin, *Collected Essays* (New York: Library of America, 1998). Paris also nurtured "black urban enclaves" where "transnational black activism" flourished. See Kevin K. Gaines, *African Americans in Ghana* (Chapel Hill: University of North Carolina Press, 2006), 29.

56. George Chauncey writes, "The government dismissed more homosexuals than Communists at the height of the McCarthy era" (Chauncey, *Why Marriage? The History Shaping Today's Debate over Gay Equality* [Cambridge, MA: Basic Books, 2004], 4–9, quote 12]; John D'Emilio, "The Homosexual Menace: The Politics of Sexuality in Cold War America," in *Passion and Power*, ed. Kathy Peiss and Christina Simmons, 226–40 (Philadelphia: Temple University Press, 1989); Allan Bérubé, *Coming Out under Fire: The History of Gay Men and Women in World War Two* (New York: Free Press, 1990); David K. Johnson, *The Lavender Scare: The Cold War Persecution of Gays and Lesbians in the Federal Government* (Chicago: University of Chicago Press, 2004); Robert J. Corber,

Homosexuality in Cold War America: Resistance and the Crisis of Masculinity (Durham, NC: Duke University Press, 1997).

57. On the fashion industry and men's place within it, see Richard Dyer, *The Culture of Queers* (New York: Routledge, 2002).

58. GLBT studies of aural performance, talking, and singing draw on a broad and interdisciplinary literature to perform queer readings of spoken and sung performances that stretch gender norms. I am not aware of an agreed-upon single method to pursue in critical listening to gender nonconformism, but some reference points in extant literature are Naomi Adele André, *Voicing Gender: Castrati, Travesti, and the Second Woman in Early-Nineteenth-Century Italian Opera* (Bloomington: Indiana University Press, 2006); Nina Sun Eidsheim, *Sensing Sound Singing and Listening as Vibrational Practice* (Durham, NC: Duke University Press, 2015); Philip Brett, Elizabeth Wood, and Gary C. Thomas, *Queering the Pitch: The New Gay and Lesbian Musicology* (New York: Routledge, 2006); Wayne Koestenbaum, *The Queen's Throat: Opera, Homosexuality, and the Mystery of Desire* (New York: Poseidon, 1993); Keith Howes, *Broadcasting It: An Encyclopaedia of Homosexuality on Film, Radio and TV in the UK, 1923–1993* (New York: Cassell, 1993); Ian Hutchby, *Confrontation Talk: Arguments, Asymmetries, and Power on Talk Radio* (Mahwah, NJ: Lawrence Erlbaum, 1996); Johanna Rendle-Short, "'I've Got a Paper-Shuffler for a Husband': Indexing Sexuality on Talk-Back Radio," *Discourse Society* 16, no. 4 (2005): 561–78; Susan J. Douglas, "Letting the Boys Be Boys: Talk Radio, Male Hysteria, and Political Discourse in the 1980s," in *Radio Reader: Essays in the Cultural History of Radio*, ed. Michele Hilmes and Jason Loviglio (New York: Routledge, 2002), 485–504; Judith Butler, *Gender Trouble: Feminism and the Subversion of Identity* (New York: Routledge, 1990).

59. Brandt interview; Michael Taylor, "Scott Beach, San Francisco Radio Commentator, Bon Vivant," *SF Gate*, 14 February 1996; obituary, *Independent*, 1 July 2006, http://www .independent.co.uk/news/obituaries/robert-carrier-406180.html; obituary, *Telegraph* (UK), 28 June 2006, http://www.telegraph.co.uk/news/obituaries/1522477/Robert-Carrier.html.

60. E. N. Brandt, interview by James J. Bohning, 1992; obituary, *Independent*, 1 July 2006, http://www.independent.co.uk/news/obituaries/robert-carrier-406180.html; obituary, *Telegraph* (UK), 28 June 2006, http://www.telegraph.co.uk/news/obituaries/1522477/ Robert-Carrier.html.

61. *Bonjour Mesdames*, winter 1955, 3524/1.1, HMRC; Taylor, "Scott Beach."

62. Herman Lebovics, *True France: The Wars over Cultural Identity, 1900–1945* (Ithaca, NY: Cornell University Press, 1992). On the post–World War II political complexities of defining terms of identity, parameters of inclusion, exclusion, and differentiation among and between metropolitan France, French citizens, and African-born French people during the era of decolonization and African independence, see, in particular, Frederick Cooper, *Citizenship between Empire and Nation, Remaking France and French Africa, 1945–1960* (Princeton, NJ: Princeton University Press, 2014); Shepard, *Invention of Decolonization*; Irwin M. Wall, *France, the United States, and the Algerian War* (Berkeley: University of California Press, 2001).

63. Rod Kedward, *France and the French* (New York: Overlook Press, 2005), 338–43.

64. Sophie Bachmann, *L'éclatement de l'ORTF: la réforme de la délivrance* (Paris: Harmattan, 1997), 17.

Chapter 6. *The Drama of Broadcast History after May 1968*

1. Pierre-Christian Renard, "À l'angle de l'Odéon," *De la Bastille à l'Arc de Triomphe*," ed. Pierre-Christian Renard (Paris: ORTF-DAEC-Variétés culturelles), 1970, 1. Direction des affaires extérieures et de la coopération, Section anglaise programme américaine, CSP 1982, 1192, cote 910122, Fonds de l'ORTF, Archives nationales, Site de Fontainebleau, Fr. [hereafter, ORTF-DAEC].

2. ORTF/DAEC programs were heard in twelve other English-speaking countries on twenty-seven stations, twelve of which were in Canada. "Analyse de la diffusion aux USA," 8 December 1971, Courrier USA, 1968 à 1972 et quelques documents datant de 1965/1966, DAEC, 1280/xre 1980, 2678, cote 20090288, Fonds ORTF, Archives Nationales, Site de Pierrefitte-sur-Seine, Fr. [hereafter, Courrier USA]. The vast literature on the sixties in the United States treats U.S. college campuses as a key locus of political and cultural action; see, for example, Allen J. Matusow, *The Unraveling of America: A History of Liberalism in the 1960s* (New York: Harper and Row, 1984); Todd Gitlin, *The Sixties: Years of Hope, Days of Rage* (New York: Bantam, 1987); David R. Farber, *The Sixties: From Memory to History* (Chapel Hill: University of North Carolina Press, 1994); M. J. Heale, "The Sixties as History," *Reviews in American History* 33, no. 1 (March 2005): 133–52.

3. This chapter is based on analysis of scripts of 234 episodes of eighteen long-form drama series produced by DAEC for U.S. audiences, which are part of the Fonds de l'ORTF in Paris.

4. Pierre Bourdieu, *Distinction: A Social Critique of the Judgment of Taste* (Cambridge, MA: Harvard University Press, 1984), xii. On U.S. public media's shortcomings, see, for example, Laurie Ouellette, *Viewers like You? How Public TV Failed the People* (New Brunswick, NJ: Rutgers University Press, 2002).

5. I find the distinction between an oppositional and an alternative culture useful in conceptualizing these dramas as resistant acts. See Raymond Williams, *Problems in Materialism and Culture: Selected Essays* (London: Verso, 1980), 40.

6. The literature on May 1968 is daunting and vast. One point of entry is Julian Jackson, "Review Article: The Mystery of May 1968," *French Historical Studies* 33, no. 4 (2010), 625–53. See also, for instance, H. R. Kedward, *France and the French: A Modern History* (Woodstock, NY: Overlook, 2006), 418–23; Pascal Ory, *L'entre-deux-Mai: histoire culturelle de la France, Mai 1968–Mai 1981* (Paris: Seuil, 1983), and Kristin Ross, *May '68 and Its Afterlives* (Chicago: University of Chicago Press, 2002). On the ORTF and May 1968, see Comité d'histoire de la radiodiffusion, ed., *Mai 68 à l'ORTF* (Paris: Documentation française/INA, 1987); Jean-Jacques Cheval, "Mai 68, un entre deux dans l'histoire des médias et de la radio en France," *Site Internet du GRER* (2009); J. J. Ledos, "Mai 68: l'ORTF dans l'œil du cyclone: souvenirs d'ancien combattant," *Gavroche* 17, no. 99–100 (1998): 21–25.

7. Jackson, "Review Article: The Mystery of May 1968"; Kedward, *France and the French*, 418–23; Ross, *May '68 and Its Afterlives*.

8. Quote from Bruno Leroux and Janine Antoine, "1944 et 1958, une liberté surveillée." In *La radio dans la vie politique française*, broadcast transcription by Taos Aït Si Slimane, http://www.fabriquedesens.net/La-radio-entre-1944-et-1958-une: France Culture, 1985.

9. Jérôme Bourdon, *Histoire de la télévision sous de Gaulle* (Paris: Anthropos/INA, 1990); Raymond Kuhn, *The Media in France* (New York: Routledge, 1995); Michèle de Bussierre, Cécile Méadel, and Caroline Ulmann-Mauriat, ed., *Radios et télévision au*

temps des "événements d'Algérie:" 1954–1962 (Paris: Harmattan, 1999); Jean K. Chalaby, *The de Gaulle Presidency and the Media: Statism and Public Communications* (New York: Palgrave, 2002), 95–96; Christian Brochand and Comité d'histoire de la radiodiffusion, *Histoire générale de la radio et de la télévision en France*, vol. 2, *1944–1974* (Paris: Documentation française, 1994). On PTT press screening, see André-Jean Tudesq, "L'utilisation gouvernementale de la radio," in *Édouard Daladier, chef de gouvernement*, ed. René Rémond and Janine Bourdin, 255–64 (Paris: Presses de la Fondation Nationale des Sciences Politiques, 1977).

10. Thierry Lefebvre, "Vers un changement de paradigme radiophonique?" in *Histoire de la radio, Ouvrez grand vos oreilles!* ed. Musée des arts et métiers and l'Institut national de l'audiovisuel (Paris: Silvana, 2012), 61.

11. Chalaby, *De Gaulle Presidency*, 87–89.

12. Kedward, *France and the French,* 422; Kuhn, *Media in France*.

13. The government cynically attacked independent broadcasters for inflaming the public "under the pretext of informing [it]." The commercial stations covering the protests earned the title of "barricades radio" *(radios barricades).* There were also independent broadcasters using shortwave and other radio communications to report from the scene. See also Lefebvre, "Vers un changement," 61–63. On *radios barricades,* see also *Le Grand Robert en-ligne,* http://www.lerobert.com/le-grand-robert/ [subscription required]. On Europe No1, see https://fr.wikipedia.org/wiki/Europe_1; Kedward, *France and the French*, 456; John L. Hess, "A General Strike to Back Students Starts," *New York Times*, 13 May 1968, 1.

14. Comité d'histoire de la radiodiffusion, ed., *Mai 68 à l'ORTF*; Cheval, "Mai 68"; Ledos, "Mai 68"; Louis Nevin, "Strikes Spread over France," *Atlanta Constitution,* 18 May 1968, 1. Quote in Don Cook, "De Gaulle Has a Way with TV," *Los Angeles Times*, 9 August 1968, B2A. On the particulars at the ORTF during the crisis, see Jean-Pierre Filiu, *Mai 68 à l'ORTF* (Paris: Nouveau Monde, 2008).

15. "La diffusion internationale des programmes radiophoniques," and Annex Bb and Cb to report, n.p. Budget figure on p. 29 of report draft, 451, 2, Dépôt d'André-Jean Tudesq, Archives départementales de la Gironde, Bordeaux, Fr.

16. Douglas Siler, email correspondence with the author, 11 June 2012 and 14 November 2014. Siler worked for the ORTF translating plays for several dramatic series in the mid-1960s.

17. Pierre Christian Renard, "À la porte de la conciergerie," *De la Bastille à l'Arc de Triomphe*, ed. Pierre-Christian Renard (Paris: ORTF-DAEC-Variétés Culturelles, 1970), 11, ORTF-DAEC.

18. Renard, "Autour de la Prison du Temple," 4.

19. Ibid., 18.

20. Ibid.

21. Ibid., 14.

22. Renard, "Au coin du Pont-Neuf," 6.

23. Renard, "Autour de la Prison du Temple," 4.

24. Bernard Véron, "La Normandie," *Légendes et merveilles*, ed. Pierre-Christian Renard (Paris: ORTF-DAEC-Variétés culturelles, 1969), 5–14.

25. Alain Franck, "Bretagne," *Légendes et merveilles*, 27–29.

26. The cemetery is the largest for U.S. soldiers in Europe. The fourteen thousand occupied graves are a fraction of those originally dug there. See http://battlefields1418.50megs.com/meuse_argonne_cemetery.htm.

27. Alain Franck, "Lorraine et Champagne," *Légendes et merveilles*, 14. The "boneyard of Douaumont" is an ossuary and memorial for the unidentified hundreds of thousands of French and German fighters who died at Verdun. The "bayonets trench" is another site, whose exact history is debated, but which sustains a legend of troops poised with bayonets as Jack described, http://www.verdun-douaumont.com/?lang=en.

28. Alain Franck, "Savoie-Dauphine," *Légendes et merveilles*, 14–15. On the event, see Julian Jackson, *France: The Dark Years, 1940–1944* (New York: Oxford University Press, 2001).

29. James B. Roberts and Alexander G. Skutt, *The Boxing Register, International Boxing Hall of Fame Official Record Book* (Ithaca, NY: McBooks, 2006), 338–41; Philip Dine, "Shaping the Colonial Body: Sport and Society in Algeria, 1870–1962," in *Algeria and France 1800–2000 Identity Memory Nostalgia*, ed. Patricia M. E. Lorcin (Syracuse, NY: Syracuse University Press, 2006), 33–48.

30. Bernard Véron, "Marcel Cerdan," *Plus haut, plus loin, plus vite*, ed. Christiane Mallarmé (Paris: ORTF-DAEC-Émission dramatique, 1970), 3, ORTF-DAEC. Emphasis added.

31. Ibid., 5.

32. Ibid., 5, 15.

33. Ibid., 18.

34. Ibid., 21.

35. Ibid., 24.

36. Dine, "Shaping the Colonial Body," 47.

37. Bernard Véron, "Alain Mimoun," in *Plus haut, plus loin, plus vite*, 10.

38. Raphaël Pujazon was born in El Campillo, Spain.

39. Véron, "Alain Mimoun," in *Plus haut, plus loin, plus vite*, 11–12. Clermont-Ferrand lies close to the geographic center of metropolitan France, giving a native son special bragging rights.

40. "Just before recording this program I met Mimoun in his lovely home, which is named, of course, Olympe" (Véron, "Alain Mimoun," in *Plus haut, plus loin, plus vite*, 30).

41. See http://en.wikipedia.org/wiki/Pierre_de_Coubertin and "Pierre, baron de Coubertin," *Encyclopædia Britannica: Encyclopædia Britannica Online Academic Edition* (Chicago: Encyclopædia Britannica, 2013), https://www.britannica.com/biography/Pierre-baron-de-Coubertin.

42. Véron, "Pierre de Coubertin," in *Plus haut, plus loin, plus vite*, 5–6.

43. Coubertin changed the bylaws of the Olympic organization specifically to permit workers' participation (ibid.).

44. Véron, "Alain Gerbault," in *Plus haut, plus loin, plus vite*, 13.

45. Véron, "Émile Allais," in *Plus haut, plus loin, plus vite*, 4–5.

46. Ibid., 5.

47. According to the *Encyclopædia Britannica*, Lenglen's "first appearance at Wimbledon in a calf-length white dress with short sleeves and without petticoat or suspender (garter) belt caused a sensation," http://www.britannica.com.proxy.lib.umich.edu/EBchecked/topic/587387/tennis/29704/Outstanding-players?anchor=ref403230. See also Larry Engelman, *The Goddess and the American Girl: The Story of Suzanne Lenglen and Helen Wills* (New York: Oxford University Press, 1988).

48. Véron, "Suzanne Lenglen," in *Plus haut, plus loin, plus vite*, 4.

49. Ibid., 8, 10.

50. On women's rights struggles in U.S. politics and in American institutions, including athletics, see for example, Nancy F. Cott, *The Grounding of Modern Feminism* (New Haven, CT: Yale University Press, 1987), and Susan K. Cahn, *Coming on Strong: Gender and Sexuality in Twentieth-Century Women's Sport* (Cambridge, MA: Harvard University Press, 1995).

51. Correspondence, Carl R. Jenkins, Program Director, to Yvette Mallet, 15 October 1969, English Language Section, DAEC, Courrier USA.

52. Miscellaneous letters dated fall 1969 from WGGL, WSHR, WILL-FM, WFPL-WFPK, English Language Section, DAEC, Courrier USA.

53. Ibid.

54. Correspondence, Ben Smith to Yvette Mallet, 4 December 1969, 2590, English Language Section, DAEC, Courrier USA.

55. "Report of Activities, February 1969;" "Radio Report of 1 June 1969," 2678, English Language Section, DAEC, Courrier USA.

56. Quote in "Report of Activities, February 1969," n.p., 2591, English Language Section, DAEC, Courrier USA.

57. The requested programs were *Actualités BFA* (Weekly from France); *The Way It Is*; *Made in France*; *Patricia in Paris*; *From France to You*; and *Weekly Review of the French Press*, 2591, English Language Section, DAEC, Courrier USA.

58. "Analyse de la diffusion aux USA," 8 December 1971, English Language Section, DAEC, Courrier USA.

59. Correspondence, Kenneth Platnick to DAEC/SLA, n.d., Ben Smith to Kenneth Platnick, 9 December 1971, English Language Section, DAEC, Courrier USA.

60. Raymond Poussard, "Rapport de fin de mission de M. Raymond Poussard, la DAEC 4 ans après sa création" (Paris: ORTF/DAEC, 1973), 45. Directeur Générale, ORTF, Action extérieure de la DAEC (Direction des affaires extérieures et de la coopération), Rapports avec l'étranger, émissions vers l'étranger 1969–72, Ministère des affaires étrangères et européens (MAEE)/Direction des Archives, Archives Diplomatiques, Site La Courneuve, Fr.; *Extrait de Journal Officiel du 25 Janvier 1969*, no. 21, 835.

61. Poussard, "Rapport de fin de mission," 5. As a measure of fiscal health, in France, worker weekly wages had exceeded Germany's for well over a decade. "B4: Europe: Money/ Wages in Industry," in *International Historical Statistics: Europe 1790–1973*, 4th ed., ed. Brian R. Mitchell (London: Macmillan Reference, 1998), 190.

62. Poussard, "Rapport de fin de mission," 45.

63. Ibid., 10.

64. Sophie Bachmann, *L'éclatement de l'ORTF: la réforme de la déliverance* (Paris: Harmattan, 1997). Scholars note that the break-up of the ORTF did not produce an immediate lessening of government manipulation of broadcast news. See Douglas A. Boyd and John Y. Benzies, "SOFIRAD: France's International Commercial Media Empire," *Journal of Communication*, no. 2 (Spring 1983): 56–69, and Jeremy Tunstall, *The Media Were American: U.S. Mass Media in Decline* (New York: Oxford University Press, 2008), 251–53.

65. These bodies were Télévision française 1 (TF1), Antenne 2, France Région 3 (FR3), Télédiffusion de France (TDF), Radio France, Société française de production, and l'Institut national de l'audiovisuel (INA).

66. For overviews of broadcast deregulation and consequences for radio in particular, see especially Kuhn, *The Media in France*; Jean-Noël Jeanneney, *Une histoire des médias: des*

origines à nos jours (Paris: Seuil, 1998); Jean-Jacques Cheval, *Les radios en France: histoire, état et enjeux* (Rennes, Fr.: Apogée, 1997). On developing radio niche markets since the 1990s, see Hervé Glevarec and Michel Pinet, "From Liberalization to Fragmentation: A Sociology of French Radio Audiences since the 1990s and the Consequences for Cultural Industries Theory," *Media, Culture and Society* 30, no. 2 (2008): 215–38.

67. On the histories of French and European pirate and community broadcasting, see, for example, René Duval, *Histoire de la radio en France* (Paris: A. Moreau, 1979); Jean-Jacques Cheval, "Des radios pirates aux radios libres," *Cahiers d'histoire de la radiodiffusion* no. 67 (January–March 2001); Peter Lewis, "'It's Only Community Radio': The British Campaign for Community Radio," in *Community Radio in the 21st Century*, ed. Janey Gordon, 7–32 (Oxford, UK: Peter Lang, 2011); John Hind and Stephen Mosco, *Rebel Radio: The Full Story of British Pirate Radio* (London: Pluto, 1985). Quote is from James Miller, "From Radios Libres to Radios Privées: The Rapid Triumph of Commercial Networks in French Local Radio," *Media, Culture and Society* 14, no. 2 (1992), 276.

Afterword

1. See, for example, Nabil Echchaibi, *Voicing Diasporas: Ethnic Radio in Paris and Berlin between Cultural Renewal and Retention* (Lanham, MD: Lexington, 2011); Steve Cannon and Hugh Dauncey, ed., *Popular Music in France from Chanson to Techno: Culture, Identity, and Society* (Burlington, VT: Ashgate, 2003). On managing French institutional and political legacies in the postcolonial Francophone media world, see Jill Campaiola, "The Moroccan Media Field: An Analysis of Elite Hybridity in Television and Film Institutions," *Communication, Culture and Critique* 7 (2014): 487–505; Annemarie Iddins, "No Concessions: Independent Media and the Reshaping of the Moroccan Public" (PhD. diss, University of Michigan, 2016).

2. Translation of de Gaulle from Julian Jackson, *France: The Dark Years, 1940–1944* (Oxford: Oxford University Press, 2001), 385. André Passeron, "L'organisation de l'année de Gaulle transcende les clivages politiques," *Le Monde*, 13 June 1990; Jonathan Fenby, "Finding His Voice While Losing His Clothes," *Guardian* (London), 18 June 1990, 19; Carolyn Marvin, *When Old Technologies Were New: Thinking about Electric Communication in the Late Nineteenth Century* (New York: Oxford University Press, 1988), 161.

3. Alan Riding, "A Landmark under Renovation Wears Its Own Face as a Mask," *New York Times*, 4 March 1991, 11; http://christojeanneclaude.net/projects/the-pont-neuf-wrapped ?view=info; quote in "Christo and Jeanne-Claude," *Journal of Contemporary Art*, www.jca -online.com/christo.html.

4. Quote in Asa Briggs, *The War of Words*, vol. 3, *The History of Broadcasting in the United Kingdom* (London: Oxford University Press, 1970), 241. On the marginal direct effects of the Appeal, see also Jackson, *Dark Years, 1940–1944*.

5. Ian Davidson, "Hero-Worship of de Gaulle Comes Back into Vogue in Paris," *Financial Times* (London), 14 June 1990, 2.

6. On FDR's radio work, see Jason Loviglio, *Radio's Intimate Public: Network Broadcasting and Mass-Mediated Democracy* (Minneapolis: University of Minnesota Press, 2005).

Selected Resources

Books

Aitken, Hugh G. J. *The Continuous Wave: Technology and American Radio, 1900–1932*. Princeton, NJ: Princeton University Press, 1985.

Brochand, Christian, and Comité d'histoire de la radiodiffusion. *Histoire générale de la radio et de la télévision en France*. 2 vols. Vol. 1, *1921–1944*. Paris: Documentation française, 1994.

———. *Histoire générale de la radio et de la télévision en France*. 2 vols. Vol. 2, *1944–1974*. Paris: Documentation française, 1994.

Cazenave, Élisabeth, and Ulmann-Mauriat. *Presse, radio et télévision an France de 1631 à nos jours*. Paris: Hachette, 1995.

Hilmes, Michele, and Michael Henry, ed. *NBC: America's Network*. Berkeley: University of California Press, 2007.

Jeanneney, Jean-Noël. *Une histoire des médias: des origines à nos jours*. Paris: Seuil, 1998.

Prot, Robert. *Dictionnaire de la radio*. Grenoble, Fr.: Presses universitaires de Grenoble–Institut national de l'audiovisuel, 1997.

Ulmann-Mauriat, Caroline. *Naissance d'un média: histoire politique de la radio en France (1921–1931)*. Paris: Harmattan, 1999.

Archives and Libraries Consulted

Wisconsin State Historical Society Archives, Madison, WI
    National Broadcasting Company Records, Central Files, 1921–1969 [NBC-WHS]
    National Association of Educational Broadcasters Records, 1925–1977 (bulk 1950–1970)
Library of Congress, Recorded Sound Section, Motion Picture, Broadcasting and Recorded Sound Division, Washington, DC [NBC-LOC]
    NBC History Files
Miller Nichols Library, University of Missouri, Kansas City, MO
    Marr Sound Archives

National Archives and Records Administration, College Park, MD [NARA]
    RG 59, Records of the Department of State, Central Decimal Files
    RG 84 Records of the Foreign Service Posts of the Department of State, 1788–ca. 1991
    RG 200 Civilian Agency Records
    RG 208 Records of the Office of War Information [OWI]
    RG 263 Records of the Central Intelligence Agency
    RG 306 Records of the United States Information Agency
    RG 457 Records of the National Security Agency/Central Security Service
    RG 469 Records of the U.S. Foreign Assistance Agencies
    Motion Picture Sound and Video Research Room
Bentley Historical Library, University of Michigan, Ann Arbor, MI
    Leland Stowe Papers, 1926–1990
Richard J. Daley Library Special Collections and University Archives, University of Illinois at Chicago.
    Lenox Riley Lohr Papers
University of Maryland, College Park, MD, Special Collections
    National Public Broadcasting Archives, National Association of Educational Broadcasters
University of Illinois, Urbana-Champaign, IL
    Harry S. Skornia Papers
University of Texas at Austin
    Historical Music Recordings Collection

FRANCE

Archives Bordeaux métropole, Bordeaux
Archives départementales de la Gironde, Bordeaux
    Dépôt d'André-Jean Tudesq
École supérieure de physique et de chimie industrielles, Paris
Centre des archives diplomatiques, La Corneuve
Archives nationales, Paris
Archives nationales, Fontainebleau
Archives nationales, Pierrefitte-sur-Seine
Bibliothèque nationale de France, Paris
    Archives de l'audiovisuel
    Archives de Madame Jacqueline Baudrier
    Fonds Pierre Crénesse
    Fonds Philippe Ragueneau
Institute national de l'audiovisuel de France (Inathèque), Paris
Inathèque médiathèque, Pessac

Index

Numbers in *italic* indicate an illustration.

DEREK W. VAILLANT is an associate professor of communication studies at the University of Michigan. He is the author of *Sounds of Reform: Progressivism and Music in Chicago, 1873–1935.*

The History of Communication

The University of Illinois Press
is a founding member of the
Association of American University Presses.

University of Illinois Press
1325 South Oak Street
Champaign, IL 61820-6903
www.press.uillinois.edu